Office for
National Statistics

CW00687221

Family Spending

Edition No.: 2019/20

Office for National Statistics

2019/20

Family spending in the UK: financial year ending 2020

Family spending in the UK: financial year ending 2020

Contents	Page No.

Statistical bulletin

Family spending in the UK: April 2019 to March 2020

Average weekly household expenditure on goods and services in the UK, by age, income, economic status, socio-economic class, household composition and region.

Contact:
Carla Kidd
wealth.and.assets.survey@ons.
gov.uk
+44 (0)1633 580088

Release date:
16 March 2021

Next release:
To be announced

Table of contents

1 . Main points

- In the financial year ending (FYE) 2020, the period immediately prior to the coronavirus (COVID-19) pandemic, average weekly household spending in the UK was £587.90, down slightly (not significantly) from FYE 2019 (£603.10 adjusted for inflation), despite average income increasing modestly during the same period.

- On average, households in the highest income decile spent almost four times as much as those in the lowest decile; however, their average disposable income was around 11 times higher, which suggests they had a greater ability to save.

- Prior to the coronavirus (COVID-19) pandemic, households with lower income spent proportionately more on essentials such as housing, food and transport than those on higher incomes; households in the lowest income decile spent 54% of their total weekly expenditure in these areas compared with 42% in the highest income decile.

- Households in the highest income decile spent almost five times as much on discretionary areas such as recreation, culture, restaurants and hotels as those in the lowest income decile, suggesting they may have had greater capacity to cut back on spending when restrictions were imposed during the coronavirus (COVID-19) pandemic.

- Households headed by people aged under 30 years spent proportionally more on housing and food (41%) than other age groups (30% to 36%), and together with those on lower incomes are among the groups most affected by labour market shocks associated with the coronavirus (COVID-19) pandemic.

2 . Family Spending data

Family spending workbook 1: Detailed expenditure and trends
Dataset | Released 16 March 2021
Detailed breakdown of average weekly household expenditure on goods and services in the UK. Data are shown by place of purchase, income group (deciles) and age of household reference person.

Family spending workbook 2: Expenditure by income
Dataset | Released 16 March 2021
Data are shown by region, age, income (including equivalised) group (deciles and quintiles), economic status, socio-economic class, housing tenure, output area classification, urban and rural areas (Great Britain only), place of purchase and household composition.

Family spending workbook 3: Expenditure by region
Dataset | Released 16 March 2021
Data are shown by region, age, income (including equivalised) group (deciles and quintiles), economic status, socio-economic class, housing tenure, output area classification, urban and rural areas (Great Britain only), place of purchase and household composition.

Family spending workbook 4: Expenditure by household characteristic
Dataset | Released 16 March 2021
Data are shown by region, age, income (including equivalised) group (deciles and quintiles), economic status, socio-economic class, housing tenure, output area classification, urban and rural areas (Great Britain only), place of purchase and household composition.

Family spending workbook 5: Expenditure on housing
Dataset | Released 16 March 2021
Data are shown by region, age, income (including equivalised) group (deciles and quintiles), economic status, socio-economic class, housing tenure, output area classification, urban and rural areas (Great Britain only), place of purchase and household composition.

3 . Measuring the data

Family spending has been designated by the UK Statistics Authority as National Statistics, in accordance with the Statistics and Registration Service Act 2007 and signifying compliance with the Code of Practice for Statistics.

Results presented in this headline release cover the financial year ending (FYE) 2020, that is, April 2019 to March 2020.

Following government guidance in relation to the coronavirus (COVID-19) pandemic, a pause in data collection led to interviews being conducted for 13 fewer days in March 2020 than planned. Final March interviews took place on Monday 16 March 2020. All households that were not interviewed as a result were treated as non-responders and data were weighted to account for reduced data collection in March 2020 compared with previous years.

Data collected in March 2020 may have covered changes to spending habits around the start of the first UK lockdown on 23 March, for example panic buying beforehand and reduced spending during lockdown when people were advised to stay at home and many businesses were closed. However, because of reduced data collection in the latter half of March, data may not accurately reflect the impact of lockdown on spending and the annual estimates reported in this release will not be significantly impacted.

Survey description

All the findings in this headline release are taken from data collected on the Living Costs and Food Survey (LCF). The LCF is a UK household survey designed to provide information on household expenditure patterns and food consumption.

The LCF is a voluntary sample survey of private households. Each individual in a selected household is asked to complete a household interview and then an expenditure diary for two weeks. The survey is continuous, interviews being spread evenly over the year to ensure that seasonal effects are covered.

Great care is taken to ensure complete confidentiality of information and to protect the identity of LCF households. Only anonymised data are supplied to users.

The LCF is reviewed every year and changes are made to keep it up to date. Therefore, year-on-year changes should be interpreted with caution.

Values reported in this headline release

This headline release uses the mean when referring to averages unless stated otherwise. Therefore, total average weekly household expenditure is equal to the total weekly expenditure of households divided by the number of households. All spending estimates are rounded to the nearest £0.10, therefore the sum of component items does not necessarily add to the totals shown.

This release discusses income decile groups. Households have been ranked in ascending order of household equivalised disposable income (Organisation for Economic Co-operation and Development-modified scale) and then divided into decile groups to examine expenditure patterns across income groups. Income deciles divide the household income distribution into 10 equal parts. Households with the smallest income lie in the first decile and those with the largest income lie in the top decile.

This release considers household expenditure by age group. The age of a household refers to the age of the person who is legally responsible for the household, known as the household reference person (HRP). Where there is more than one person who is legally responsible in the household, the HRP is the person with the highest income. If there is more than one person with the same income, the eldest member of the household becomes the HRP.

Quality

More quality and methodology information on strengths, limitations, appropriate uses, and how the data were created is available in the Living Costs and Food Survey technical report and QMI.

4 . Related links

Personal and economic well-being in Great Britain: January 2021
Article | Last revised 21 January 2021
Estimates looking across multiple sources for personal and economic well-being to understand the impact of the coronavirus (COVID-19) pandemic on people and households in Great Britain. Covers the period from March 2020 to December 2020.

Average household income, UK: financial year 2020
Article | Last revised 21 January 2021
Final estimates of average household income in the UK, with analysis of how these measures have changed over time, accounting for inflation and household composition.

Definition of total housing expenditure

Costs which are included in the COICOP classification of housing expenditure:

- Actual rentals for housing
  - net rent (gross rent *less* housing benefit, rebates and allowances received)
  - second dwelling rent
- Maintenance and repair of dwelling
  - central heating maintenance and repair
  - house maintenance and repair
  - paint, wallpaper, timber
  - equipment hire, small materials
- Water supply and miscellaneous services relating to dwelling
  - water charges
  - other regular housing payments including service charge for rent
  - refuse collection, including skip hire.

Housing costs which are included elsewhere in the COICOP classification:

- Household Insurances
  - structural insurance
  - contents insurance
  - insurance for household appliances.

Housing costs which are included as 'other expenditure items' but excluded from COICOP classification:

- Housing: mortgage interest payments etc
  - mortgage interest payments
  - mortgage protection premiums
  - council tax, domestic rates
  - council tax, mortgage, insurance (second dwelling).

Housing costs which are included as 'other items recorded' and are excluded from COICOP classification:

- Purchase or alteration of dwellings (contracted out), mortgages
  - outright purchase of houses, flats etc including deposits
  - capital repayment of mortgage
  - central heating installation
  - DIY improvements: double glazing, kitchen units, sheds etc
  - home improvements (contracted out)
  - bathroom fittings
  - purchase of materials for capital improvements
  - purchase of second dwelling.

Tables in reports on the Living Costs and Food Survey, financial year ending 2018 to financial year ending 2020

2019-20 tables		Table numbers in reports for		
		2019-20	2018-19	2017-18
Detailed expenditure and place of purchase				
A1	Detailed expenditure with full-method standard errors	A1	A1	A1
	Expenditure on alcoholic drink by type of premises	..	..	..
A2	Expenditure on food by place of purchase	A2	A2	A2
	Expenditure on selected items by place of purchase	..	..	..
A3	Expenditure on clothing and footwear by place of purchase	A3	A3	A3
Expenditure by income				
A4	Main items by gross income decile	A4	A4	A4
A5	Percentage on main items by gross income decile	A5	A5	A5
A6	Detailed expenditure by gross income decile	A6	A6	A6
A7	Main items by disposable income decile	A7	A7	A7
A8	Percentage on main items by disposable income decile	A8	A8	A8
Expenditure by age and income				
A9	Main items by age of Household Reference Person	A9	A9	A9
A10	Main items as a percentage by age of Household Reference Person	A10	A10	A10
A11	Detailed expenditure by age of Household Reference Person	A11	A11	A11
A12	HRP aged under 30 by gross income quintile group	A12	A12	A12
A12DE	HRP aged under 30 by equivalised disposable income quintile group	A12DE	A12DE	A12DE
A13	HRP aged 30 and under 50 by gross income quintile group	A13	A13	A13
A13DE	HRP aged 30 and under 50 by equivalised disposable income quintile group	A13DE	A13DE	A13DE
A14	HRP aged 50 and under 65 by gross income quintile group	A14	A14	A14
A14DE	HRP aged 50 and under 65 by equivalised disposable income quintile group	A14DE	A14DE	A14DE
A15	HRP aged 65 and under 75 by gross income quintile group	A15	A15	A15
A15DE	HRP aged 65 and under 75 by equivalised disposable income quintile group	A15DE	A15DE	A15DE
A16	HRP aged 75 or over by gross income quintile group	A16	A16	A16
A16DE	HRP aged 75 or over by equivalised disposable income quintile group	A16DE	A16DE	A16DE
Expenditure by socio-economic characteristics				
A17	Expenditure by economic activity status of Household Reference Person (HRP)	A17	A17	A17
A18	HRP is a full-time employee by gross income quintile group	A18	A18	A18
A18DE	HRP is a full-time employee by equivalised disposable income quintile group	A18DE	A18DE	A18DE
A19	HRP is self-employed by gross income quintile group	A19	A19	A19
A19DE	HRP is self-employed by equivalised disposable income quintile group	A19DE	A19DE	A19DE
A20	Expenditure by number of persons working	A20	A20	A20

Tables in reports on the Living Costs and Food Survey, financial year ending 2018 to financial year ending 2020

		Table numbers in reports for		
2019-20 tables		**2019-20**	**2018-19**	**2017-18**
A21	Expenditure by age HRP completed continuous full-time education	A21	A21	A21
A22	Expenditure by socio-economic class of HRP	A22	A22	A22
Expenditure by composition, income and tenure				
A23	Expenditure by household composition	A23	A23	A23
..	1 adult retired households mainly dependent on state pensions by gross income quintile group	..	..	..
..	1 adult retired households not mainly dependent on state pensions by gross income quintile group	..	..	..
A26	1 adult non-retired by gross income quintile group	A26	A26	A26
..	1 adult with children by gross income quintile group	..	..	..
..	2 adults with children by gross income quintile group	..	..	..
A29	2 adults non-retired by gross income quintile group	A29	A29	A29
..	2 adults retired mainly dependent on state pensions by gross income quintile group	..	..	..
..	2 adults retired not mainly dependent on state pensions by gross income quintile group	..	..	..
A32	Household expenditure by tenure	A32	A32	A32
Expenditure by region				
A33	Main items of expenditure by region	A33	A33	A33
A34	Main items as a percentage of expenditure by region	A34	A34	A34
A35	Detailed expenditure by region	A35	A35	A35
A36	Expenditure by urban/rural areas (GB only)	A36	A36	A36
Household income[2]				
..	Income by household composition	..	..	..
..	Income by age of HRP	..	..	..
..	Income by income group	..	..	..
..	Income by household tenure	..	..	..
..	Income by regions	..	..	..
..	Income by GB urban/rural areas	..	..	..
..	Income by socio-economic class	..	..	..
..	Income 1970 to 2014	..	..	..
Households characteristics and ownership of durable goods				
A45	Percentage with durable goods 1970 to financial year ending 2019	A45	A45	A45
A46	Percentage with durable goods by income group and household composition	A46	A46	A46
A47	Percentage with cars	A47	A47	A47
A48	Percentage with durable goods by UK countries and regions	A48	A48	A48

Tables in reports on the Living Costs and Food Survey, financial year ending 2018 to financial year ending 2020

2019-20 tables		Table numbers in reports for		
		2019-20	2018-19	2017-18
A49	Percentage by size, composition, age, in each income group	A49	A49	A49
A50	Percentage by economic activity, tenure and socio-economic class in each income group	A50	A50	A50
Output Area Classification				
A51	Expenditure by OAC supergroup	A51	A51	A51
A52	Expenditure by OAC group	A52	A52	A52
..	Average gross weekly household income by OAC supergroup[2]	..	..	..
Further tables by household characteristics				
A56	Households with children	A56	..	..
A57	Households without children	A57	..	..
Methodology				
..	Household characteristics	..	..	..
..	Person characteristics	..	..	..
Housing (formerly chapter 2)				
2.2	Housing expenditure	2.2	2.2	2.2
2.3	Housing expenditure by gross income decile group	2.3	2.3	2.3
2.4	Housing expenditure by age of household reference person	2.4	2.4	2.4
2.5	Housing expenditure by countries and regions	2.5	2.5	2.5
2.6	Housing expenditure by socio-economic classification of household reference person	2.6	2.6	2.6
2.7	Housing expenditure by household composition	2.7	2.7	2.7
2.8	Expenditure on rent by renters	2.8	2.8	2.8
2.9	Expenditure on mortgages by mortgage holders	2.9	2.9	2.9
2.10	Expenditure on rent and mortgages by renters and mortgage holders by gross income decile group	2.10	2.10	2.10
2.11	Expenditure on rent and mortgages by renters and mortgage holders by countries and regions	2.11	2.11	2.11
Equivalised income tables (formerly chapter 3) - tables report on gross incomes before 2012				
3.1	Detailed household expenditure by disposable income decile group	3.1	3.1	3.1
3.1E	Detailed household expenditure by disposable equivalised income decile group (OECD-modified scale)	3.1E	3.1E	3.1E
3.2	Percentage of total expenditure by disposable income decile group	3.2	3.2	3.2
3.2E	Percentage of total expenditure by disposable equivalised income decile group (OECD-modified scale)	3.2E	3.2E	3.2E
3.3	1 adult non-retired households by disposable income quintile group	3.3	3.3	3.3
3.3E	1 adult non-retired households by equivalised disposable income quintile group (OECD-modified scale)	3.3E	3.3E	3.3E
..	1 person retired households not mainly dependent on state pensions by disposable income quintile group	..	..	..

Tables in reports on the Living Costs and Food Survey, financial year ending 2018 to financial year ending 2020

2019-20 tables		Table numbers in reports for		
		2019-20	**2018-19**	**2017-18**
..	1 person retired households not mainly dependent on state pensions by equivalised disposable income quintile group (OECD-modified scale)	..	..	..
..	2 adult households with children by disposable income quintile group	..	.. ..	
..	2 adult households with children by equivalised disposable income quintile group (OECD-modified scale)	..	..	..
..	1 adult households with children by disposable income quintile group			
..	1 adult households with children by equivalised disposable income quintile group (OECD-modified scale)	..	..	..
		..	..	..
3.7	2 adult non-retired households by disposable income quintile group	3.7	3.7	3.7
3.7E	2 adult non-retired households by equivalised disposable income quintile group (OECD-modified scale)	3.7E	3.7E	3.7E
..	1 person retired households mainly dependent on state pensions by disposable income quintile group	..	..	..
..	1 person retired households mainly dependent on state pensions by equivalised disposable income quintile group (OECD-modified scale)	..	..	..
..	2 adult retired households mainly dependent on state pensions by disposable income quintile group	..	..	..
..	2 adult retired households mainly dependent on state pensions by equivalised disposable income quintile group (OECD-modified scale)	..	..	..
..	2 adult retired households not mainly dependent on state pensions by disposable income quintile group	..	..	..
..	2 adult retired households not mainly dependent on state pensions by equivalised disposable income quintile group (OECD-modified scale)	..	..	..
..	Income and source of income by disposable income quintile group	..	..	..
..	Income and source of income by equivalised disposable income quintile group (OECD-modified scale)	..	..	..
3.12	Percentage of households by composition in each disposable and equivalised disposable income decile group (OECD-modified scale)	3.12	3.12	3.12

Trends in household expenditure (formerly chapter 4)

4.1	COICOP main items 2001/02 to 2019/20	4.1	4.1	4.1
4.2	COICOP as a percentage of total expenditure 2001/02 to 2019/20	4.2	4.2	4.2
4.3	Household expenditure 2001/02 to 2019/20 COICOP based on current prices	4.3	4.3	4.3
..	FES main items 1995/96 - 2011	..	..	..
..	FES as a percentage of total expenditure 1995/96 - 2011	..	..	..

Notes:

.. Tables do not appear in these publications.

1. A subset of tables was produced for the financial year ending 2015 to cover the change from reporting on a calendar year basis to a financial year. They can be accessed using the links to 2015-16 tables. Otherwise, Where no hyperlink is given, the URL address is longer than Excel permits. Tables can be downloaded from our archived release page: http://webarchive.nationalarchives.gov.uk/20160129144222/http://www.ons.gov.uk/ons/rel/family-spending/family-spending/index.html

2. From 2014-15 onwards, Family Spending no longer includes tables reporting solely on income. See the survey methodology for details of ONS' preferred income measure.

Source: Office for National Statistics

Background notes

Impact of the coronavirus (COVID-19) pandemic on the Living Costs and Food Survey (LCF) for the financial year ending 2020

Following Government guidance in relation to the coronavirus (COVID-19) pandemic, a pause in data collection led to interviews being conducted for 13 fewer days in March 2020 than planned. Final March interviews took place on Monday March 16th. All households that were not interviewed as a result were treated as non-responders and data were weighted to account for reduced data collection in March 2020 compared to previous years.

Data collected in March 2020 may have covered changes to spending habits around the start of the first UK lockdown on March 23rd, for example panic buying beforehand and reduced spending during lockdown when people were advised to stay at home and many businesses were closed. However, due to reduced data collection in the latter half of March data may not accurately reflect the impact of lockdown on spending and the annual estimates reported in this release will not be significantly impacted.

Housing expenditure tables

Table 2.2

Housing expenditure

UK, financial year ending 2017 to financial year ending 2020

	2018-19			2019-20		
	£ per week	% of total expend-iture	% of housing expend-iture	£ per week	% of total expend-iture	% of housing expend-iture
Weighted number of households (thousands)	27,480			27,820		
Total number of households in sample	5,480			5,440		
Total number of persons in sample	12,790			12,670		
Total number of adults in sample	9,980			9,880		
Weighted average number of persons per household	2.4			2.4		
Commodity or service						
Primary dwelling						
Rent	**50.20**	**6**	**28**	**52.50**	**6**	**30**
Gross rent	50.20	6	28	52.50	6	30
less housing benefit, rebates and						
allowances received	12.90	2	7	12.40	1	7
Net rent[1]	37.30	4	21	40.10	5	23
Mortgage	**49.40**	**6**	**27**	**51.50**	**6**	**29**
Mortgage interest payments	20.80	2	12	22.30	3	13
Mortgage protection premiums	1.10	0~	1	1.00	0~	1
Capital repayment of mortgage	27.60	3	15	28.20	3	16
Outright purchase, including deposits	**[0.10]**	**0~**	**0~**	**[0.80]**	**0~**	**0~**
Secondary dwelling	**17.40**	**2**	**10**	**4.50**	**1**	**3**
Rent	..	0~	0~	..	0~	0~
Council tax, mortgage, insurance						
(secondary dwelling)	0.80	0~	0~	1.10	0~	1
Purchase of second dwelling	16.50	2	9	3.40	0~	2
Charges	**34.30**	**4**	**19**	**36.40**	**4**	**21**
Council tax, domestic rates	24.50	3	14	26.00	3	15
Water charges	8.10	1	5	8.20	1	5
Other regular housing payments including						
service charge for rent	**1.50**	**0~**	**1**	**2.10**	**0~**	**1**
Refuse collection, including skip hire	0.10	0~	0~	0.10	0~	0~
Moving house	**2.40**	**0~**	**1**	**2.00**	**0~**	**1**
Property transaction - purchase and sale	1.20	0~	1	0.90	0~	1
Property transaction - sale only	0.50	0~	0~	0.40	0~	0~
Property transaction - purchase only	0.50	0~	0~	0.40	0~	0~
Property transaction - other payments	0.20	0~	0~	0.20	0~	0~
Maintenance and repair of dwelling	**7.50**	**1**	**4**	**8.00**	**1**	**5**
Central heating repairs	0.80	0~	0~	1.20	0~	1
House maintenance etc.	4.60	1	3	4.70	1	3
Paint, wallpaper, timber	1.20	0~	1	1.20	0~	1
Equipment hire, small materials	0.90	0~	0~	0.80	0~	0~
Alterations and improvements to dwelling	**26.40**	**3**	**15**	**28.10**	**3**	**16**
Central heating installation	1.60	0~	1	1.40	0~	1
DIY improvements: double glazing,						
kitchen units, sheds etc.	1.30	0~	1	1.40	0~	1
Home improvements - contracted out	22.50	3	13	24.50	3	14
Bathroom fittings	0.70	0~	0~	0.40	0~	0~
Purchase of materials for Capital Improvements	0.30	0~	0~	0.40	0~	0~
Household insurances	**5.10**	**1**	**3**	**4.90**	**1**	**3**
Structure	2.40	0~	1	2.30	0~	1
Contents	2.30	0~	1	2.10	0~	1
Household appliances[2]	0.50	0~	0~	0.50	0~	0~
Housing expenditure	**180.00**	**21**	**100**	**176.40**	**21**	**100**
Total expenditure[3]	**843.30**			**842.50**		

Please see background notes for symbols and conventions used in this report.

1 The figure included in total expenditure is net rent as opposed to gross rent.

2 From FYE 2019, information about insurance for household appliances was collected in the questionnaire in addition to the diary. In previous years, this was based on diary data only.

3 This total includes all categories recorded in the LCF, including those outside the 'COICOP' total expenditure.

Source: Office for National Statistics

Table 2.3

Housing expenditure by gross income decile group

UK, financial year ending 2020

	Gross income decile group										
	1	2	3	4	5	6	7	8	9	10	All
Weighted number of households (thousands)	2,780	2,780	2,780	2,780	2,780	2,780	2,780	2,780	2,780	2,780	27,820
Total number of households in sample	550	550	570	580	570	560	530	530	520	480	5,440
Total number of persons in sample	710	870	1,090	1,220	1,300	1,420	1,460	1,510	1,530	1,560	12,670
Total number of adults in sample	620	720	880	980	1,030	1,080	1,100	1,150	1,190	1,140	9,880
Weighted average number of persons per household	1.3	1.6	1.9	2.1	2.3	2.5	2.8	2.8	3.0	3.3	2.4

Commodity or service	Average weekly household expenditure (£)										
Primary dwelling											
Rent	**74.30**	**57.50**	**58.90**	**49.50**	**45.80**	**51.50**	**45.30**	**44.10**	**45.80**	**52.50**	**52.50**
Gross rent	74.30	57.50	58.90	49.50	45.80	51.50	45.30	44.10	45.80	52.50	52.50
less housing benefit, rebates and allowances received	47.10	31.70	19.30	11.50	5.30	.1.80	3.50	[0.70]	..	..	12.40
Net rent[1]	27.20	25.70	39.70	38.10	40.50	49.70	41.80	43.40	43.10	52.40	40.10
Mortgage	**5.90**	**5.90**	**10.10**	**12.90**	**26.90**	**41.70**	**61.00**	**82.70**	**106.10**	**161.50**	**51.50**
Mortgage interest payments	3.70	2.80	4.30	4.90	11.50	16.70	26.10	36.30	46.20	70.10	22.30
Mortgage protection premiums	..	..	0.30	0.30	0.60	1.00	1.50	1.30	2.10	3.10	1.00
Capital repayment of mortgage	[2.20]	3.00	5.50	7.70	14.80	23.90	33.40	45.00	57.80	88.30	28.20
Outright purchase, including deposits	:	:	:	..	:	:	:	..	..	..	**[0.80]**
Secondary dwelling	..	..	..	[1.50]	[2.20]	[3.20]	..	[2.70]	4.10	14.10	4.50
Rent	:	:	:	:	:	:	:	:	:	..	..
Council tax, mortgage, insurance (secondary dwelling)	:	..	:	..	..	..	..	..	..	[5.20]	1.10
Purchase of second dwelling	..	..	..	..	..	..	..	[2.00]	[3.00]	8.90	3.40
Charges	**22.10**	**24.60**	**29.90**	**33.80**	**36.70**	**38.20**	**40.40**	**41.70**	**43.30**	**53.90**	**36.40**
Council tax, domestic rates	12.90	16.00	20.80	25.30	26.90	27.30	29.50	30.80	32.80	38.10	26.00
Water charges	6.10	6.50	7.20	7.30	7.80	8.60	9.50	9.20	9.10	10.50	8.20
Other regular housing payments including service charge for rent	3.00	2.10	1.70	1.10	1.90	2.10	1.20	1.80	1.30	5.20	2.10
Refuse collection, including skip hire	..	..	..	..	..	..	..	..	..	..	0.10
Moving house	..	..	**[1.10]**	**[1.10]**	**1.90**	**1.30**	**2.30**	**4.70**	**2.40**	**3.90**	**2.00**
Property transaction - purchase and sale	..	..	..	..	[1.10]	..	[1.40]	[1.40]	[1.30]	[1.90]	0.90
Property transaction - sale only	..	..	..	..	..	..	..	..	..	..	0.40
Property transaction - purchase only	:	:	..	..	..	[0.50]	..	[2.10]	[0.50]	..	0.40
Property transaction - other payments	..	:	..	..	..	[0.40]	..	0.60	[0.40]	[0.40]	0.20
Maintenance and repair of dwelling	**2.60**	**3.30**	**4.70**	**5.60**	**6.60**	**7.10**	**11.00**	**10.50**	**10.20**	**18.10**	**8.00**
Central heating repairs	0.30	0.40	1.10	0.80	1.10	1.00	1.40	1.10	1.40	3.60	1.20
House maintenance etc.	1.70	1.50	2.80	3.20	2.90	4.50	6.80	4.60	6.20	12.70	4.70
Paint, wallpaper, timber	0.60	0.40	0.60	1.00	1.40	1.20	2.10	1.90	1.80	1.10	1.20
Equipment hire, small materials	..	[1.00]	0.20	0.60	1.20	0.30	0.70	2.90	0.80	0.60	0.80
Alterations and improvements to dwelling	**11.70**	**9.20**	**16.30**	**18.60**	**20.90**	**17.30**	**32.60**	**33.30**	**36.10**	**85.50**	**28.10**
Central heating installation	..	..	[1.00]	[1.40]	[1.70]	[1.00]	[1.10]	[1.40]	[2.20]	[1.80]	1.40
DIY improvements: double glazing, kitchen units, sheds etc.	..	..	..	..	..	[1.30]	[3.00]	..	[0.90]	[6.10]	1.40
Home improvements - contracted out	9.30	8.20	13.40	15.70	18.60	15.00	27.60	29.60	32.10	75.40	24.50
Bathroom fittings	..	..	..	..	[0.20]	..	[0.90]	[1.50]	[0.30]	[0.30]	0.40
Purchase of materials for capital improvements	:	..	..	..	..	..	..	..	..	..	0.40
Household insurances	**2.60**	**3.30**	**3.40**	**4.60**	**5.00**	**4.80**	**5.50**	**5.30**	**6.20**	**8.30**	**4.90**
Structure	1.10	1.50	1.50	1.90	2.00	2.30	2.60	2.60	3.10	4.10	2.30
Contents	1.20	1.60	1.50	1.90	1.90	2.10	2.30	2.30	2.70	3.70	2.10
Household appliances[2]	0.40	0.20	0.30	0.80	1.20	0.40	0.60	0.40	0.40	0.50	0.50
Housing expenditure	**72.60**	**74.40**	**105.30**	**116.60**	**140.80**	**163.30**	**210.00**	**224.70**	**257.70**	**399.20**	**176.40**
Total expenditure[3]	**267.70**	**311.90**	**420.70**	**517.00**	**647.20**	**753.00**	**914.40**	**1,101.30**	**1,293.50**	**2,200.70**	**842.50**

Please see background notes for symbols and conventions used in this report.

1 The figure included in total expenditure is net rent as opposed to gross rent.

2 From FYE 2019, information about insurance for household appliances was collected in the questionnaire in addition to the diary. In previous years, this was based on diary data only.

3 This total includes all categories recorded in the LCF, including those outside the 'COICOP' total expenditure.

Source: Office for National Statistics

Table 2.4

Housing expenditure by age of household reference person

UK, financial year ending 2020

	Under 30	30 to 49	50 to 64	65 to 74	75 or over	All
Weighted number of households (thousands)	2,480	9,280	7,820	4,240	3,990	27,820
Total number of households in sample	390	1,790	1,530	980	750	5,440
Total number of persons in sample	940	5,400	3,460	1,710	1,160	12,670
Total number of adults in sample	700	3,280	3,050	1,690	1,160	9,880
Weighted average number of persons per household	2.4	3.0	2.4	1.8	1.5	2.4
Commodity or service	Average weekly household expenditure (£)					
Primary dwelling						
Rent	**131.30**	**65.20**	**38.50**	**31.20**	**24.10**	**52.50**
Gross rent	131.30	65.20	38.50	31.20	24.10	52.50
less housing benefit, rebates and allowances received	8.70	10.80	12.00	15.30	16.00	12.40
Net rent[1]	122.60	54.40	26.50	15.90	8.10	40.10
Mortgage	**41.50**	**95.20**	**52.00**	**7.90**	**[1.30]**	**51.50**
Mortgage interest payments	20.50	43.00	19.30	4.00	[0.50]	22.30
Mortgage protection premiums	0.90	1.90	1.00	[0.20]	..	1.00
Capital repayment of mortgage	20.10	50.30	31.70	3.70	..	28.20
Outright purchase, including deposits	..	..	..	..	:	**[0.80]**
Secondary dwelling	..	**4.40**	**9.60**	**[1.70]**	..	**4.50**
Rent	:	..	:	:	:	..
Council tax, mortgage, insurance (secondary dwelling)	:	1.50	[1.80]	..	:	1.10
Purchase of second dwelling	..	2.90	7.80	[1.30]	..	3.40
Charges	**29.90**	**36.60**	**38.10**	**37.20**	**36.10**	**36.40**
Council tax, domestic rates	20.70	26.00	27.70	27.20	24.80	26.00
Water charges	7.20	8.30	8.70	8.30	7.20	8.20
Other regular housing payments including service charge for rent	2.00	2.10	1.70	1.60	4.00	2.10
Refuse collection, including skip hire	..	..	..	..	..	0.10
Moving house	**3.00**	**2.20**	**2.30**	**1.00**	..	**2.00**
Property transaction - purchase and sale	[0.90]	1.20	0.90	..	..	0.90
Property transaction - sale only	..	[0.30]	[0.90]	..	:	0.40
Property transaction - purchase only	[1.10]	0.40	[0.40]	..	..	0.40
Property transaction - other payments	0.90	0.30	0.20	..	..	0.20
Maintenance and repair of dwelling	**3.80**	**6.90**	**11.40**	**9.60**	**4.60**	**8.00**
Central heating repairs	0.10	0.90	1.90	1.60	0.90	1.20
House maintenance etc.	2.50	3.90	6.20	6.50	3.20	4.70
Paint, wallpaper, timber	1.00	1.40	1.50	1.20	0.30	1.20
Equipment hire, small materials	[0.20]	0.80	1.70	0.40	0.20	0.80
Alterations and improvements to dwelling	**7.50**	**33.70**	**37.50**	**23.40**	**14.70**	**28.10**
Central heating installation	..	1.10	1.90	[0.90]	2.10	1.40
DIY improvements: double glazing, kitchen units, sheds etc.	..	1.60	1.30	[1.10]	[2.00]	1.40
Home improvements - contracted out	6.20	30.00	33.10	20.50	10.50	24.50
Bathroom fittings	..	0.60	0.50	[0.40]	..	0.40
Purchase of materials for capital improvements	:	..	[0.60]	..	..	0.40
Household insurances	**2.40**	**4.40**	**5.70**	**5.70**	**5.30**	**4.90**
Structure	0.80	2.10	2.70	2.60	2.50	2.30
Contents	1.00	2.00	2.40	2.30	2.20	2.10
Household appliances[2]	0.60	0.30	0.60	0.90	0.50	0.50
Housing expenditure	**211.00**	**240.00**	**183.30**	**102.80**	**71.90**	**176.40**
Total expenditure[3]	**800.80**	**1,031.80**	**972.00**	**609.80**	**422.30**	**842.50**

Please see background notes for symbols and conventions used in this report.

1 The figure included in total expenditure is net rent as opposed to gross rent.

2 From FYE 2019, information about insurance for household appliances was collected in the questionnaire in addition to the diary. In previous years, this was based on diary data only.

3 This total includes all categories recorded in the LCF, including those outside the 'COICOP' total expenditure.

Source: Office for National Statistics

Table 2.5

Housing expenditure by countries and regions

UK, financial year ending 2020

Commodity or service	United Kingdom	England	North East	North West	Yorkshire and the Humber	East Midlands	West Midlands
	K02000001	E92000001	E12000001	E12000002	E12000003	E12000004	E12000005
Weighted number of households (thousands)	27,820	23,220	1,210	3,190	2,400	2,030	2,460
Total number of households in sample	5,440	4,030	250	570	450	410	420
Total number of persons in sample	12,670	9,530	560	1,290	1,030	980	980
Total number of adults in sample	9,880	7,410	440	1,010	800	760	790
Weighted average number of persons per household	2.4	2.4	2.2	2.3	2.3	2.3	2.4
Commodity or service	Average weekly household expenditure (£)						
Primary dwelling							
Rent	**52.50**	**55.00**	**41.30**	**39.90**	**34.00**	**35.90**	**44.10**
Gross rent	52.50	55.00	41.30	39.90	34.00	35.90	44.10
less housing benefit, rebates and allowances received	12.40	12.30	13.90	11.00	9.50	7.30	8.50
Net rent[1]	40.10	42.70	27.40	28.90	24.40	28.50	35.60
Mortgage	**51.50**	**54.20**	**27.70**	**45.80**	**43.60**	**45.60**	**46.10**
Mortgage interest payments	22.30	23.60	11.20	18.80	16.70	19.30	19.30
Mortgage protection premiums	1.00	1.10	[0.60]	0.90	0.80	1.20	1.10
Capital repayment of mortgage	28.20	29.50	15.90	26.00	26.00	25.10	25.80
Outright purchase, including deposits	**[0.80]**	**[1.00]**	:	..	..	..	:
Secondary dwelling	**4.50**	**4.90**	..	**[3.20]**	..	**[20.20]**	..
Rent	..	:	:	:	:	:	:
Council tax, mortgage, insurance (secondary dwelling)	1.10	1.20	:	:	:	:	:
Purchase of second dwelling	3.40	3.70	..	..	..	..	..
Charges	**36.40**	**37.90**	**35.40**	**34.40**	**33.30**	**33.60**	**36.50**
Council tax, domestic rates	26.00	26.80	24.40	24.20	23.40	25.40	25.20
Water charges	8.20	8.60	8.90	9.20	8.10	7.40	8.20
Other regular housing payments including service charge for rent	2.10	2.40	[1.60]	0.80	1.70	0.70	3.10
Refuse collection, including skip hire	0.10	0.10	..	..	..	..	:
Moving house	**2.00**	**2.10**	..	**2.00**	**1.90**	**3.00**	**[0.80]**
Property transaction - purchase and sale	0.90	0.90	..	[1.20]	..	..	..
Property transaction - sale only	0.40	0.40	..	..	..	..	..
Property transaction - purchase only	0.40	0.50	:	[0.50]	..	[1.60]	..
Property transaction - other payments	0.20	0.30	..	[0.10]	..	..	..
Maintenance and repair of dwelling	**8.00**	**7.90**	**4.50**	**6.90**	**4.90**	**7.30**	**6.90**
Central heating repairs	1.20	1.20	0.60	0.60	0.70	1.10	0.60
House maintenance etc.	4.70	4.80	2.90	4.80	2.30	4.10	5.00
Paint, wallpaper, timber	1.20	1.10	[0.80]	1.20	1.10	1.40	1.00
Equipment hire, small materials	0.80	0.80	[0.20]	0.30	0.80	0.70	0.30
Alterations and improvements to dwelling	**28.10**	**29.50**	**16.00**	**16.90**	**14.30**	**21.80**	**28.20**
Central heating installation	1.40	1.50	..	[1.30]	[1.10]	[2.80]	[1.20]
DIY improvements: double glazing, kitchen units, sheds etc.	1.40	1.50	..	..	..	..	..
Home improvements - contracted out	24.50	25.60	12.60	13.80	11.90	17.70	24.10
Bathroom fittings	0.40	0.40	..	..	[0.20]	..	..
Purchase of materials for capital improvements	0.40	0.50	:	..	..	..	..
Household insurances	**4.90**	**4.90**	**4.10**	**4.80**	**4.50**	**4.60**	**4.60**
Structure	2.30	2.30	1.80	2.10	2.10	2.20	2.20
Contents	2.10	2.10	1.90	1.90	2.00	2.00	1.90
Household appliances[2]	0.50	0.50	0.40	0.80	0.30	0.40	0.50
Housing expenditure	**176.40**	**184.90**	**116.60**	**143.20**	**129.50**	**164.80**	**160.90**
Total expenditure[3]	**842.50**	**869.80**	**649.90**	**751.20**	**693.40**	**809.60**	**790.80**

Table 2.5

Housing expenditure by countries and regions

UK, financial year ending 2020

	East	London	South East	South West	Wales	Scotland	Northern Ireland
	E12000006	E12000007	E12000008	E12000009	W92000004	S92000003	N92000002
Weighted number of households (thousands)	2,580	3,240	3,700	2,410	1,400	2,430	780
Total number of households in sample	450	390	610	500	250	790	370
Total number of persons in sample	1,070	1,010	1,450	1,160	570	1,730	840
Total number of adults in sample	850	740	1,120	910	450	1,390	630
Weighted average number of persons per household	2.4	2.8	2.4	2.3	2.2	2.2	2.4
Commodity or service	Average weekly household expenditure (£)						
Primary dwelling							
Rent	**50.90**	**126.40**	**53.50**	**41.30**	**36.80**	**43.30**	**34.30**
Gross rent	50.90	126.40	53.50	41.30	36.80	43.30	34.30
less housing benefit, rebates and allowances received	9.70	27.90	10.40	9.30	12.80	12.30	13.00
Net rent[1]	41.10	98.50	43.10	32.00	24.00	31.00	21.20
Mortgage	**62.50**	**65.90**	**73.20**	**50.60**	**45.30**	**34.90**	**34.00**
Mortgage interest payments	28.10	31.60	32.90	21.30	17.90	14.80	12.50
Mortgage protection premiums	1.00	1.10	1.40	1.10	0.90	0.80	1.60
Capital repayment of mortgage	33.40	33.20	38.80	28.20	26.50	19.30	20.00
Outright purchase, including deposits	:	..	..	..	:	:	:
Secondary dwelling	..	[5.70]	[4.40]	[4.70]	[4.40]	[2.20]	..
Rent	:	:	:	:	..	:	:
Council tax, mortgage, insurance (secondary dwelling)	..	..	..	..	..	..	..
Purchase of second dwelling	..	..	[3.30]	..	..	..	..
Charges	**38.70**	**41.60**	**43.20**	**39.40**	**33.80**	**31.60**	**13.40**
Council tax, domestic rates	28.90	27.10	31.40	28.20	24.90	23.40	12.50
Water charges	8.70	8.60	8.60	9.00	8.70	6.70	:
Other regular housing payments including service charge for rent	1.10	5.90	3.10	2.10	..	1.40	0.80
Refuse collection, including skip hire	..	:	..	..	:	..	:
Moving house	**[1.90]**	**2.20**	**2.20**	**3.50**	**[3.30]**	**[0.70]**	..
Property transaction - purchase and sale	..	..	..	..	..	..	..
Property transaction - sale only	..	..	..	..	..	..	..
Property transaction - purchase only	..	..	[0.60]	..	..	..	..
Property transaction - other payments	..	[0.60]	[0.30]	[0.50]	..	..	..
Maintenance and repair of dwelling	**8.50**	**6.80**	**11.00**	**11.20**	**10.90**	**8.10**	**5.10**
Central heating repairs	1.70	1.40	1.80	1.50	2.90	0.70	0.80
House maintenance etc.	4.80	4.30	7.20	5.60	4.90	4.40	2.70
Paint, wallpaper, timber	1.30	[0.90]	1.00	1.20	1.60	1.80	1.50
Equipment hire, small materials	0.70	[0.20]	1.00	2.90	1.50	1.30	[0.20]
Alterations and improvements to dwelling	**38.50**	**14.20**	**60.00**	**39.70**	**25.40**	**23.30**	**8.50**
Central heating installation	[1.60]	[1.30]	..	[2.20]	..	[0.70]	..
DIY improvements: double glazing, kitchen units, sheds etc.	..	..	..	[2.40]	..	[0.60]	..
Home improvements - contracted out	35.60	11.30	54.30	34.00	21.30	21.70	6.30
Bathroom fittings	[0.80]	..	..	[0.30]	..	[0.30]	..
Purchase of materials for capital improvements	..	..	..	..	..	:	:
Household insurances	**5.00**	**4.50**	**6.10**	**4.90**	**6.60**	**4.60**	**4.00**
Structure	2.40	2.10	2.80	2.20	2.50	2.20	2.00
Contents	2.20	1.90	2.70	2.30	2.10	2.10	1.80
Household appliances[2]	0.40	0.50	0.50	0.40	2.00	0.30	[0.20]
Housing expenditure	**197.90**	**244.20**	**244.20**	**186.30**	**153.70**	**136.50**	**89.20**
Total expenditure[3]	**913.00**	**1,008.20**	**1,098.20**	**861.10**	**712.80**	**715.10**	**659.60**

Please see background notes for symbols and conventions used in this report.

1 The figure included in total expenditure is net rent as opposed to gross rent.

2 From FYE 2019, information about insurance for household appliances was collected in the questionnaire in addition to the diary. In previous years, this was based on diary data only.

3 This total includes all categories recorded in the LCF, including those outside the 'COICOP' total expenditure.

Source: Office for National Statistics

Table 2.6

Housing expenditure by socio-economic classification of household reference person

UK, financial year ending 2020

	Large employers and higher managerial	Higher professional	Lower managerial & professional	Inter-mediate	Small employers	Lower supervisory
Weighted number of households (thousands)	1,100	3,150	5,390	1,930	1,910	1,500
Total number of households in sample	200	570	1,030	390	350	290
Total number of persons in sample	570	1,530	2,720	940	920	810
Total number of adults in sample	410	1,100	2,000	720	690	560
Weighted average number of persons per household	2.9	2.7	2.6	2.5	2.8	2.7
Commodity or service	Average weekly household expenditure (£)					
Primary dwelling						
Rent	**39.70**	**53.80**	**45.10**	**58.60**	**58.90**	**61.60**
Gross rent	39.70	53.80	45.10	58.60	58.90	61.60
less housing benefit, rebates and allowances received	..	0.60	2.20	6.50	13.70	8.50
Net rent[1]	36.90	53.30	42.90	52.10	45.20	53.10
Mortgage	**144.60**	**114.60**	**86.70**	**51.20**	**62.90**	**53.80**
Mortgage interest payments	62.70	50.10	38.10	21.70	26.30	22.00
Mortgage protection premiums	2.60	1.80	1.70	1.00	1.40	1.60
Capital repayment of mortgage	79.30	62.60	46.90	28.50	35.10	30.20
Outright purchase, including deposits	:	..	..	:	:	:
Secondary dwelling	..	[5.60]	6.70	..	[3.80]	..
Rent	:	:	:	..	:	:
Council tax, mortgage, insurance (secondary dwelling)	..	..	[2.10]	..	..	..
Purchase of second dwelling	..	[4.70]	4.70	..	[2.80]	..
Charges	**46.50**	**44.40**	**40.00**	**34.20**	**38.20**	**34.90**
Council tax, domestic rates	34.80	32.20	29.30	25.60	27.80	25.70
Water charges	9.20	9.10	8.70	7.60	8.90	8.40
Other regular housing payments including service charge for rent	2.30	2.90	1.90	0.90	1.30	0.80
Refuse collection, including skip hire	..	..	..	..	..	..
Moving house	**[3.00]**	**3.20**	**2.80**	**3.20**	**2.60**	**[2.30]**
Property transaction - purchase and sale	..	1.70	[0.80]	..	[1.80]	..
Property transaction - sale only	..	..	[1.00]	..	..	..
Property transaction - purchase only	..	[0.50]	0.60	..	..	..
Property transaction - other payments	..	0.70	0.40	[0.60]	..	..
Maintenance and repair of dwelling	**14.70**	**11.10**	**9.50**	**5.20**	**13.30**	**12.30**
Central heating repairs	3.20	2.50	1.40	0.40	1.60	0.60
House maintenance etc.	9.20	6.70	6.30	3.30	5.70	4.20
Paint, wallpaper, timber	[1.20]	1.40	1.20	1.10	3.30	2.50
Equipment hire, small materials	[1.10]	0.50	0.60	0.40	[2.70]	5.00
Alterations and improvements to dwelling	**61.10**	**57.80**	**37.60**	**32.80**	**16.50**	**32.50**
Central heating installation	..	2.00	1.70	[1.10]	..	..
DIY improvements: double glazing, kitchen units, sheds etc.	..	..	3.10	[0.90]	..	..
Home improvements - contracted out	54.30	53.70	32.20	30.70	14.10	29.10
Bathroom fittings	..	..	[0.30]	..	..	..
Purchase of materials for capital improvements	..	..	..	:	..	..
Household insurances	**7.90**	**6.20**	**5.50**	**4.90**	**4.60**	**4.30**
Structure	3.90	3.00	2.50	2.20	2.30	2.00
Contents	3.60	2.90	2.30	2.20	2.00	1.90
Household appliances[2]	0.40	0.40	0.60	0.50	0.30	0.40
Housing expenditure	**321.80**	**296.40**	**235.40**	**184.40**	**187.20**	**195.10**
Total expenditure[3]	**1,694.30**	**1,430.90**	**1,096.80**	**827.80**	**778.70**	**837.80**

Table 2.6

Housing expenditure by socio-economic classification of household reference person

UK, financial year ending 2020

	Semi-routine	Routine	Long-term term unemployed[1]	Students	Occupation not stated[2] and not classifiable	All groups
Weighted number of households (thousands)	2,060	1,850	440	380	8,110	27,820
Total number of households in sample	410	360	90	70	1,700	5,440
Total number of persons in sample	1,060	900	190	180	2,850	12,670
Total number of adults in sample	740	650	120	140	2,750	9,880
Weighted average number of persons per household	2.7	2.5	2.3	2.7	1.7	2.4

Commodity or service	Average weekly household expenditure (£)					
Primary dwelling						
Rent	**78.70**	**72.90**	**108.40**	**193.10**	**33.10**	**52.50**
Gross rent	78.70	72.90	108.40	193.10	33.10	52.50
less housing benefit, rebates and						
allowances received	13.50	20.10	68.10	[9.60]	21.90	12.40
Net rent[1]	65.20	52.80	40.30	183.50	11.20	40.10
Mortgage	**25.30**	**32.20**	..	**[25.40]**	**2.90**	**51.50**
Mortgage interest payments	10.40	11.80	..	[11.50]	1.70	22.30
Mortgage protection premiums	0.80	1.00	:	..	..	1.00
Capital repayment of mortgage	14.20	19.50	..	[13.50]	1.10	28.20
Outright purchase, including deposits	:	:	:	:	..	**[0.80]**
Secondary dwelling	..	..	:	..	**[0.70]**	**4.50**
Rent	:	:	:	:	:	..
Council tax, mortgage, insurance						
(secondary dwelling)	..	..	:	..	..	1.10
Purchase of second dwelling	..	..	:	:	[0.40]	3.40
Charges	**29.80**	**31.50**	**15.60**	**21.00**	**34.80**	**36.40**
Council tax, domestic rates	21.60	21.70	9.10	11.60	23.80	26.00
Water charges	7.80	7.80	6.50	6.80	7.60	8.20
Other regular housing payments including						
service charge for rent	0.50	1.90	..	[2.70]	3.30	2.10
Refuse collection, including skip hire	:	..	:	:	[0.10]	0.10
Moving house	..	**[1.70]**	:	..	**1.10**	**2.00**
Property transaction - purchase and sale	..	..	:	..	[0.70]	0.90
Property transaction - sale only	..	..	:	:	..	0.40
Property transaction - purchase only	..	..	:	:	..	0.40
Property transaction - other payments	..	..	:	..	..	0.20
Maintenance and repair of dwelling	**3.00**	**3.50**	**[0.80]**	**[5.20]**	**6.20**	**8.00**
Central heating repairs	0.50	0.50	..	..	1.00	1.20
House maintenance etc.	1.10	1.10	..	..	4.40	4.70
Paint, wallpaper, timber	1.00	1.40	..	:	0.50	1.20
Equipment hire, small materials	0.50	0.50	..	..	0.30	0.80
Alterations and improvements to dwelling	**8.80**	**12.00**	..	..	**17.90**	**28.10**
Central heating installation	..	..	..	..	1.30	1.40
DIY improvements: double glazing,						
kitchen units, sheds etc.	..	..	:	..	1.70	1.40
Home improvements - contracted out	7.70	7.40	..	..	14.50	24.50
Bathroom fittings	..	..	:	..	0.20	0.40
Purchase of materials for capital improvements	..	..	:	:	..	0.40
Household insurances	**3.00**	**2.90**	**[1.10]**	**1.90**	**5.10**	**4.90**
Structure	1.20	1.30	[0.50]	[0.50]	2.30	2.30
Contents	1.30	1.30	[0.50]	1.10	2.10	2.10
Household appliances[2]	0.50	0.30	..	..	0.70	0.50
Housing expenditure	**137.00**	**158.10**	**61.00**	**251.40**	**80.00**	**176.40**
Total expenditure[3]	**645.00**	**657.40**	**267.50**	**834.30**	**473.10**	**842.50**

Note: Changes to categories of socio-economic classification were made from 2011.

Please see background notes for symbols and conventions used in this report.

1 The figure included in total expenditure is net rent as opposed to gross rent.

2 From FYE 2019, information about insurance for household appliances was collected in the questionnaire in addition to the diary. In previous years, this was based on diary data only.

3 This total includes all categories recorded in the LCF, including those outside the 'COICOP' total expenditure.

Source: Office for National Statistics

Table 2.7

Housing expenditure by household composition

UK, financial year ending 2020

Commodity or service	Retired households		Non-retired		Retired and non-retired households			
	One Person	Two adults	One Person	Two adults	One adult with children	Two adults with children	Three or more adults without children	with children
Weighted number of households (thousands)	3,540	3,240	4,370	6,220	1,160	5,690	2,520	1,080
Total number of households in sample	670	760	840	1,190	270	1,120	410	170
Total number of persons in sample	670	1,530	840	2,390	730	4,290	1,370	850
Total number of adults in sample	670	1,530	840	2,390	270	2,240	1,370	570
Weighted average number of persons per household	1.0	2.0	1.0	2.0	2.7	3.8	3.4	5.0

Commodity or service	Average weekly household expenditure (£)							
Primary dwelling								
Rent	**36.40**	**14.20**	**60.90**	**50.50**	**103.20**	**60.50**	**73.40**	**53.00**
Gross rent	36.40	14.20	60.90	50.50	103.20	60.50	73.40	53.00
less housing benefit, rebates &								
allowances received	24.10	7.90	18.30	4.20	38.70	7.50	8.50	[16.70]
Net rent[1]	12.20	6.20	42.60	46.30	64.50	53.00	64.90	36.40
Mortgage	**[1.70]**	**3.60**	**36.80**	**60.10**	**25.40**	**109.50**	**50.20**	**93.40**
Mortgage interest payments	[1.20]	1.90	16.00	25.50	10.90	48.50	18.30	42.30
Mortgage protection premiums	..	..	0.50	1.20	0.50	2.10	1.10	3.00
Capital repayment of mortgage	..	[1.50]	20.30	33.30	14.00	58.90	30.80	48.20
Outright purchase, including deposits	:	:	..	..	:	..	:	:
Secondary dwelling	..	**[0.90]**	**[2.20]**	**3.60**	..	**12.90**	**[4.20]**	..
Rent	:	:	:	:	:	:	..	:
Council tax, mortgage, insurance								
(secondary dwelling)	..	..	..	[1.20]	..	[2.40]	..	:
Purchase of second dwelling	..	..	[1.40]	[2.40]	..	10.40	..	..
Charges	**29.80**	**42.40**	**26.50**	**40.10**	**22.60**	**40.30**	**42.70**	**40.10**
Council tax, domestic rates	19.00	31.70	17.50	29.10	15.30	30.00	30.70	29.20
Water charges	6.00	9.10	6.00	8.30	7.10	9.40	10.30	10.50
Other regular housing payments								
including service charge for rent	4.70	1.60	3.00	2.50	[0.20]	0.80	1.80	..
Refuse collection, including skip hire	..	..	..	..	:	..	..	..
Moving house	..	**[1.60]**	**1.80**	**3.10**	..	**2.80**	**[1.40]**	..
Property transaction - purchase and sale	..	..	[0.60]	1.10	..	1.90	..	:
Property transaction - sale only	:	..	..	[0.70]	..	..	..	:
Property transaction - purchase only	:	..	[0.50]	0.80	..	[0.30]	..	..
Property transaction - other payments	..	..	[0.20]	0.50	..	0.30	..	..
Maintenance and repair of dwelling	**4.10**	**8.20**	**5.30**	**10.70**	**1.50**	**9.10**	**10.70**	**9.60**
Central heating repairs	0.60	1.40	1.10	1.70	[0.20]	0.80	2.70	[0.50]
House maintenance etc.	3.10	5.70	3.00	5.80	[0.70]	5.90	5.80	[2.10]
Paint, wallpaper, timber	[0.30]	0.60	1.00	1.90	[0.50]	1.40	1.60	[1.70]
Equipment hire, small materials	..	0.40	0.20	1.30	..	1.00	0.60	5.30
Alterations and improvements to dwelling	**7.60**	**32.60**	**12.10**	**30.30**	**6.50**	**50.30**	**32.20**	**32.00**
Central heating installation	[1.30]	1.50	1.50	1.60	..	1.70	..	..
DIY improvements: double glazing,								
kitchen units, sheds etc.	..	[3.70]	..	0.80	..	1.10	..	..
Home improvements - contracted out	6.10	26.50	10.00	27.20	[5.70]	45.70	25.30	28.20
Bathroom fittings	..	..	..	0.20	..	1.10	[0.30]	..
Purchase of materials for								
capital improvements	:	..	..	..	..	..	..	..
Household insurances	**4.90**	**5.80**	**3.10**	**5.50**	**2.00**	**5.20**	**5.90**	**5.60**
Structure	2.10	2.80	1.40	2.50	0.80	2.50	2.70	2.70
Contents	1.90	2.50	1.50	2.40	1.00	2.30	2.40	2.10
Household appliances[2]	1.00	0.40	0.10	0.70	0.20	0.30	0.80	0.80
Housing expenditure	**61.20**	**101.30**	**130.70**	**202.70**	**125.30**	**283.40**	**212.10**	**221.50**
Total expenditure[3]	**308.90**	**633.10**	**517.30**	**976.50**	**474.50**	**1,198.20**	**1,283.10**	**1,260.10**

Please see background notes for symbols and conventions used in this report.

1 The figure included in total expenditure is net rent as opposed to gross rent.

2 From FYE 2019, information about insurance for household appliances was collected in the questionnaire in addition to the diary. In previous years, this was based on diary data only.

3 This total includes all categories recorded in the LCF, including those outside the 'COICOP' total expenditure.

Source: Office for National Statistics

Table 2.8

Expenditure on rent[1] by renters

UK, financial year ending 2018 to financial year ending 2020

	2017-18 $£^2$	2017-18 % of total expenditure	2018-19 $£^2$	2018-19 % of total expenditure	2019-20 $£^2$	2019-20 % of total expenditure
Weighted number of households (thousands)	9,100		9,200		9,360	
Total number of households in sample	1,710		1,740		1,740	
Total number of persons in sample	4,030		4,060		4,030	
Total number of adults in sample	2,900		2,910		2,900	
Weighted average number of persons per household	2.4		2.4		2.4	
Total expenditure for renters	**601.40**		**581.10**		**610.10**	
Rent	**149.60**	**24.9**	**149.80**	**25.8**	**156.00**	**25.6**
Gross rent	149.60	24.9	149.80	25.8	156.00	25.6
less housing benefit, rebates and						
allowances received	41.80	6.9	38.50	6.6	36.80	6.0
Net rent[3]	107.80	17.9	111.40	19.2	119.20	19.5

Please see background notes for symbols and conventions used in this report.

1 Primary dwelling.

2 Average weekly household expenditure (£).

3 The figure included in total expenditure is net rent as opposed to gross rent.

Source: Office for National Statistics

Table 2.9

Expenditure on mortgages[1] by mortgage holders

UK, financial year ending 2018 to financial year ending 2020

	2017-18 $£^2$	2017-18 % of total expenditure	2018-19 $£^2$	2018-19 % of total expenditure	2019-20 $£^2$	2019-20 % of total expenditure
Weighted number of households (thousands)	8,260		8,340		8,360	
Total number of households in sample	1,640		1,660		1,600	
Total number of persons in sample	4,760		4,740		4,620	
Total number of adults in sample	3,330		3,330		3,220	
Weighted average number of persons per household	2.9		2.9		2.9	
Total expenditure for mortgage payers	**1,224.70**		**1,232.10**		**1,271.40**	
Mortgage	**156.50**	**12.8**	**162.10**	**13.2**	**169.20**	**13.3**
Mortgage interest payments	68.00	5.6	68.10	5.5	73.10	5.8
Mortgage protection premiums	3.30	0.3	3.50	0.3	3.40	0.3
Capital repayment of mortgage	85.20	7.0	90.50	7.3	92.60	7.3

Please see background notes for symbols and conventions used in this report.

1 Primary dwelling.

2 Average weekly household expenditure (£).

Source: Office for National Statistics

Table 2.10

Expenditure on rent and mortgages[1] by renters and mortgage holders

by gross income decile group

UK, financial year ending 2020

| | Gross income decile group | | | | | | | | | | |
	1	2	3	4	5	6	7	8	9	10	All
Weighted number of households (thousands)	1,620	1,330	1,270	1,030	950	940	730	590	510	400	9,360
Total number of households in sample	330	270	250	190	180	170	130	100	80	60	1,740
Total number of persons in sample	430	470	530	510	490	490	390	300	240	190	4,030
Total number of adults in sample	360	350	370	330	320	330	280	220	200	140	2,900
Weighted average number of persons per hous	1.3	1.8	2.1	2.6	2.6	2.8	3.0	3.1	3.0	3.6	2.4

Commodity or service	Average weekly household expenditure (£)										
Rent for renters	**128.00**	**120.60**	**128.60**	**134.40**	**134.00**	**152.20**	**172.90**	**206.60**	**250.60**	**365.30**	**156.00**
Gross rent	128.00	120.60	128.60	134.40	134.00	152.20	172.90	206.60	250.60	365.30	156.00
less housing benefit, rebates and											
allowances received	81.20	66.70	42.00	31.10	15.60	5.40	13.30	[3.20]	..	..	36.80
Net rent[2]	46.80	54.00	86.60	103.30	118.40	146.80	159.60	203.30	235.50	364.40	119.20

| | Gross income decile group | | | | | | | | | | |
	1	2	3	4	5	6	7	8	9	10	All
Weighted number of households (thousands)	130	180	290	340	640	860	1,180	1,430	1,570	1,740	8,360
Total number of households in sample	30	30	60	70	130	180	220	280	300	300	1,600
Total number of persons in sample	50	60	130	150	320	460	640	840	940	1,050	4,620
Total number of adults in sample	30	40	90	110	220	320	430	580	660	720	3,220
Weighted average number of persons per hous	1.8	2.0	2.0	2.0	2.5	2.6	3.0	2.9	3.2	3.5	2.9

Commodity or service	Average weekly household expenditure (£)										
Mortgage for mortgage holders	**126.30**	**91.70**	**95.10**	**102.20**	**113.80**	**131.10**	**142.50**	**158.50**	**185.90**	**257.00**	**169.20**
Mortgage interest payments	78.20	43.00	40.60	38.70	48.70	52.40	60.90	69.50	80.90	111.60	73.10
Mortgage protection premiums	..	..	2.40	2.00	2.50	3.20	3.40	2.50	3.70	5.00	3.40
Capital repayment of mortgage	[48.00]	47.10	52.10	61.40	62.50	75.40	78.20	86.50	101.20	140.40	92.60

Please see background notes for symbols and conventions used in this report.

1 Primary dwelling.

2 The figure included in total expenditure is net rent as opposed to gross rent.

Source: Office for National Statistics

Table 2.11

Expenditure on rent and mortgages[1] by renters and mortgage holders, by countries and regions

UK, financial year ending 2020

	United Kingdom	England	North East	North West	Yorks & the Humber	East Midlands	West Midlands	East	London	South East	South West	Wales	Scotland	Northern Ireland
	K02000001	E92000001	E12000001	E12000002	E12000003	E12000004	E12000005	E12000006	E12000007	E12000008	E12000009	W92000004	S92000003	N92000002
Weighted number of households (thousands)	9,360	7,770	450	1,060	710	660	800	770	1,550	1,080	690	410	910	280
Total number of households in sample	1,740	1,260	90	180	130	120	130	130	180	170	140	70	280	130
Total number of persons in sample	4,030	3,010	200	380	280	320	290	300	500	400	350	170	590	270
Total number of adults in sample	2,900	2,140	150	280	200	210	210	220	350	290	240	120	450	190
Weighted average number of persons per household	2.4	2.4	2.1	2.1	2.1	2.4	2.3	2.3	2.9	2.5	2.4	2.0	2.1	2.2
Commodity or service						*Average weekly household expenditure (£)*								
Rent by renters	**156.00**	**164.50**	**110.30**	**120.10**	**115.00**	**110.60**	**136.00**	**171.50**	**263.40**	**182.90**	**144.20**	**125.10**	**115.70**	**96.50**
Gross rent	156.00	164.50	110.30	120.10	115.00	110.60	136.00	171.50	263.40	182.90	144.20	125.10	115.70	96.50
less housing benefit, rebates and allowances received	36.80	36.90	37.20	33.10	32.30	22.70	26.10	32.70	58.10	35.50	32.30	43.50	32.90	36.70
Net rent[2]	119.20	127.60	73.20	87.10	82.70	88.00	109.90	138.80	205.30	147.40	111.80	81.50	82.80	59.80
Weighted number of households (thousands)	8,360	7,100	300	1,000	780	630	690	810	910	1,240	760	440	610	210
Total number of households in sample	1,600	1,230	60	180	140	130	120	140	110	200	150	70	200	90
Total number of persons in sample	4,620	3,590	170	530	420	370	330	420	320	610	420	210	540	290
Total number of adults in sample	3,220	2,520	120	370	300	270	240	300	220	410	300	140	370	180
Weighted average number of persons per household	2.9	2.9	2.7	2.9	3.0	2.8	2.8	3.0	3.1	3.0	2.7	2.8	2.7	3.1
Commodity or service						*Average weekly household expenditure (£)*								
Mortgage by mortgage holders	**169.20**	**174.80**	**113.50**	**146.40**	**133.80**	**147.50**	**163.30**	**197.70**	**227.60**	**214.10**	**159.20**	**144.40**	**137.40**	**123.20**
Mortgage interest payments	73.10	76.20	45.90	60.10	51.30	62.40	68.30	89.20	109.80	96.20	67.00	57.10	58.30	45.10
Mortgage protection premiums	3.40	3.40	[2.30]	3.00	2.60	3.80	3.80	2.80	3.60	4.10	3.40	2.80	3.20	5.60
Capital repayment of mortgage	92.60	95.20	65.30	83.30	80.00	81.30	91.20	105.70	114.30	113.80	88.80	84.50	75.80	72.50

Please see background notes for symbols and conventions used in this report.

1 Primary dwelling.

2 The figure included in total expenditure is net rent as opposed to gross rent.

Source: Office for National Statistics

25

Equivalised income tables

Table 3.1

Detailed household expenditure by disposable income decile group

UK, financial year ending 2020

		Lowest ten per cent	Second decile group	Third decile group	Fourth decile group	Fifth decile group	Sixth decile group	Seventh decile group	Eighth decile group	Ninth decile group	Highest ten per cent	All house- holds
Lower boundary of group (£ per week)			224	321	413	510	624	750	892	1064	1386	
Weighted number of households (thousands)		2,780	2,780	2,780	2,790	2,780	2,780	2,780	2,780	2,790	2,780	27,820
Total number of households in sample		560	550	570	560	570	550	540	530	520	480	5,440
Total number of persons in sample		720	860	1,020	1,180	1,350	1,400	1,490	1,540	1,520	1,600	12,670
Total number of adults in sample		630	710	840	960	1,030	1,070	1,110	1,170	1,190	1,190	9,880
Weighted average number of persons per household		1.3	1.6	1.8	2.1	2.4	2.5	2.8	2.9	3.0	3.4	2.4
Commodity or service		Average weekly household expenditure (£)										
1	**Food & non-alcoholic drinks**	**35.00**	**40.40**	**47.00**	**54.40**	**60.20**	**64.60**	**72.60**	**79.00**	**83.10**	**100.80**	**63.70**
1.1	Food	32.10	37.00	43.00	50.00	55.20	59.10	66.50	72.10	76.20	92.50	58.40
1.1.1	Bread, rice and cereals	3.20	3.60	4.20	4.80	5.70	6.00	6.90	7.30	7.70	9.20	5.80
1.1.2	Pasta products	0.20	0.30	0.30	0.30	0.40	0.50	0.50	0.60	0.70	0.80	0.50
1.1.3	Buns, cakes, biscuits etc.	2.40	2.80	3.20	3.70	4.00	4.20	4.60	5.00	5.10	6.20	4.10
1.1.4	Pastry (savoury)	0.40	0.50	0.60	0.70	0.90	1.10	1.10	1.30	1.40	1.60	1.00
1.1.5	Beef (fresh, chilled or frozen)	1.10	1.20	1.20	1.70	1.90	2.10	2.10	2.20	2.20	3.10	1.90
1.1.6	Pork (fresh, chilled or frozen)	0.30	0.40	0.30	0.70	0.40	0.60	0.60	0.70	0.80	0.70	0.50
1.1.7	Lamb (fresh, chilled or frozen)	0.20	0.40	0.40	0.50	0.70	0.60	1.10	1.00	0.90	1.10	0.70
1.1.8	Poultry (fresh, chilled or frozen)	1.00	1.40	1.60	2.10	2.00	2.30	3.00	3.40	3.50	4.10	2.40
1.1.9	Bacon and ham	0.50	0.70	0.60	0.80	0.70	0.90	0.90	0.90	1.00	1.30	0.80
1.1.10	Other meat and meat preparations	4.30	4.60	5.40	6.00	6.00	6.90	7.20	7.90	8.30	9.50	6.60
1.1.11	Fish and fish products	1.60	1.90	2.30	2.50	3.20	3.00	3.30	4.20	4.20	5.40	3.20
1.1.12	Milk	1.40	1.70	1.90	2.00	2.20	2.30	2.30	2.50	2.40	2.60	2.10
1.1.13	Cheese and curd	1.10	1.30	1.60	1.70	2.00	2.20	2.60	3.00	3.20	3.50	2.20
1.1.14	Eggs	0.40	0.50	0.60	0.70	0.70	0.70	0.90	0.90	1.00	1.30	0.80
1.1.15	Other milk products	1.40	1.50	1.80	1.90	2.40	2.40	2.60	2.80	3.00	3.60	2.30
1.1.16	Butter	0.30	0.30	0.30	0.40	0.40	0.40	0.60	0.50	0.70	0.80	0.50
1.1.17	Margarine, other vegetable fats and peanut butter	0.40	0.50	0.60	0.60	0.60	0.60	0.70	0.70	0.80	0.70	0.60
1.1.18	Cooking oils and fats	0.20	0.20	0.30	0.30	0.30	0.40	0.50	0.60	0.50	0.60	0.40
1.1.19	Fresh fruit	2.30	2.50	2.90	3.50	3.60	4.10	4.50	4.70	4.90	7.10	4.00
1.1.20	Other fresh, chilled or frozen fruits	0.20	0.20	0.40	0.40	0.40	0.40	0.50	0.60	0.60	0.90	0.50
1.1.21	Dried fruit and nuts	0.40	0.40	0.60	0.80	1.00	0.70	1.50	1.00	1.10	1.60	0.90
1.1.22	Preserved fruit and fruit based products	0.10	0.10	0.10	0.20	0.20	0.20	0.20	0.20	0.20	0.20	0.20
1.1.23	Fresh vegetables	2.20	2.60	3.10	3.60	4.00	4.20	5.30	5.60	6.30	7.80	4.50
1.1.24	Dried vegetables	[0.00]	[0.00]	0.00~	[0.00]	0.10	0.00~	0.10	0.10	0.10	0.10	0.10
1.1.25	Other preserved or processed vegetables	0.80	1.10	1.30	1.40	2.00	2.00	2.10	2.20	3.00	3.60	2.00
1.1.26	Potatoes	0.40	0.50	0.60	0.70	0.70	0.70	0.80	0.90	0.80	0.90	0.70
1.1.27	Other tubers and products of tuber vegetables	1.00	1.30	1.50	1.60	1.80	2.10	1.80	2.30	2.20	2.40	1.80
1.1.28	Sugar and sugar products	0.20	0.20	0.30	0.30	0.40	0.40	0.50	0.50	0.50	0.60	0.40
1.1.29	Jams, marmalades	0.20	0.20	0.20	0.30	0.40	0.30	0.40	0.30	0.40	0.50	0.30
1.1.30	Chocolate	1.20	1.40	1.70	1.80	2.30	2.30	2.40	3.10	3.30	3.90	2.30
1.1.31	Confectionery products	0.40	0.50	0.70	0.80	0.70	0.90	1.10	1.00	1.00	1.00	0.80
1.1.32	Edible ices and ice cream	0.40	0.50	0.60	0.70	0.70	0.70	0.90	0.80	0.90	1.30	0.70
1.1.33	Other food products	1.50	1.90	1.90	2.40	2.50	3.00	2.80	3.30	3.70	4.60	2.80
1.2	Non-alcoholic drinks	2.90	3.40	3.90	4.50	5.00	5.50	6.10	6.80	6.80	8.20	5.30
1.2.1	Coffee	0.70	0.60	0.80	0.90	1.00	1.30	1.20	1.10	1.50	1.70	1.10
1.2.2	Tea	0.40	0.30	0.50	0.50	0.50	0.40	0.50	0.50	0.60	0.70	0.50
1.2.3	Cocoa and powdered chocolate	0.10	0.10	0.10	0.10	0.10	0.10	0.10	0.10	0.20	0.20	0.10
1.2.4	Fruit and vegetable juices (inc. fruit squash)	0.50	0.70	0.70	0.80	1.00	1.00	1.20	1.40	1.40	1.80	1.10
1.2.5	Mineral or spring waters	0.20	0.20	0.20	0.30	0.40	0.40	0.50	0.50	0.40	0.50	0.40
1.2.6	Soft drinks (inc. fizzy and ready to drink fruit drinks)	1.20	1.50	1.60	1.90	2.10	2.30	2.60	3.20	2.70	3.30	2.20

Note: The commodity and service categories are not comparable to those in publications before 2001-02.

The numbering system is sequential, it does not use actual COICOP codes.

Please see background notes for symbols and conventions used in this report.

Table 3.1
Detailed household expenditure by disposable income decile group (cont.)
UK, financial year ending 2020

Commodity or service	Lowest ten per cent	Second decile group	Third decile group	Fourth decile group	Fifth decile group	Sixth decile group	Seventh decile group	Eighth decile group	Ninth decile group	Highest ten per cent	All house-holds
					Average weekly household expenditure (£)						
2 Alcoholic drink, tobacco & narcotics	**8.80**	**8.70**	**8.80**	**9.80**	**12.40**	**13.70**	**13.10**	**15.30**	**18.60**	**20.10**	**12.90**
2.1 Alcoholic drinks	4.80	4.90	6.10	6.80	8.30	8.70	9.70	11.90	14.40	17.30	9.30
2.1.1 Spirits and liqueurs (brought home)	1.20	1.50	1.60	2.00	2.40	2.50	2.30	2.70	3.30	3.20	2.30
2.1.2 Wines, fortified wines (brought home)	2.10	2.20	3.00	3.10	4.10	3.80	4.90	5.40	7.20	10.00	4.60
2.1.3 Beer, lager, ciders and perry (brought home)	1.60	1.30	1.50	1.80	1.80	2.40	2.50	3.70	3.90	4.10	2.50
2.1.4 Alcopops (brought home)	..	..	..	..	..	..	..	..	[0.10]	..	0.00~
2.2 Tobacco and narcotics	4.00	3.80	2.70	3.00	4.10	5.00	3.40	3.50	4.20	2.80	3.60
2.2.1 Cigarettes	3.10	2.80	1.90	2.10	2.60	3.70	2.40	2.10	3.50	1.80	2.60
2.2.2 Cigars, other tobacco products and narcotics	0.90	1.00	0.90	0.90	1.50	1.30	1.00	1.30	0.70	1.00	1.10
3 Clothing & footwear	**8.70**	**9.10**	**12.00**	**15.50**	**18.10**	**22.40**	**29.10**	**31.50**	**36.60**	**50.80**	**23.40**
3.1 Clothing	7.00	7.50	9.80	12.30	14.50	17.50	23.90	26.10	28.60	39.40	18.70
3.1.1 Men's outer garments	1.30	1.60	2.90	1.70	2.90	4.70	6.10	7.20	7.20	10.50	4.60
3.1.2 Men's under garments	0.30	0.20	0.40	0.50	0.60	0.50	0.60	0.50	0.80	1.10	0.60
3.1.3 Women's outer garments	3.10	3.50	3.50	6.20	5.90	7.60	9.90	11.40	12.90	16.10	8.00
3.1.4 Women's under garments	0.90	0.50	0.70	1.10	1.10	0.90	1.30	1.30	1.90	2.50	1.20
3.1.5 Boys' outer garments (5-15)	[0.10]	[0.10]	0.50	0.60	0.80	0.50	1.30	0.90	0.90	2.20	0.80
3.1.6 Girls' outer garments (5-15)	[0.20]	0.50	0.60	0.70	1.00	0.70	1.30	1.40	1.50	2.00	1.00
3.1.7 Infants' outer garments (under 5)	[0.20]	0.30	0.40	0.40	0.60	0.80	0.80	0.90	0.70	1.80	0.70
3.1.8 Children's under garments (under 16)	0.10	0.20	0.30	0.30	0.40	0.40	0.50	0.70	0.60	0.70	0.40
3.1.9 Accessories	0.20	0.30	0.40	0.60	0.70	0.80	1.00	1.20	1.40	1.40	0.80
3.1.10 Haberdashery and clothing hire	0.30	0.10	0.10	0.10	0.30	0.40	0.70	0.30	0.40	0.30	0.30
3.1.11 Dry cleaners, laundry and dyeing	[0.20]	[0.10]	..	..	[0.20]	[0.20]	[0.20]	0.20	[0.40]	0.80	0.20
3.2 Footwear	1.80	1.60	2.20	3.20	3.60	4.90	5.10	5.40	8.00	11.40	4.70
4 Housing (net)[1], fuel & power	**58.60**	**60.00**	**74.20**	**74.80**	**85.10**	**86.40**	**88.60**	**94.20**	**87.00**	**121.00**	**83.00**
4.1 Actual rentals for housing	73.90	56.50	58.80	50.00	52.70	44.20	46.30	47.60	41.30	54.00	52.50
4.1.1 Gross rent	73.90	56.50	58.80	50.00	52.70	44.20	46.30	47.60	41.30	53.90	52.50
4.1.2 *less housing benefit, rebates & allowances rec'd*	46.10	29.70	19.00	13.40	6.20	2.00	2.50	2.60	..	..	12.40
4.1.3 Net rent[2]	27.80	26.80	39.70	36.60	46.50	42.20	43.80	45.00	39.30	53.80	40.10
4.1.4 Second dwelling rent	:	:	:	:	:	:	:	:	..	..	..
4.2 Maintenance and repair of dwelling	2.60	3.20	4.80	5.00	5.70	9.70	9.40	9.90	10.40	19.00	8.00
4.3 Water supply and miscellaneous services relating to the dwelling	9.10	8.80	8.40	9.20	9.50	10.80	10.50	11.20	10.60	15.80	10.40
4.4 Electricity, gas and other fuels	19.10	21.10	21.20	24.00	23.40	23.80	24.80	28.10	26.80	32.30	24.50
4.4.1 Electricity	10.20	11.00	11.00	12.50	11.90	12.00	12.80	13.40	14.10	15.90	12.50
4.4.2 Gas	7.90	9.00	9.20	9.90	10.30	10.80	10.60	12.10	11.20	13.80	10.50
4.4.3 Other fuels	1.00	1.10	1.10	1.60	1.20	1.00	1.50	2.60	1.50	2.60	1.50

Note: The commodity and service categories are not comparable to those in publications before 2001-02.

The numbering system is sequential, it does not use actual COICOP codes.

Please see background notes for symbols and conventions used in this report.

1 Excluding mortgage interest payments, council tax and Northern Ireland rates.

2 The figure included in total expenditure is net rent as opposed to gross rent.

Table 3.1
Detailed household expenditure by disposable income decile group (cont.)
UK, financial year ending 2020

Commodity or service	Lowest ten per cent	Second decile group	Third decile group	Fourth decile group	Fifth decile group	Sixth decile group	Seventh decile group	Eighth decile group	Ninth decile group	Highest ten per cent	All house-holds
	Average weekly household expenditure (£)										
5 Household goods & services	**13.30**	**18.90**	**21.50**	**29.70**	**30.90**	**34.10**	**36.20**	**48.50**	**55.70**	**76.60**	**36.50**
5.1 Furniture and furnishings, carpets and other floor coverings	6.50	8.70	11.80	16.30	16.10	17.00	19.60	27.20	32.50	45.40	20.10
5.1.1 Furniture and furnishings	4.90	6.90	9.50	12.50	13.20	14.70	16.20	22.90	28.00	37.20	16.60
5.1.2 Floor coverings	1.70	1.80	2.40	3.90	3.00	2.30	3.40	4.30	4.50	8.20	3.50
5.2 Household textiles	0.90	0.90	0.60	1.20	1.60	1.90	2.00	3.20	3.30	4.00	2.00
5.3 Household appliances	1.00	2.40	1.90	2.70	2.90	3.30	2.50	4.00	3.20	4.70	2.90
5.4 Glassware, tableware and household utensils	0.50	0.60	0.90	1.50	1.50	1.90	2.20	2.50	2.60	4.20	1.80
5.5 Tools and equipment for house and garden	0.50	1.80	1.70	2.20	3.00	3.50	3.60	4.40	4.80	4.20	3.00
5.6 Goods and services for routine household maintenance	3.90	4.40	4.60	5.70	5.80	6.50	6.40	7.20	9.20	14.20	6.80
5.6.1 Cleaning materials	1.50	1.70	2.30	2.40	2.60	3.00	2.70	3.00	3.50	4.10	2.70
5.6.2 Household goods and hardware	0.90	1.10	1.40	1.50	1.80	2.00	2.20	2.20	2.60	2.90	1.90
5.6.3 Domestic services, carpet cleaning, hire/repair of furniture/furnishings	1.40	1.60	0.90	1.70	1.40	1.50	1.50	2.00	3.20	7.20	2.20
6 Health	**4.30**	**5.30**	**5.00**	**5.90**	**7.30**	**8.10**	**8.80**	**9.00**	**12.50**	**15.80**	**8.20**
6.1 Medical products, appliances and equipment	2.30	3.40	2.90	2.60	4.80	3.80	5.50	5.40	7.80	6.40	4.50
6.1.1 Medicines, prescriptions, healthcare products etc.	1.30	2.20	1.70	1.90	2.70	2.40	2.80	2.80	4.80	3.80	2.60
6.1.2 Spectacles, lenses, accessories and repairs	1.00	1.20	1.20	0.70	2.10	1.40	2.70	2.50	3.00	2.60	1.80
6.2 Hospital services	2.00	1.90	2.20	3.30	2.60	4.40	3.30	3.60	4.70	9.30	3.70
7 Transport	**22.80**	**27.10**	**42.50**	**52.50**	**63.50**	**91.30**	**91.50**	**106.20**	**137.60**	**181.40**	**81.60**
7.1 Purchase of vehicles	6.20	7.60	12.40	14.10	18.10	33.90	29.00	33.70	46.40	61.40	26.30
7.1.1 Purchase of new cars and vans	..	[3.10]	[3.10]	4.70	5.70	9.70	6.20	10.50	14.30	20.60	7.90
7.1.2 Purchase of second hand cars or vans	5.30	4.50	8.40	9.30	11.70	19.30	21.50	22.30	30.00	39.80	17.20
7.1.3 Purchase of motorcycles and other vehicles	:	..	..	..	[0.70]	..	[1.30]	..	[2.00]	[1.00]	1.20
7.2 Operation of personal transport	10.70	13.20	20.40	26.30	31.00	36.50	40.30	46.10	51.50	60.20	33.60
7.2.1 Spares and accessories	[1.70]	0.60	1.80	3.20	1.90	2.60	2.20	2.80	2.40	4.90	2.40
7.2.2 Petrol, diesel and other motor oils	6.70	9.10	12.90	16.70	19.50	25.30	26.00	33.00	35.30	38.10	22.30
7.2.3 Repairs and servicing	1.70	2.60	4.20	4.60	6.60	6.10	8.10	7.50	9.00	11.80	6.20
7.2.4 Other motoring costs	0.80	0.90	1.50	1.80	3.00	2.50	4.10	2.80	4.80	5.40	2.80
7.3 Transport services	5.90	6.40	9.80	12.10	14.40	20.80	22.20	26.30	39.70	59.90	21.70
7.3.1 Rail and tube fares	1.00	0.80	1.20	1.90	2.50	3.90	5.00	5.10	10.40	14.60	4.60
7.3.2 Bus and coach fares	1.00	0.80	1.30	1.50	1.60	2.10	1.50	1.40	1.80	2.40	1.50
7.3.3 Combined fares	..	..	..	..	[0.40]	..	..	[1.40]	..	1.70	0.60
7.3.4 Other travel and transport	3.70	4.60	6.80	8.50	9.80	14.60	15.20	18.40	27.00	41.20	15.00
8 Communication	**10.40**	**14.10**	**15.80**	**19.20**	**20.10**	**23.20**	**22.90**	**26.00**	**27.90**	**33.90**	**21.40**
8.1 Postal services	0.50	0.50	0.60	0.50	0.70	0.70	0.60	0.60	0.80	1.20	0.70
8.2 Telephone and telefax equipment	[0.20]	[0.50]	[0.60]	[1.70]	0.80	[1.40]	0.90	1.20	3.10	4.70	1.50
8.3 Telephone and telefax services[3]	3.80	4.60	5.50	6.30	7.30	9.60	9.80	11.40	11.40	13.90	8.40
8.4 Internet subscription fees (ex. combined packages)	0.40	0.60	0.60	0.60	0.80	0.70	0.80	1.00	0.80	0.70	0.70
8.5 Combined telecom services[4]	5.50	7.90	8.60	10.00	10.50	10.90	10.80	11.90	11.90	13.30	10.10

Note: The commodity and service categories are not comparable to those in publications before 2001-02.

The numbering system is sequential, it does not use actual COICOP codes.

Please see background notes for symbols and conventions used in this report.

3 For FYE 2019 onwards, excludes payments made as part of a combined bill.

4 New for FYE 2019. This encompasses all telecoms bills that include more than one service. Due to the nature of combined packages, this also includes packages that includes television services.

Table 3.1

Detailed household expenditure by disposable income decile group (cont.)

UK, financial year ending 2020

Commodity or service	Lowest ten per cent	Second decile group	Third decile group	Fourth decile group	Fifth decile group	Sixth decile group	Seventh decile group	Eighth decile group	Ninth decile group	Highest ten per cent	All house-holds
	Average weekly household expenditure (£)										
9 Recreation & culture	**31.00**	**33.70**	**42.60**	**52.70**	**57.40**	**68.60**	**82.30**	**94.80**	**126.70**	**158.00**	**74.80**
9.1 Audio-visual, photographic and information processing equipment	1.40	1.60	3.30	4.60	2.70	5.60	4.60	6.30	7.70	7.00	4.50
9.1.1 Audio equipment and accessories, CD players	0.50	0.40	0.50	1.40	0.60	1.20	1.20	0.60	2.10	2.50	1.10
9.1.2 TV, video and computers	0.90	1.10	2.70	3.20	1.60	4.20	2.60	5.70	3.10	3.90	2.90
9.1.3 Photographic, cine and optical equipment	..	..	..	..	..	..	..	..	..	[0.60]	0.50
9.2 Other major durables for recreation and culture	..	..	[1.90]	..	[2.50]	[2.50]	[2.00]	[2.50]	3.00	3.10	2.00
9.3 Other recreational items and equipment, gardens and pets	6.50	8.30	9.00	11.50	11.50	13.40	16.10	24.30	21.50	33.50	15.50
9.3.1 Games, toys and hobbies	0.80	1.40	1.70	1.90	3.20	4.20	3.40	4.90	4.70	5.80	3.20
9.3.2 Computer software and games	..	[1.00]	[0.30]	0.80	1.10	0.50	1.50	0.70	2.10	1.40	1.00
9.3.3 Equipment for sport, camping and open-air recreation	[0.60]	[0.30]	[0.90]	0.30	1.20	0.80	1.40	2.30	1.80	7.40	1.70
9.3.4 Horticultural goods, garden equipment and plants	1.30	1.70	1.90	2.90	2.20	3.00	2.90	3.90	3.40	4.70	2.80
9.3.5 Pets and pet food	3.10	3.90	4.20	5.60	3.80	5.00	6.90	12.40	9.50	14.10	6.80
9.4 Recreational and cultural services	9.20	9.00	10.60	13.70	15.00	17.70	20.10	25.20	34.10	43.30	19.80
9.4.1 Sports admissions, subscriptions, leisure class fees and equipment hire	1.80	2.30	3.20	4.80	6.00	5.50	6.70	10.20	16.90	20.80	7.80
9.4.2 Cinema, theatre and museums etc.	1.80	1.30	0.80	1.60	1.70	3.00	4.40	4.20	5.50	9.00	3.30
9.4.3 TV, video, satellite rental, cable subscriptions and TV licences[5]	2.90	3.10	3.30	3.90	4.40	4.90	5.10	5.60	6.10	7.30	4.70
9.4.4 Miscellaneous entertainments	0.50	0.40	0.50	0.60	0.80	1.50	2.00	2.40	2.40	3.30	1.40
9.4.5 Development of film, deposit for film development, passport photos, holiday and school photos	..	..	..	..	[0.20]	[0.20]	[0.20]	[0.20]	0.20	0.30	0.20
9.4.6 Gambling payments	2.20	1.80	2.80	2.60	2.00	2.50	1.80	2.70	3.00	2.60	2.40
9.5 Newspapers, books and stationery	3.10	3.20	3.90	4.60	4.60	5.90	5.60	5.40	7.10	11.50	5.50
9.5.1 Books	0.80	0.40	0.50	1.10	0.80	1.20	1.30	1.40	2.20	2.60	1.20
9.5.2 Diaries, address books, cards etc.	0.80	1.20	1.20	1.50	1.90	2.40	2.60	2.50	2.90	6.50	2.40
9.5.3 Newspapers	1.00	1.10	1.40	1.40	1.20	1.30	1.00	0.90	1.20	1.40	1.20
9.5.4 Magazines and periodicals	0.50	0.50	0.70	0.50	0.70	0.90	0.70	0.60	0.80	1.00	0.70
9.6 Package holidays	10.70	11.40	14.00	16.60	21.10	23.60	33.90	31.10	53.30	59.60	27.50
9.6.1 Package holidays - UK	[0.90]	[1.10]	[1.00]	2.60	1.70	1.50	1.80	[1.40]	3.30	4.00	1.90
9.6.2 Package holidays - abroad	9.90	10.30	13.00	14.00	19.40	22.10	32.10	29.80	50.10	55.60	25.60
10 Education	..	..	[1.10]	[2.70]	[1.70]	1.30	6.10	4.80	7.30	18.90	4.50
10.1 Education fees	..	..	..	..	..	[1.20]	4.50	4.40	6.30	18.10	4.10
10.2 Payments for school trips, other ad-hoc expenditure	..	..	..	..	[0.20]	..	[1.60]	[0.40]	1.00	[0.80]	0.50
11 Restaurants & hotels	**16.00**	**20.20**	**24.40**	**32.70**	**45.20**	**48.30**	**59.00**	**71.00**	**85.10**	**126.90**	**52.90**
11.1 Catering services	13.50	16.20	19.50	26.50	36.10	39.30	47.00	56.80	64.50	93.70	41.30
11.1.1 Restaurant and café meals	7.10	8.30	9.60	13.80	18.80	19.10	22.60	26.60	30.00	46.00	20.20
11.1.2 Alcoholic drinks (away from home)	2.60	2.70	3.50	5.50	6.00	7.40	9.30	12.70	14.10	19.20	8.30
11.1.3 Take away meals eaten at home	2.30	3.00	3.00	3.30	5.40	5.90	6.60	7.80	8.40	10.40	5.60
11.1.4 Other take-away and snack food	1.40	1.80	2.50	3.10	3.80	5.00	5.90	7.30	9.30	12.60	5.30
11.1.5 Contract catering (food) and canteens	[0.10]	0.50	0.80	0.80	2.00	1.80	2.50	2.50	2.80	5.40	1.90
11.2 Accommodation services	2.50	4.00	4.90	6.20	9.10	9.00	12.10	14.20	20.50	33.20	11.60
11.2.1 Holiday in the UK	1.60	2.40	3.40	4.30	6.20	5.50	7.50	8.90	10.30	12.60	6.30
11.2.2 Holiday abroad	[0.90]	1.60	1.50	2.00	2.70	3.40	4.20	5.20	10.20	20.50	5.20
11.2.3 Room hire	:	..	..	:	..	..	..	..	:	..	0.10

Note: The commodity and service categories are not comparable to those in publications before 2001-02.

The numbering system is sequential, it does not use actual COICOP codes.

Please see background notes for symbols and conventions used in this report.

5 For FYE 2019 onwards, excludes payments made as part of a combined bill.

Table 3.1

Detailed household expenditure by disposable income decile group (cont.)

UK, financial year ending 2020

Commodity or service	Lowest ten per cent	Second decile group	Third decile group	Fourth decile group	Fifth decile group	Sixth decile group	Seventh decile group	Eighth decile group	Ninth decile group	Highest ten per cent	All house-holds
					Average weekly household expenditure (£)						
12 Miscellaneous goods & services	**19.90**	**20.10**	**26.90**	**35.10**	**39.80**	**46.00**	**49.10**	**60.40**	**65.50**	**94.10**	**45.70**
12.1 Personal care	6.10	6.30	7.80	10.80	11.50	14.60	14.00	17.90	19.50	25.70	13.40
12.1.1 Hairdressing, beauty treatment	1.90	2.30	2.40	3.60	3.40	5.00	4.30	7.00	6.50	7.50	4.40
12.1.2 Toilet paper	0.60	0.70	0.80	0.90	0.90	1.10	1.20	1.20	1.00	1.30	1.00
12.1.3 Toiletries and soap	1.30	1.30	1.70	2.10	2.40	2.60	3.20	3.10	3.60	5.20	2.60
12.1.4 Baby toiletries and accessories (disposable)	0.20	0.40	0.40	0.40	0.60	0.70	0.70	0.70	0.80	0.70	0.60
12.1.5 Hair products, cosmetics and related electrical appliances	2.00	1.70	2.60	3.80	4.20	5.20	4.60	5.90	7.60	10.90	4.80
12.2 Personal effects	1.40	1.20	1.50	4.90	3.10	4.70	4.80	4.60	6.60	9.70	4.20
12.3 Social protection	..	..	[1.20]	[3.60]	4.10	3.20	3.10	5.10	3.10	13.40	3.70
12.4 Insurance	7.60	10.50	14.00	13.90	16.90	19.90	21.60	24.40	27.90	36.20	19.30
12.4.1 Household insurances - structural, contents and appliances	2.70	3.30	3.90	3.90	4.80	5.10	5.40	5.30	6.30	8.40	4.90
12.4.2 Medical insurance premiums[6]	0.80	1.10	0.70	1.00	1.30	1.70	2.00	3.60	4.60	6.80	2.40
12.4.3 Vehicle insurance including boat insurance	3.90	5.60	8.80	8.10	10.00	12.00	13.20	14.50	15.70	19.20	11.10
12.4.4 Non-package holiday, other travel insurance[7]	0.30	0.50	0.60	0.90	0.80	1.00	0.90	1.00	1.30	1.80	0.90
12.5 Other services	4.50	2.00	2.40	1.90	4.30	3.60	5.60	8.50	8.40	9.20	5.00
12.5.1 Moving house	[0.50]	[1.00]	1.20	1.30	2.30	1.70	2.60	4.50	4.20	4.70	2.40
12.5.2 Bank, building society, post office, credit card charges	0.20	0.20	0.20	0.30	0.40	0.60	0.60	0.80	0.80	1.20	0.50
12.5.3 Other services and professional fees	[3.80]	[0.80]	0.90	0.20	1.60	1.20	2.40	3.20	3.30	3.20	2.10
1-12 All expenditure groups	**229.70**	**258.30**	**321.80**	**384.90**	**441.70**	**508.20**	**559.20**	**640.70**	**743.50**	**998.20**	**508.50**
13 Other expenditure items	**25.00**	**31.10**	**36.80**	**43.20**	**64.00**	**72.80**	**89.50**	**104.30**	**132.90**	**193.70**	**79.30**
13.1 Housing: mortgage interest payments, council tax etc.	18.10	19.10	25.40	28.90	40.80	49.00	57.50	71.10	81.50	113.20	50.40
13.2 Licences, fines and transfers	1.30	1.70	2.20	2.80	3.40	4.40	4.40	4.30	5.20	8.30	3.80
13.3 Holiday spending	[1.50]	..	[2.10]	[3.50]	8.30	8.20	12.00	10.00	27.50	46.40	12.10
13.4 Money transfers and credit	4.10	8.60	7.10	8.10	11.50	11.30	15.60	19.00	18.70	25.90	13.00
13.4.1 Money, cash gifts given to children	..	..	..	..	..	[0.30]	[1.00]	..	[0.60]	[0.20]	0.30
13.4.2 Cash gifts and donations	3.90	8.00	6.00	6.90	10.80	9.80	13.10	17.30	16.90	23.80	11.70
13.4.3 Club instalment payments (child) and interest on credit cards	[0.20]	0.50	0.90	0.70	0.70	1.20	1.50	1.40	1.30	1.90	1.00
Total expenditure	**254.70**	**289.40**	**358.60**	**428.20**	**505.70**	**581.00**	**648.70**	**745.00**	**876.40**	**1191.90**	**587.90**
14 Other items recorded											
14.1 Life assurance and contributions to pension funds	2.80	3.90	7.20	11.00	18.20	23.80	34.10	45.30	63.30	137.50	34.70
14.2 Other insurance inc. friendly societies	0.80	1.20	1.30	1.70	1.80	2.00	2.80	3.40	3.30	5.30	2.40
14.3 Income tax, payments *less* refunds	13.10	23.00	19.70	32.90	52.20	68.30	92.70	128.20	187.10	435.60	105.20
14.4 National insurance contributions	1.30	3.10	8.20	14.30	23.30	36.00	49.10	62.60	84.60	122.30	40.50
14.5 Purchase or alteration of dwellings, mortgages	15.40	14.60	17.80	29.90	35.20	51.50	80.00	85.20	103.40	172.60	60.60
14.6 Savings and investments	[0.90]	1.20	1.80	3.60	4.90	5.10	14.80	10.60	14.80	34.10	9.20
14.7 Pay off loan to clear other debt	..	..	[0.80]	[1.00]	1.50	2.60	4.00	3.40	2.00	6.20	2.20
14.8 Windfall receipts from gambling etc[8]	1.30	1.00	1.60	1.00	0.40	3.20	0.80	1.20	1.50	1.50	1.30

Note: The commodity and service categories are not comparable to those in publications before 2001-02.

The numbering system is sequential, it does not use actual COICOP codes.

Please see background notes for symbols and conventions used in this report.

6 For FYE 2019, critical illness cover, personal accident insurance and other medical insurance are included here. They were not included in previous years.

7 For FYE 2019, information about insurance for non-package holiday and other travel insurance was collected in the questionnaire in addition to the diary. In previous years, this was based on diary data only.

8 Expressed as an income figure as opposed to an expenditure figure.

Source: Office for National Statistics

Table 3.1E

Detailed household expenditure by equivalised disposable income decile group (OECD-modified scale)

UK, financial year ending 2020

	Lowest ten per cent	Second decile group	Third decile group	Fourth decile group	Fifth decile group	Sixth decile group	Seventh decile group	Eighth decile group	Ninth decile group	Highest ten per cent	All house- holds
Lower boundary of group (£ per week)		182	240	296	342	398	462	529	629	781	
Weighted number of households (thousands)	2,780	2,780	2,780	2,790	2,780	2,780	2,780	2,780	2,790	2,770	27,820
Total number of households in sample	550	560	580	560	570	540	530	520	520	510	5,440
Total number of persons in sample	1,090	1,260	1,320	1,310	1,360	1,290	1,350	1,260	1,250	1,200	12,670
Total number of adults in sample	770	890	970	1,010	1,030	1,030	1,110	1,050	1,020	1,010	9,880
Weighted average number of persons per household	2.0	2.3	2.2	2.4	2.4	2.4	2.5	2.5	2.5	2.4	2.4

Commodity or service	Average weekly household expenditure (£)										
1 Food & non-alcoholic drinks	**44.90**	**51.60**	**55.10**	**60.50**	**62.50**	**65.40**	**72.40**	**70.60**	**74.30**	**79.70**	**63.70**
1.1 Food	40.90	47.30	50.30	55.20	57.30	59.70	66.70	64.70	68.40	73.30	58.40
1.1.1 Bread, rice and cereals	4.30	4.90	5.20	5.70	5.80	6.20	6.80	6.50	6.50	6.70	5.80
1.1.2 Pasta products	0.40	0.40	0.40	0.40	0.40	0.50	0.60	0.50	0.60	0.50	0.50
1.1.3 Buns, cakes, biscuits etc.	2.90	3.60	3.80	4.10	4.50	4.10	4.60	4.70	4.20	4.60	4.10
1.1.4 Pastry (savoury)	0.60	0.80	0.80	0.90	1.10	1.00	1.20	1.10	1.00	1.20	1.00
1.1.5 Beef (fresh, chilled or frozen)	1.50	1.30	1.50	1.80	1.70	2.10	2.00	2.10	2.10	2.70	1.90
1.1.6 Pork (fresh, chilled or frozen)	0.40	0.40	0.50	0.50	0.50	0.60	0.60	0.70	0.60	0.50	0.50
1.1.7 Lamb (fresh, chilled or frozen)	0.40	0.70	0.50	0.60	0.90	0.60	0.80	0.80	0.80	0.90	0.70
1.1.8 Poultry (fresh, chilled or frozen)	1.70	1.90	2.00	2.10	2.20	2.90	3.10	2.90	3.00	2.80	2.40
1.1.9 Bacon and ham	0.60	0.60	0.70	0.80	0.80	0.90	0.90	0.90	0.90	1.00	0.80
1.1.10 Other meat and meat preparations	4.60	5.60	6.40	6.70	6.80	6.60	7.80	7.10	7.30	7.40	6.60
1.1.11 Fish and fish products	1.80	2.30	2.20	3.00	2.80	3.10	3.60	3.80	4.10	4.80	3.20
1.1.12 Milk	1.90	2.20	2.30	2.20	2.30	2.10	2.30	2.10	1.90	2.00	2.10
1.1.13 Cheese and curd	1.40	1.70	1.80	2.00	2.00	2.20	2.50	2.60	3.00	2.80	2.20
1.1.14 Eggs	0.60	0.70	0.60	0.70	0.60	0.80	0.80	0.80	0.90	1.00	0.80
1.1.15 Other milk products	1.70	1.90	2.00	2.10	2.30	2.50	2.50	2.60	2.50	3.30	2.30
1.1.16 Butter	0.30	0.40	0.40	0.40	0.40	0.50	0.60	0.50	0.50	0.70	0.50
1.1.17 Margarine, other vegetable fats and peanut butter	0.50	0.60	0.60	0.70	0.60	0.70	0.70	0.60	0.70	0.60	0.60
1.1.18 Cooking oils and fats	0.30	0.30	0.30	0.40	0.40	0.40	0.40	0.40	0.50	0.50	0.40
1.1.19 Fresh fruit	2.80	2.90	3.30	3.60	3.70	4.00	4.50	4.40	5.20	5.70	4.00
1.1.20 Other fresh, chilled or frozen fruits	0.30	0.40	0.30	0.40	0.40	0.50	0.50	0.70	0.70	0.60	0.50
1.1.21 Dried fruit and nuts	0.40	0.60	0.70	0.80	1.30	0.80	1.00	1.10	1.10	1.40	0.90
1.1.22 Preserved fruit and fruit based products	0.10	0.10	0.20	0.10	0.20	0.20	0.20	0.20	0.20	0.20	0.20
1.1.23 Fresh vegetables	2.90	3.20	3.30	3.70	3.80	4.50	5.40	4.90	6.20	6.60	4.50
1.1.24 Dried vegetables	0.00~	[0.00]	0.00~	0.00~	0.00~	0.10	0.10	0.10	0.10	0.10	0.10
1.1.25 Other preserved or processed vegetables	1.20	1.30	1.70	1.50	1.80	2.00	2.20	2.20	2.60	3.10	2.00
1.1.26 Potatoes	0.60	0.60	0.70	0.80	0.70	0.70	0.80	0.80	0.70	0.70	0.70
1.1.27 Other tubers and products of tuber vegetables	1.40	1.70	1.90	2.00	1.90	1.90	2.00	1.80	1.90	1.70	1.80
1.1.28 Sugar and sugar products	0.40	0.40	0.30	0.40	0.30	0.50	0.50	0.40	0.30	0.40	0.40
1.1.29 Jams, marmalades	0.20	0.30	0.20	0.30	0.40	0.30	0.40	0.40	0.40	0.40	0.30
1.1.30 Chocolate	1.50	1.70	2.20	2.10	2.50	2.20	2.70	2.60	2.80	3.00	2.30
1.1.31 Confectionery products	0.60	0.80	0.90	0.90	1.00	0.90	0.80	0.90	0.80	0.70	0.80
1.1.32 Edible ices and ice cream	0.60	0.60	0.70	0.80	0.70	0.60	0.80	0.80	0.90	0.90	0.70
1.1.33 Other food products	2.00	2.60	2.10	2.50	2.60	2.90	3.00	3.00	3.50	3.60	2.80
1.2 Non-alcoholic drinks	4.00	4.30	4.80	5.30	5.20	5.70	5.80	6.00	5.90	6.40	5.30
1.2.1 Coffee	0.70	0.80	0.80	0.90	0.90	1.40	1.10	1.30	1.20	1.70	1.10
1.2.2 Tea	0.40	0.40	0.50	0.50	0.40	0.50	0.40	0.60	0.50	0.70	0.50
1.2.3 Cocoa and powdered chocolate	0.10	0.10	0.10	0.10	0.10	0.10	0.10	0.20	0.10	0.10	0.10
1.2.4 Fruit and vegetable juices (inc. fruit squash)	0.80	0.80	1.00	1.00	1.10	1.10	1.10	1.20	1.30	1.30	1.10
1.2.5 Mineral or spring waters	0.20	0.30	0.30	0.40	0.40	0.30	0.50	0.40	0.30	0.40	0.40
1.2.6 Soft drinks (inc. fizzy and ready to drink fruit drinks)	1.80	1.90	2.20	2.30	2.40	2.30	2.50	2.40	2.50	2.10	2.20

Note: The commodity and service categories are not comparable to those in publications before 2001-02.

The numbering system is sequential, it does not use actual COICOP codes.

Please see background notes for symbols and conventions used in this report.

Table 3.1E

Detailed household expenditure by equivalised disposable income decile group (OECD-modified scale) (cont.)

UK, financial year ending 2020

Commodity or service	Lowest ten per cent	Second decile group	Third decile group	Fourth decile group	Fifth decile group	Sixth decile group	Seventh decile group	Eighth decile group	Ninth decile group	Highest ten per cent	All house-holds
					Average weekly household expenditure (£)						
2 Alcoholic drink, tobacco & narcotics	**9.50**	**9.10**	**10.50**	**12.10**	**12.20**	**11.70**	**14.50**	**15.40**	**16.00**	**18.50**	**12.90**
2.1 Alcoholic drinks	5.20	5.20	6.90	7.40	7.80	8.90	10.00	12.20	12.70	16.60	9.30
2.1.1 Spirits and liqueurs (brought home)	1.30	1.60	1.90	2.30	2.10	2.30	2.30	2.80	3.10	3.10	2.30
2.1.2 Wines, fortified wines (brought home)	1.90	2.20	3.00	3.60	3.50	4.20	4.40	6.10	6.30	10.30	4.60
2.1.3 Beer, lager, ciders and perry (brought home)	2.00	1.40	2.10	1.40	2.20	2.50	3.40	3.20	3.30	3.10	2.50
2.1.4 Alcopops (brought home)	..	[0.00]	..	..	..	..	..	..	..	..	0.00~
2.2 Tobacco and narcotics	4.40	3.90	3.50	4.70	4.40	2.70	4.40	3.20	3.30	1.90	3.60
2.2.1 Cigarettes	3.00	2.90	2.50	3.30	3.10	1.40	3.10	2.50	2.50	1.50	2.60
2.2.2 Cigars, other tobacco products and narcotics	1.30	1.00	1.00	1.40	1.30	1.30	1.30	0.70	0.80	[0.40]	1.10
3 Clothing & footwear	**12.50**	**14.40**	**13.60**	**15.60**	**22.10**	**25.90**	**25.90**	**31.30**	**31.10**	**41.40**	**23.40**
3.1 Clothing	9.70	11.60	10.90	12.10	17.50	21.40	21.40	24.60	24.70	32.60	18.70
3.1.1 Men's outer garments	2.10	2.20	2.70	2.30	4.40	5.40	6.10	5.60	5.90	9.50	4.60
3.1.2 Men's under garments	0.30	0.40	0.40	0.40	0.50	0.50	0.50	0.80	0.70	0.90	0.60
3.1.3 Women's outer garments	3.70	4.90	4.10	5.00	7.00	10.20	8.30	11.30	11.60	14.10	8.00
3.1.4 Women's under garments	0.70	1.00	0.70	1.10	1.10	1.10	1.30	1.60	1.70	1.90	1.20
3.1.5 Boys' outer garments (5-15)	0.40	0.60	0.80	0.50	1.10	0.80	0.80	1.00	0.60	1.30	0.80
3.1.6 Girls' outer garments (5-15)	0.90	1.00	0.70	0.60	1.00	1.10	1.50	1.20	1.10	1.00	1.00
3.1.7 Infants' outer garments (under 5)	0.40	0.50	0.40	0.70	0.40	0.80	0.90	0.70	0.70	1.30	0.70
3.1.8 Children's under garments (under 16)	0.30	0.40	0.40	0.40	0.50	0.30	0.50	0.80	0.30	0.40	0.40
3.1.9 Accessories	0.30	0.40	0.50	0.40	0.90	0.70	1.00	1.30	1.40	1.10	0.80
3.1.10 Haberdashery and clothing hire	0.30	0.10	0.20	0.60	0.30	0.50	0.20	0.30	0.20	0.50	0.30
3.1.11 Dry cleaners, laundry and dyeing	[0.20]	[0.10]	[0.10]	..	[0.20]	..	[0.40]	[0.20]	0.50	0.70	0.20
3.2 Footwear	2.80	2.80	2.70	3.40	4.60	4.50	4.50	6.70	6.40	8.80	4.70
4 Housing (net)[1], fuel & power	**64.70**	**75.70**	**70.30**	**82.40**	**82.00**	**82.80**	**86.30**	**88.80**	**85.20**	**111.70**	**83.00**
4.1 Actual rentals for housing	83.30	72.20	52.70	53.20	48.20	39.30	44.70	44.60	39.00	48.00	52.50
4.1.1 Gross rent	83.30	72.20	52.70	53.20	48.20	39.30	44.70	44.60	39.00	48.00	52.50
4.1.2 *less housing benefit, rebates & allowances rec'd*	52.30	31.90	19.80	9.80	4.20	0.90	3.70	0.50	0.50	[0.20]	12.40
4.1.3 Net rent[2]	31.00	40.30	32.90	43.40	44.10	38.50	41.00	44.00	38.50	47.80	40.10
4.1.4 Second dwelling rent	:	:	:	:	:	:	:	..	:	:	..
4.2 Maintenance and repair of dwelling	2.60	3.20	5.40	5.40	5.40	10.40	9.10	9.00	9.30	20.00	8.00
4.3 Water supply and miscellaneous services relating to the dwelling	8.50	9.90	8.50	9.10	9.10	10.00	11.70	10.90	11.20	14.90	10.40
4.4 Electricity, gas and other fuels	22.60	22.30	23.40	24.40	23.40	23.80	24.50	24.80	26.30	29.00	24.50
4.4.1 Electricity	11.90	11.80	12.30	12.30	12.00	12.50	12.30	12.20	13.00	14.30	12.50
4.4.2 Gas	9.80	9.60	10.00	10.30	10.20	9.90	10.90	10.80	11.20	12.30	10.50
4.4.3 Other fuels	1.00	1.00	1.10	1.80	1.20	1.40	1.30	1.80	2.10	2.40	1.50

Note: The commodity and service categories are not comparable to those in publications before 2001-02.

The numbering system is sequential, it does not use actual COICOP codes.

Please see background notes for symbols and conventions used in this report.

1 Excluding mortgage interest payments, council tax and Northern Ireland rates.

2 The figure included in total expenditure is net rent as opposed to gross rent.

Table 3.1E

Detailed household expenditure by equivalised disposable income decile group (OECD-modified scale) (cont.)

UK, financial year ending 2020

Commodity or service	Lowest ten per cent	Second decile group	Third decile group	Fourth decile group	Fifth decile group	Sixth decile group	Seventh decile group	Eighth decile group	Ninth decile group	Highest ten per cent	All house-holds
					Average weekly household expenditure (£)						
5 Household goods & services	**16.00**	**19.80**	**26.30**	**32.40**	**28.60**	**37.40**	**42.20**	**43.10**	**49.90**	**69.40**	**36.50**
5.1 Furniture and furnishings, carpets and other floor coverings	8.40	9.20	14.50	18.20	15.00	18.80	24.40	23.90	26.20	42.50	20.10
5.1.1 Furniture and furnishings	6.30	7.90	10.70	13.60	12.90	15.80	20.70	20.90	21.70	35.50	16.60
5.1.2 Floor coverings	2.10	1.30	3.80	4.70	2.10	3.00	3.70	3.00	4.50	7.00	3.50
5.2 Household textiles	1.00	0.90	1.10	1.70	1.20	2.20	2.40	2.80	2.50	3.80	2.00
5.3 Household appliances	1.40	2.10	2.10	2.80	2.20	3.90	3.50	2.30	4.50	3.80	2.90
5.4 Glassware, tableware and household utensils	0.60	1.10	1.00	1.70	1.50	1.90	2.30	2.10	3.20	3.00	1.80
5.5 Tools and equipment for house and garden	0.80	1.80	2.00	2.50	3.00	3.60	3.30	4.60	4.60	3.60	3.00
5.6 Goods and services for routine household maintenance	3.80	4.80	5.50	5.60	5.80	7.10	6.30	7.30	8.90	12.80	6.80
5.6.1 Cleaning materials	1.80	2.30	2.50	2.40	2.70	3.00	3.10	3.10	2.80	3.20	2.70
5.6.2 Household goods and hardware	1.20	1.30	1.70	1.60	1.60	2.20	2.30	2.10	2.40	2.20	1.90
5.6.3 Domestic services, carpet cleaning, hire/repair of furniture/furnishings	0.80	1.20	1.30	1.60	1.50	1.90	0.90	2.20	3.70	7.40	2.20
6 Health	**2.70**	**5.60**	**6.60**	**6.30**	**5.70**	**9.20**	**6.70**	**10.50**	**11.60**	**17.10**	**8.20**
6.1 Medical products, appliances and equipment	1.90	3.40	3.50	3.60	3.30	4.60	4.30	5.80	6.70	7.80	4.50
6.1.1 Medicines, prescriptions, healthcare products etc.	1.60	1.70	2.20	2.50	2.20	2.50	3.30	2.60	4.40	3.40	2.60
6.1.2 Spectacles, lenses, accessories and repairs	[0.30]	1.70	1.30	1.10	1.10	2.10	1.00	3.20	2.30	4.40	1.80
6.2 Hospital services	[0.80]	2.20	3.10	2.70	2.40	4.50	2.50	4.70	4.90	9.30	3.70
7 Transport	**30.10**	**39.60**	**52.10**	**58.70**	**65.30**	**82.40**	**92.40**	**111.90**	**128.60**	**155.30**	**81.60**
7.1 Purchase of vehicles	7.90	9.60	19.00	18.50	19.00	29.80	28.30	38.00	39.40	53.40	26.30
7.1.1 Purchase of new cars and vans	..	[2.50]	[2.90]	4.90	3.70	13.10	7.60	10.00	10.40	21.90	7.90
7.1.2 Purchase of second hand cars or vans	5.90	6.80	10.40	13.50	14.70	16.00	20.20	26.80	27.80	30.10	17.20
7.1.3 Purchase of motorcycles and other vehicles	..	..	..	..	..	..	..	..	..	[1.50]	1.20
7.2 Operation of personal transport	14.80	18.90	23.50	26.70	32.60	37.40	39.70	43.40	52.10	47.20	33.60
7.2.1 Spares and accessories	1.20	1.90	1.80	1.80	2.20	2.70	2.70	2.00	4.60	3.20	2.40
7.2.2 Petrol, diesel and other motor oils	10.20	12.50	15.50	17.90	20.90	26.00	26.80	30.30	33.90	28.50	22.30
7.2.3 Repairs and servicing	2.40	2.80	4.80	5.40	6.50	5.70	6.40	8.00	9.40	10.80	6.20
7.2.4 Other motoring costs	1.00	1.60	1.40	1.60	3.00	2.90	3.80	3.10	4.20	4.80	2.80
7.3 Transport services	7.50	11.10	9.60	13.50	13.60	15.30	24.40	30.50	37.10	54.70	21.70
7.3.1 Rail and tube fares	1.20	1.40	1.20	2.00	2.30	3.10	4.90	7.10	10.80	12.50	4.60
7.3.2 Bus and coach fares	1.70	1.30	1.20	1.70	1.80	1.50	1.90	1.70	1.40	1.10	1.50
7.3.3 Combined fares	..	..	..	..	..	..	..	[0.60]	[1.10]	[1.10]	0.60
7.3.4 Other travel and transport	4.10	8.20	7.20	9.50	9.30	10.10	16.70	21.10	23.80	39.90	15.00
8 Communication	**13.40**	**16.20**	**18.00**	**20.50**	**19.90**	**23.40**	**24.20**	**25.00**	**25.30**	**27.60**	**21.40**
8.1 Postal services	0.50	0.40	0.50	0.70	0.60	0.60	0.90	0.60	0.90	1.00	0.70
8.2 Telephone and telefax equipment	0.50	[0.60]	0.70	[2.00]	0.50	1.70	1.60	2.30	1.10	4.10	1.50
8.3 Telephone and telefax services[3]	5.10	6.50	7.10	7.50	8.00	9.40	9.80	9.50	10.80	9.80	8.40
8.4 Internet subscription fees (ex. combined packages)	0.60	0.70	0.60	0.60	0.70	0.50	0.70	0.70	1.00	0.70	0.70
8.5 Combined telecom services[4]	6.80	8.10	9.10	9.60	10.10	11.10	11.20	11.90	11.50	12.00	10.10

Note: The commodity and service categories are not comparable to those in publications before 2001-02.

The numbering system is sequential, it does not use actual COICOP codes.

Please see background notes for symbols and conventions used in this report.

3 For FYE 2019 onwards, excludes payments made as part of a combined bill.

4 New for FYE 2019. This encompasses all telecoms bills that include more than one service. Due to the nature of combined packages, this also includes packages that includes television services.

Table 3.1E
Detailed household expenditure by equivalised disposable income decile group (OECD-modified scale) (cont.)
UK, financial year ending 2020

Commodity or service	Lowest ten per cent	Second decile group	Third decile group	Fourth decile group	Fifth decile group	Sixth decile group	Seventh decile group	Eighth decile group	Ninth decile group	Highest ten per cent	All house-holds
	Average weekly household expenditure (£)										
9 Recreation & culture	**31.90**	**40.30**	**47.50**	**51.50**	**59.70**	**73.50**	**79.00**	**99.20**	**115.10**	**150.40**	**74.80**
9.1 Audio-visual, photographic and information processing equipment	1.80	2.10	2.90	2.90	3.60	6.80	4.50	6.70	8.00	5.60	4.50
9.1.1 Audio equipment and accessories, CD players	0.80	0.90	0.40	0.70	1.00	1.10	1.00	1.30	2.00	1.70	1.10
9.1.2 TV, video and computers	1.00	1.10	2.40	2.20	1.90	5.50	3.50	4.60	3.30	3.40	2.90
9.1.3 Photographic, cine and optical equipment	..	..	..	:	..	..	..	..	..	..	0.50
9.2 Other major durables for recreation and culture	..	..	..	..	[2.30]	[2.70]	[0.80]	[1.90]	[2.90]	[4.80]	2.00
9.3 Other recreational items and equipment, gardens and pets	7.50	9.90	11.80	12.60	12.40	14.80	17.10	18.40	22.00	29.00	15.50
9.3.1 Games, toys and hobbies	1.40	2.00	2.70	3.30	3.00	3.80	3.70	3.50	4.70	4.00	3.20
9.3.2 Computer software and games	[0.70]	1.60	0.80	0.60	1.20	1.30	0.70	1.40	0.70	1.00	1.00
9.3.3 Equipment for sport, camping and open-air recreation	0.50	0.70	0.90	0.50	1.50	0.70	1.00	2.30	2.30	6.70	1.70
9.3.4 Horticultural goods, garden equipment and plants	1.20	1.50	2.40	2.60	2.40	3.00	2.60	3.50	4.60	4.10	2.80
9.3.5 Pets and pet food	3.60	4.20	5.00	5.50	4.40	6.00	9.20	7.80	9.60	13.20	6.80
9.4 Recreational and cultural services	10.00	11.50	12.60	13.90	15.80	18.10	24.10	24.70	26.90	40.30	19.80
9.4.1 Sports admissions, subscriptions, leisure class fees and equipment hire	2.90	3.10	3.90	4.80	4.90	6.30	9.20	10.80	11.00	21.20	7.80
9.4.2 Cinema, theatre and museums etc.	1.80	1.50	1.80	1.90	2.00	2.40	5.30	3.90	5.50	7.40	3.30
9.4.3 TV, video, satellite rental, cable subscriptions and TV licences[5]	3.20	3.20	3.70	4.20	4.40	4.70	5.30	5.20	6.00	6.70	4.70
9.4.4 Miscellaneous entertainments	0.40	0.90	0.60	0.80	1.90	1.80	1.60	2.00	1.90	2.50	1.40
9.4.5 Development of film, deposit for film development, passport photos, holiday and school photos	..	..	..	[0.20]	[0.20]	[0.20]	[0.20]	[0.30]	0.20	0.30	0.20
9.4.6 Gambling payments	1.70	2.70	2.60	2.10	2.40	2.60	2.60	2.70	2.30	2.20	2.40
9.5 Newspapers, books and stationery	3.00	3.50	4.40	4.40	5.10	5.10	5.70	6.60	7.00	10.20	5.50
9.5.1 Books	0.70	0.70	0.70	0.80	0.80	1.20	1.10	1.80	2.20	2.40	1.20
9.5.2 Diaries, address books, cards etc.	0.90	1.10	1.90	1.80	2.30	2.00	2.60	2.60	3.10	5.30	2.40
9.5.3 Newspapers	0.80	1.00	1.20	1.10	1.40	1.20	1.30	1.10	1.00	1.70	1.20
9.5.4 Magazines and periodicals	0.50	0.70	0.50	0.60	0.60	0.70	0.60	1.10	0.70	0.80	0.70
9.6 Package holidays	9.40	11.30	15.10	16.60	20.40	26.00	26.80	40.90	48.20	60.60	27.50
9.6.1 Package holidays - UK	[0.80]	[1.20]	1.30	[1.90]	1.70	1.60	[1.50]	[2.10]	2.90	4.20	1.90
9.6.2 Package holidays - abroad	8.60	10.10	13.80	14.70	18.70	24.50	25.40	38.80	45.40	56.40	25.60
10 Education	**[0.90]**	**1.90**	**[0.90]**	**3.90**	**4.20**	**3.10**	**3.80**	**7.10**	**4.70**	**14.70**	**4.50**
10.1 Education fees	..	[1.50]	..	[3.60]	[2.60]	[2.60]	3.50	6.60	4.30	14.30	4.10
10.2 Payments for school trips, other ad-hoc expenditure	..	[0.40]	..	..	[1.60]	..	[0.40]	[0.50]	[0.40]	..	0.50
11 Restaurants & hotels	**22.00**	**24.40**	**30.90**	**32.40**	**44.30**	**48.90**	**63.50**	**74.50**	**80.60**	**107.20**	**52.90**
11.1 Catering services	18.70	20.90	24.60	26.50	36.00	41.10	50.90	57.00	63.00	74.30	41.30
11.1.1 Restaurant and café meals	8.30	10.00	11.60	12.60	17.70	20.30	24.90	27.30	31.00	38.10	20.20
11.1.2 Alcoholic drinks (away from home)	3.10	3.00	4.20	4.80	5.90	8.00	11.40	11.90	14.30	16.50	8.30
11.1.3 Take away meals eaten at home	3.90	4.20	4.30	4.10	5.40	5.80	6.10	7.90	7.00	7.30	5.60
11.1.4 Other take-away and snack food	2.70	2.80	3.20	3.80	4.70	4.80	6.40	7.20	8.20	8.90	5.30
11.1.5 Contract catering (food) and canteens	0.60	1.00	1.30	1.10	2.20	2.20	2.10	2.70	2.50	3.50	1.90
11.2 Accommodation services	3.30	3.50	6.30	5.90	8.30	7.80	12.60	17.50	17.60	32.90	11.60
11.2.1 Holiday in the UK	2.10	2.50	3.80	4.10	6.70	5.20	7.70	9.00	9.80	11.90	6.30
11.2.2 Holiday abroad	[1.20]	1.00	2.50	1.80	1.50	2.60	4.50	8.40	7.80	20.80	5.20
11.2.3 Room hire	..	..	..	:	..	..	..	..	..	..	0.10

Note: The commodity and service categories are not comparable to those in publications before 2001-02.

The numbering system is sequential, it does not use actual COICOP codes.

Please see background notes for symbols and conventions used in this report.

5 For FYE 2019 onwards, excludes payments made as part of a combined bill.

Table 3.1E

Detailed household expenditure by equivalised disposable income decile group (OECD-modified scale) (cont.)

UK, financial year ending 2020

Commodity or service	Lowest ten per cent	Second decile group	Third decile group	Fourth decile group	Fifth decile group	Sixth decile group	Seventh decile group	Eighth decile group	Ninth decile group	Highest ten per cent	All house-holds
	Average weekly household expenditure (£)										
12 Miscellaneous goods & services	**19.70**	**27.40**	**28.00**	**33.40**	**41.20**	**49.80**	**49.50**	**62.40**	**60.60**	**84.90**	**45.70**
12.1 Personal care	6.90	9.40	8.70	11.10	12.10	14.00	15.60	16.70	19.00	20.60	13.40
12.1.1 Hairdressing, beauty treatment	1.90	2.70	2.20	3.60	3.80	4.70	5.20	5.70	6.90	7.20	4.40
12.1.2 Toilet paper	0.70	0.90	1.00	1.10	0.90	1.10	1.00	1.00	1.00	1.00	1.00
12.1.3 Toiletries and soap	1.60	2.00	1.90	2.20	2.40	2.80	3.10	3.30	3.40	3.80	2.60
12.1.4 Baby toiletries and accessories (disposable)	0.50	0.60	0.60	0.60	0.60	0.60	0.60	0.50	0.60	0.50	0.60
12.1.5 Hair products, cosmetics and related electrical appliances	2.30	3.20	2.90	3.60	4.40	4.80	5.60	6.20	7.20	8.20	4.80
12.2 Personal effects	1.20	2.20	1.60	1.80	2.90	5.00	5.20	7.20	5.10	10.00	4.20
12.3 Social protection	..	[0.50]	1.90	2.60	2.80	7.60	3.60	4.60	[1.30]	12.00	3.70
12.4 Insurance	10.10	10.40	13.80	15.70	19.40	18.40	20.50	24.60	28.40	31.60	19.30
12.4.1 Household insurances - structural, contents and appliances	2.80	3.00	4.30	4.00	4.20	5.00	4.80	6.40	6.50	8.10	4.90
12.4.2 Medical insurance premiums[6]	1.10	0.60	0.70	1.20	1.30	1.70	1.50	2.70	4.90	7.90	2.40
12.4.3 Vehicle insurance including boat insurance	5.90	6.40	8.00	9.90	13.20	11.10	13.10	14.60	15.40	13.50	11.10
12.4.4 Non-package holiday, other travel insurance[7]	0.20	0.40	0.80	0.60	0.70	0.70	1.10	0.90	1.60	2.10	0.90
12.5 Other services	1.10	4.80	2.10	2.20	4.00	4.80	4.50	9.20	6.90	10.70	5.00
12.5.1 Moving house	0.80	[0.70]	[0.40]	1.30	2.80	2.40	1.60	4.30	3.40	6.60	2.40
12.5.2 Bank, building society, post office, credit card charges	0.30	0.20	0.40	0.30	0.40	0.50	0.50	0.70	0.90	1.20	0.50
12.5.3 Other services and professional fees	[0.10]	3.90	1.20	0.60	0.80	1.90	2.30	4.30	2.60	2.90	2.10
1-12 All expenditure groups	**268.40**	**326.00**	**359.90**	**409.50**	**447.90**	**513.40**	**560.50**	**639.80**	**683.10**	**878.10**	**508.50**
13 Other expenditure items	**30.50**	**33.60**	**44.90**	**53.10**	**61.50**	**78.70**	**78.60**	**99.90**	**117.60**	**195.20**	**79.30**
13.1 Housing: mortgage interest payments, council tax etc.	20.20	23.20	28.40	35.20	41.40	49.10	56.00	66.80	79.50	104.50	50.40
13.2 Licences, fines and transfers	1.80	2.10	2.60	3.00	3.60	4.10	4.30	4.40	5.10	7.00	3.80
13.3 Holiday spending	..	[3.20]	[6.30]	..	[5.90]	14.20	7.70	14.10	14.60	50.10	12.10
13.4 Money transfers and credit	7.30	5.10	7.60	10.90	10.70	11.30	10.50	14.60	18.30	33.60	13.00
13.4.1 Money, cash gifts given to children	..	..	..	..	..	..	..	..	..	[1.20]	0.30
13.4.2 Cash gifts and donations	7.00	4.00	6.80	9.40	9.60	9.90	8.70	12.70	17.00	31.60	11.70
13.4.3 Club instalment payments (child) and interest on credit cards	0.30	1.00	0.70	0.90	1.00	1.40	1.70	1.60	1.00	0.80	1.00
Total expenditure	**298.90**	**359.70**	**404.80**	**462.60**	**509.40**	**592.10**	**639.10**	**739.70**	**800.70**	**1073.20**	**587.90**
14 Other items recorded											
14.1 Life assurance and contributions to pension funds	4.40	5.10	9.90	15.40	17.50	25.50	33.70	44.40	68.20	123.10	34.70
14.2 Other insurance inc. friendly societies	0.70	1.10	1.50	1.70	2.00	2.10	2.70	3.40	4.00	4.20	2.40
14.3 Income tax, payments *less* refunds	30.50	8.50	22.80	34.90	51.00	73.50	96.40	133.10	185.70	416.70	105.20
14.4 National insurance contributions	3.00	5.70	10.00	19.50	25.70	38.00	50.80	66.60	81.90	103.50	40.50
14.5 Purchase or alteration of dwellings, mortgages	19.30	15.20	32.60	30.60	45.30	68.90	70.70	65.60	112.70	144.80	60.60
14.6 Savings and investments	0.80	0.80	3.40	4.30	2.00	4.50	6.50	21.50	11.10	36.80	9.20
14.7 Pay off loan to clear other debt	[0.30]	[0.80]	[1.20]	2.10	1.70	2.80	1.70	2.50	5.10	[3.60]	2.20
14.8 Windfall receipts from gambling etc[8]	0.90	1.30	1.20	1.10	0.90	0.70	1.40	1.20	3.60	1.00	1.30

Note: The commodity and service categories are not comparable to those in publications before 2001-02.

The numbering system is sequential, it does not use actual COICOP codes.

Please see background notes for symbols and conventions used in this report.

6 For FYE 2019, critical illness cover, personal accident insurance and other medical insurance are included here. They were not included in previous years.

7 For FYE 2019, information about insurance for non-package holiday and other travel insurance was collected in the questionnaire in addition to the diary. In previous years, this was based on diary data only.

8 Expressed as an income figure as opposed to an expenditure figure.

Source: Office for National Statistics

Table 3.2

Detailed household expenditure as a percentage of total expenditure by disposable income decile group

UK, financial year ending 2020

	Lowest ten per cent	Second decile group	Third decile group	Fourth decile group	Fifth decile group	Sixth decile group	Seventh decile group	Eighth decile group	Ninth decile group	Highest ten per cent	All house-holds
Lower boundary of group (£ per week)		224	321	413	510	624	750	892	1064	1386	
Weighted number of households (thousands)	2,780	2,780	2,780	2,790	2,780	2,780	2,780	2,780	2,790	2,780	27,820
Total number of households in sample	560	550	570	560	570	550	540	530	520	480	5,440
Total number of persons in sample	720	860	1,020	1,180	1,350	1,400	1,490	1,540	1,520	1,600	12,670
Total number of adults in sample	630	710	840	960	1,030	1,070	1,110	1,170	1,190	1,190	9,880
Weighted average number of persons per household	1.3	1.6	1.8	2.1	2.4	2.5	2.8	2.9	3.0	3.4	2.4

Commodity or service	Percentage of total expenditure										

		Lowest ten per cent	Second	Third	Fourth	Fifth	Sixth	Seventh	Eighth	Ninth	Highest ten	All house-holds
1	**Food & non-alcoholic drinks**	**13.8**	**14.0**	**13.1**	**12.7**	**11.9**	**11.1**	**11.2**	**10.6**	**9.5**	**8.5**	**10.8**
1.1	Food	12.6	12.8	12.0	11.7	10.9	10.2	10.2	9.7	8.7	7.8	9.9
1.1.1	Bread, rice and cereals	1.3	1.2	1.2	1.1	1.1	1.0	1.1	1.0	0.9	0.8	1.0
1.1.2	Pasta products	0.1	0.1	0.1	0.1	0.1	0.1	0.1	0.1	0.1	0.1	0.1
1.1.3	Buns, cakes, biscuits etc.	0.9	1.0	0.9	0.9	0.8	0.7	0.7	0.7	0.6	0.5	0.7
1.1.4	Pastry (savoury)	0.2	0.2	0.2	0.2	0.2	0.2	0.2	0.2	0.2	0.1	0.2
1.1.5	Beef (fresh, chilled or frozen)	0.4	0.4	0.3	0.4	0.4	0.4	0.3	0.3	0.3	0.3	0.3
1.1.6	Pork (fresh, chilled or frozen)	0.1	0.1	0.1	0.2	0.1	0.1	0.1	0.1	0.1	0.1	0.1
1.1.7	Lamb (fresh, chilled or frozen)	0.1	0.1	0.1	0.1	0.1	0.1	0.2	0.1	0.1	0.1	0.1
1.1.8	Poultry (fresh, chilled or frozen)	0.4	0.5	0.5	0.5	0.4	0.4	0.5	0.5	0.4	0.3	0.4
1.1.9	Bacon and ham	0.2	0.2	0.2	0.2	0.1	0.2	0.1	0.1	0.1	0.1	0.1
1.1.10	Other meat and meat preparations	1.7	1.6	1.5	1.4	1.2	1.2	1.1	1.1	0.9	0.8	1.1
1.1.11	Fish and fish products	0.6	0.6	0.6	0.6	0.6	0.5	0.5	0.6	0.5	0.5	0.5
1.1.12	Milk	0.6	0.6	0.5	0.5	0.4	0.4	0.4	0.3	0.3	0.2	0.4
1.1.13	Cheese and curd	0.4	0.4	0.5	0.4	0.4	0.4	0.4	0.4	0.4	0.3	0.4
1.1.14	Eggs	0.2	0.2	0.2	0.2	0.1	0.1	0.1	0.1	0.1	0.1	0.1
1.1.15	Other milk products	0.5	0.5	0.5	0.4	0.5	0.4	0.4	0.4	0.3	0.3	0.4
1.1.16	Butter	0.1	0.1	0.1	0.1	0.1	0.1	0.1	0.1	0.1	0.1	0.1
1.1.17	Margarine, other vegetable fats and peanut butter	0.2	0.2	0.2	0.1	0.1	0.1	0.1	0.1	0.1	0.1	0.1
1.1.18	Cooking oils and fats	0.1	0.1	0.1	0.1	0.1	0.1	0.1	0.1	0.1	0.0~	0.1
1.1.19	Fresh fruit	0.9	0.9	0.8	0.8	0.7	0.7	0.7	0.6	0.6	0.6	0.7
1.1.20	Other fresh, chilled or frozen fruits	0.1	0.1	0.1	0.1	0.1	0.1	0.1	0.1	0.1	0.1	0.1
1.1.21	Dried fruit and nuts	0.2	0.1	0.2	0.2	0.2	0.1	0.2	0.1	0.1	0.1	0.2
1.1.22	Preserved fruit and fruit based products	0.0~	0.0~	0.0~	0.0~	0.0~	0.0~	0.0~	0.0~	0.0~	0.0~	0.0~
1.1.23	Fresh vegetables	0.9	0.9	0.9	0.8	0.8	0.7	0.8	0.7	0.7	0.7	0.8
1.1.24	Dried vegetables	[0.0]	[0.0]	0.0~	[0.0]	0.0~	0.0~	0.0~	0.0~	0.0~	0.0~	0.0~
1.1.25	Other preserved or processed vegetables	0.3	0.4	0.4	0.3	0.4	0.3	0.3	0.3	0.3	0.3	0.3
1.1.26	Potatoes	0.2	0.2	0.2	0.2	0.1	0.1	0.1	0.1	0.1	0.1	0.1
1.1.27	Other tubers and products of tuber vegetables	0.4	0.4	0.4	0.4	0.4	0.4	0.3	0.3	0.3	0.2	0.3
1.1.28	Sugar and sugar products	0.1	0.1	0.1	0.1	0.1	0.1	0.1	0.1	0.1	0.0~	0.1
1.1.29	Jams, marmalades	0.1	0.1	0.1	0.1	0.1	0.0~	0.1	0.0~	0.0~	0.0~	0.1
1.1.30	Chocolate	0.5	0.5	0.5	0.4	0.4	0.4	0.4	0.4	0.4	0.3	0.4
1.1.31	Confectionery products	0.2	0.2	0.2	0.2	0.1	0.2	0.2	0.1	0.1	0.1	0.1
1.1.32	Edible ices and ice cream	0.2	0.2	0.2	0.2	0.1	0.1	0.1	0.1	0.1	0.1	0.1
1.1.33	Other food products	0.6	0.7	0.5	0.6	0.5	0.5	0.4	0.4	0.4	0.4	0.5
1.2	Non-alcoholic drinks	1.2	1.2	1.1	1.0	1.0	1.0	0.9	0.9	0.8	0.7	0.9
1.2.1	Coffee	0.3	0.2	0.2	0.2	0.2	0.2	0.2	0.1	0.2	0.1	0.2
1.2.2	Tea	0.1	0.1	0.1	0.1	0.1	0.1	0.1	0.1	0.1	0.1	0.1
1.2.3	Cocoa and powdered chocolate	0.0~	0.0~	0.0~	0.0~	0.0~	0.0~	0.0~	0.0~	0.0~	0.0~	0.0~
1.2.4	Fruit and vegetable juices (inc. fruit squash)	0.2	0.3	0.2	0.2	0.2	0.2	0.2	0.2	0.2	0.2	0.2
1.2.5	Mineral or spring waters	0.1	0.1	0.1	0.1	0.1	0.1	0.1	0.1	0.0~	0.0~	0.1
1.2.6	Soft drinks (inc. fizzy and ready to drink fruit drinks)	0.5	0.5	0.5	0.4	0.4	0.4	0.4	0.4	0.3	0.3	0.4

Note: The commodity and service categories are not comparable to those in publications before 2001-02.

The numbering system is sequential, it does not use actual COICOP codes.

Please see background notes for symbols and conventions used in this report.

Table 3.2
Detailed household expenditure as a percentage of total expenditure by disposable income decile group (cont.)
UK, financial year ending 2020

Commodity or service	Lowest ten per cent	Second decile group	Third decile group	Fourth decile group	Fifth decile group	Sixth decile group	Seventh decile group	Eighth decile group	Ninth decile group	Highest ten per cent	All house-holds
					Percentage of total expenditure						
2 Alcoholic drink, tobacco & narcotics	**3.5**	**3.0**	**2.5**	**2.3**	**2.5**	**2.4**	**2.0**	**2.1**	**2.1**	**1.7**	**2.2**
2.1 Alcoholic drinks	1.9	1.7	1.7	1.6	1.6	1.5	1.5	1.6	1.6	1.5	1.6
2.1.1 Spirits and liqueurs (brought home)	0.5	0.5	0.4	0.5	0.5	0.4	0.4	0.4	0.4	0.3	0.4
2.1.2 Wines, fortified wines (brought home)	0.8	0.7	0.8	0.7	0.8	0.6	0.7	0.7	0.8	0.8	0.8
2.1.3 Beer, lager, ciders and perry (brought home)	0.6	0.4	0.4	0.4	0.4	0.4	0.4	0.5	0.4	0.3	0.4
2.1.4 Alcopops (brought home)	..	..	..	..	..	..	..	..	[0.0]	..	0.0~
2.2 Tobacco and narcotics	1.6	1.3	0.8	0.7	0.8	0.9	0.5	0.5	0.5	0.2	0.6
2.2.1 Cigarettes	1.2	1.0	0.5	0.5	0.5	0.6	0.4	0.3	0.4	0.2	0.4
2.2.2 Cigars, other tobacco products and narcotics	0.4	0.4	0.2	0.2	0.3	0.2	0.2	0.2	0.1	0.1	0.2
3 Clothing & footwear	**3.4**	**3.2**	**3.4**	**3.6**	**3.6**	**3.9**	**4.5**	**4.2**	**4.2**	**4.3**	**4.0**
3.1 Clothing	2.7	2.6	2.7	2.9	2.9	3.0	3.7	3.5	3.3	3.3	3.2
3.1.1 Men's outer garments	0.5	0.6	0.8	0.4	0.6	0.8	0.9	1.0	0.8	0.9	0.8
3.1.2 Men's under garments	0.1	0.1	0.1	0.1	0.1	0.1	0.1	0.1	0.1	0.1	0.1
3.1.3 Women's outer garments	1.2	1.2	1.0	1.5	1.2	1.3	1.5	1.5	1.5	1.4	1.4
3.1.4 Women's under garments	0.4	0.2	0.2	0.3	0.2	0.2	0.2	0.2	0.2	0.2	0.2
3.1.5 Boys' outer garments (5-15)	[0.0]	[0.0]	0.1	0.1	0.2	0.1	0.2	0.1	0.1	0.2	0.1
3.1.6 Girls' outer garments (5-15)	[0.1]	0.2	0.2	0.2	0.2	0.1	0.2	0.2	0.2	0.2	0.2
3.1.7 Infants' outer garments (under 5)	[0.1]	0.1	0.1	0.1	0.1	0.1	0.1	0.1	0.1	0.1	0.1
3.1.8 Children's under garments (under 16)	0.1	0.1	0.1	0.1	0.1	0.1	0.1	0.1	0.1	0.1	0.1
3.1.9 Accessories	0.1	0.1	0.1	0.1	0.1	0.1	0.2	0.2	0.2	0.1	0.1
3.1.10 Haberdashery and clothing hire	0.1	0.0~	0.0~	0.0~	0.1	0.1	0.1	0.0~	0.0~	0.0~	0.1
3.1.11 Dry cleaners, laundry and dyeing	[0.1]	[0.0]	..	..	[0.0]	[0.0]	[0.0]	0.0~	[0.0]	0.1	0.0~
3.2 Footwear	0.7	0.6	0.6	0.7	0.7	0.8	0.8	0.7	0.9	1.0	0.8
4 Housing (net)[1], fuel & power	**23.0**	**20.7**	**20.7**	**17.5**	**16.8**	**14.9**	**13.7**	**12.6**	**9.9**	**10.1**	**14.1**
4.1 Actual rentals for housing	29.0	19.5	16.4	11.7	10.4	7.6	7.1	6.4	4.7	4.5	8.9
4.1.1 Gross rent	29.0	19.5	16.4	11.7	10.4	7.6	7.1	6.4	4.7	4.5	8.9
4.1.2 *less housing benefit, rebates & allowances rec'd*	18.1	10.3	5.3	3.1	1.2	0.4	0.4	0.4	..	..	2.1
4.1.3 Net rent[2]	10.9	9.3	11.1	8.5	9.2	7.3	6.8	6.0	4.5	4.5	6.8
4.1.4 Second dwelling rent	:	:	:	:	:	:	:	:	:	..	..
4.2 Maintenance and repair of dwelling	1.0	1.1	1.3	1.2	1.1	1.7	1.5	1.3	1.2	1.6	1.4
4.3 Water supply and miscellaneous services relating to the dwelling	3.6	3.0	2.4	2.2	1.9	1.9	1.6	1.5	1.2	1.3	1.8
4.4 Electricity, gas and other fuels	7.5	7.3	5.9	5.6	4.6	4.1	3.8	3.8	3.1	2.7	4.2
4.4.1 Electricity	4.0	3.8	3.1	2.9	2.4	2.1	2.0	1.8	1.6	1.3	2.1
4.4.2 Gas	3.1	3.1	2.6	2.3	2.0	1.9	1.6	1.6	1.3	1.2	1.8
4.4.3 Other fuels	0.4	0.4	0.3	0.4	0.2	0.2	0.2	0.4	0.2	0.2	0.3

Note: The commodity and service categories are not comparable to those in publications before 2001-02.

The numbering system is sequential, it does not use actual COICOP codes.

Please see background notes for symbols and conventions used in this report.

1 Excluding mortgage interest payments, council tax and Northern Ireland rates.

2 The figure included in total expenditure is net rent as opposed to gross rent.

Table 3.2
Detailed household expenditure as a percentage of total expenditure by disposable income decile group (cont.)
UK, financial year ending 2020

Commodity or service		Lowest ten per cent	Second decile group	Third decile group	Fourth decile group	Fifth decile group	Sixth decile group	Seventh decile group	Eighth decile group	Ninth decile group	Highest ten per cent	All house-holds
						Percentage of total expenditure						
5	**Household goods & services**	**5.2**	**6.5**	**6.0**	**6.9**	**6.1**	**5.9**	**5.6**	**6.5**	**6.4**	**6.4**	**6.2**
5.1	Furniture and furnishings, carpets and other floor coverings	2.6	3.0	3.3	3.8	3.2	2.9	3.0	3.6	3.7	3.8	3.4
	5.1.1 Furniture and furnishings	1.9	2.4	2.6	2.9	2.6	2.5	2.5	3.1	3.2	3.1	2.8
	5.1.2 Floor coverings	0.7	0.6	0.7	0.9	0.6	0.4	0.5	0.6	0.5	0.7	0.6
5.2	Household textiles	0.3	0.3	0.2	0.3	0.3	0.3	0.3	0.4	0.4	0.3	0.3
5.3	Household appliances	0.4	0.8	0.5	0.6	0.6	0.6	0.4	0.5	0.4	0.4	0.5
5.4	Glassware, tableware and household utensils	0.2	0.2	0.2	0.3	0.3	0.3	0.3	0.3	0.3	0.4	0.3
5.5	Tools and equipment for house and garden	0.2	0.6	0.5	0.5	0.6	0.6	0.6	0.6	0.5	0.4	0.5
5.6	Goods and services for routine household maintenance	1.5	1.5	1.3	1.3	1.1	1.1	1.0	1.0	1.1	1.2	1.2
	5.6.1 Cleaning materials	0.6	0.6	0.6	0.6	0.5	0.5	0.4	0.4	0.4	0.3	0.5
	5.6.2 Household goods and hardware	0.4	0.4	0.4	0.4	0.3	0.3	0.3	0.3	0.3	0.2	0.3
	5.6.3 Domestic services, carpet cleaning, hire/repair of furniture/furnishings	0.5	0.6	0.2	0.4	0.3	0.3	0.2	0.3	0.4	0.6	0.4
6	**Health**	**1.7**	**1.8**	**1.4**	**1.4**	**1.5**	**1.4**	**1.3**	**1.2**	**1.4**	**1.3**	**1.4**
6.1	Medical products, appliances and equipment	0.9	1.2	0.8	0.6	0.9	0.7	0.8	0.7	0.9	0.5	0.8
	6.1.1 Medicines, prescriptions, healthcare products etc.	0.5	0.8	0.5	0.4	0.5	0.4	0.4	0.4	0.5	0.3	0.4
	6.1.2 Spectacles, lenses, accessories and repairs	0.4	0.4	0.3	0.2	0.4	0.2	0.4	0.3	0.3	0.2	0.3
6.2	Hospital services	0.8	0.7	0.6	0.8	0.5	0.7	0.5	0.5	0.5	0.8	0.6
7	**Transport**	**9.0**	**9.4**	**11.9**	**12.3**	**12.6**	**15.7**	**14.1**	**14.3**	**15.7**	**15.2**	**13.9**
7.1	Purchase of vehicles	2.4	2.6	3.5	3.3	3.6	5.8	4.5	4.5	5.3	5.2	4.5
	7.1.1 Purchase of new cars and vans	..	[1.1]	[0.9]	1.1	1.1	1.7	1.0	1.4	1.6	1.7	1.3
	7.1.2 Purchase of second hand cars or vans	2.1	1.5	2.3	2.2	2.3	3.3	3.3	3.0	3.4	3.3	2.9
	7.1.3 Purchase of motorcycles and other vehicles	:	..	..	..	[0.1]	..	[0.2]	..	[0.2]	[0.1]	0.2
7.2	Operation of personal transport	4.2	4.6	5.7	6.1	6.1	6.3	6.2	6.2	5.9	5.0	5.7
	7.2.1 Spares and accessories	[0.7]	0.2	0.5	0.8	0.4	0.5	0.3	0.4	0.3	0.4	0.4
	7.2.2 Petrol, diesel and other motor oils	2.6	3.1	3.6	3.9	3.9	4.4	4.0	4.4	4.0	3.2	3.8
	7.2.3 Repairs and servicing	0.6	0.9	1.2	1.1	1.3	1.0	1.2	1.0	1.0	1.0	1.1
	7.2.4 Other motoring costs	0.3	0.3	0.4	0.4	0.6	0.4	0.6	0.4	0.5	0.4	0.5
7.3	Transport services	2.3	2.2	2.7	2.8	2.8	3.6	3.4	3.5	4.5	5.0	3.7
	7.3.1 Rail and tube fares	0.4	0.3	0.3	0.4	0.5	0.7	0.8	0.7	1.2	1.2	0.8
	7.3.2 Bus and coach fares	0.4	0.3	0.4	0.3	0.3	0.4	0.2	0.2	0.2	0.2	0.3
	7.3.3 Combined fares	..	..	..	..	[0.1]	..	..	[0.2]	..	0.1	0.1
	7.3.4 Other travel and transport	1.4	1.6	1.9	2.0	1.9	2.5	2.3	2.5	3.1	3.5	2.5
8	**Communication**	**4.1**	**4.9**	**4.4**	**4.5**	**4.0**	**4.0**	**3.5**	**3.5**	**3.2**	**2.8**	**3.6**
8.1	Postal services	0.2	0.2	0.2	0.1	0.1	0.1	0.1	0.1	0.1	0.1	0.1
8.2	Telephone and telefax equipment	[0.1]	[0.2]	[0.2]	[0.4]	0.2	[0.2]	0.1	0.2	0.4	0.4	0.3
8.3	Telephone and telefax services[3]	1.5	1.6	1.5	1.5	1.5	1.7	1.5	1.5	1.3	1.2	1.4
8.4	Internet subscription fees (ex. combined packages)	0.2	0.2	0.2	0.1	0.2	0.1	0.1	0.1	0.1	0.1	0.1
8.5	Combined telecom services[4]	2.2	2.7	2.4	2.3	2.1	1.9	1.7	1.6	1.4	1.1	1.7

Note: The commodity and service categories are not comparable to those in publications before 2001-02.

The numbering system is sequential, it does not use actual COICOP codes.

Please see background notes for symbols and conventions used in this report.

3 For FYE 2019 onwards, excludes payments made as part of a combined bill.

4 New for FYE 2019. This encompasses all telecoms bills that include more than one service. Due to the nature of combined packages, this also includes packages that includes television services.

Table 3.2
Detailed household expenditure as a percentage of total expenditure by disposable income decile group (cont.)
UK, financial year ending 2020

	Lowest ten per cent	Second decile group	Third decile group	Fourth decile group	Fifth decile group	Sixth decile group	Seventh decile group	Eighth decile group	Ninth decile group	Highest ten per cent	All house-holds
Commodity or service	Percentage of total expenditure										
9 Recreation & culture	**12.2**	**11.6**	**11.9**	**12.3**	**11.4**	**11.8**	**12.7**	**12.7**	**14.5**	**13.3**	**12.7**
9.1 Audio-visual, photographic and information processing equipment	0.5	0.6	0.9	1.1	0.5	1.0	0.7	0.8	0.9	0.6	0.8
9.1.1 Audio equipment and accessories, CD players	0.2	0.1	0.1	0.3	0.1	0.2	0.2	0.1	0.2	0.2	0.2
9.1.2 TV, video and computers	0.3	0.4	0.7	0.7	0.3	0.7	0.4	0.8	0.4	0.3	0.5
9.1.3 Photographic, cine and optical equipment	..	..	..	..	..	..	..	..	..	[0.1]	0.1
9.2 Other major durables for recreation and culture	..	..	[0.5]	..	[0.5]	[0.4]	[0.3]	[0.3]	0.3	0.3	0.3
9.3 Other recreational items and equipment, gardens and pets	2.5	2.9	2.5	2.7	2.3	2.3	2.5	3.3	2.4	2.8	2.6
9.3.1 Games, toys and hobbies	0.3	0.5	0.5	0.4	0.6	0.7	0.5	0.7	0.5	0.5	0.5
9.3.2 Computer software and games	..	[0.3]	[0.1]	0.2	0.2	0.1	0.2	0.1	0.2	0.1	0.2
9.3.3 Equipment for sport, camping and open-air recreation	[0.2]	[0.1]	[0.2]	0.1	0.2	0.1	0.2	0.3	0.2	0.6	0.3
9.3.4 Horticultural goods, garden equipment and plants	0.5	0.6	0.5	0.7	0.4	0.5	0.5	0.5	0.4	0.4	0.5
9.3.5 Pets and pet food	1.2	1.3	1.2	1.3	0.7	0.9	1.1	1.7	1.1	1.2	1.2
9.4 Recreational and cultural services	3.6	3.1	3.0	3.2	3.0	3.0	3.1	3.4	3.9	3.6	3.4
9.4.1 Sports admissions, subscriptions, leisure class fees and equipment hire	0.7	0.8	0.9	1.1	1.2	0.9	1.0	1.4	1.9	1.7	1.3
9.4.2 Cinema, theatre and museums etc.	0.7	0.5	0.2	0.4	0.3	0.5	0.7	0.6	0.6	0.8	0.6
9.4.3 TV, video, satellite rental, cable subscriptions and TV licences[5]	1.1	1.1	0.9	0.9	0.9	0.8	0.8	0.7	0.7	0.6	0.8
9.4.4 Miscellaneous entertainments	0.2	0.1	0.1	0.1	0.2	0.3	0.3	0.3	0.3	0.3	0.2
9.4.5 Development of film, deposit for film development, passport photos, holiday and school photos	..	..	..	..	[0.0]	[0.0]	[0.0]	[0.0]	0.0~	0.0~	0.0~
9.4.6 Gambling payments	0.9	0.6	0.8	0.6	0.4	0.4	0.3	0.4	0.3	0.2	0.4
9.5 Newspapers, books and stationery	1.2	1.1	1.1	1.1	0.9	1.0	0.9	0.7	0.8	1.0	0.9
9.5.1 Books	0.3	0.1	0.1	0.3	0.2	0.2	0.2	0.2	0.2	0.2	0.2
9.5.2 Diaries, address books, cards etc.	0.3	0.4	0.3	0.4	0.4	0.4	0.4	0.3	0.3	0.5	0.4
9.5.3 Newspapers	0.4	0.4	0.4	0.3	0.2	0.2	0.2	0.1	0.1	0.1	0.2
9.5.4 Magazines and periodicals	0.2	0.2	0.2	0.1	0.1	0.2	0.1	0.1	0.1	0.1	0.1
9.6 Package holidays	4.2	3.9	3.9	3.9	4.2	4.1	5.2	4.2	6.1	5.0	4.7
9.6.1 Package holidays - UK	[0.3]	[0.4]	[0.3]	0.6	0.3	0.3	0.3	[0.2]	0.4	0.3	0.3
9.6.2 Package holidays - abroad	3.9	3.6	3.6	3.3	3.8	3.8	4.9	4.0	5.7	4.7	4.4
10 Education	..	..	[0.3]	[0.6]	[0.3]	0.2	0.9	0.6	0.8	1.6	**0.8**
10.1 Education fees	..	..	..	..	..	[0.2]	0.7	0.6	0.7	1.5	0.7
10.2 Payments for school trips, other ad-hoc expenditure	..	..	..	..	[0.0]	..	[0.2]	[0.1]	0.1	[0.1]	0.1
11 Restaurants & hotels	**6.3**	**7.0**	**6.8**	**7.6**	**8.9**	**8.3**	**9.1**	**9.5**	**9.7**	**10.6**	**9.0**
11.1 Catering services	5.3	5.6	5.4	6.2	7.1	6.8	7.2	7.6	7.4	7.9	7.0
11.1.1 Restaurant and café meals	2.8	2.9	2.7	3.2	3.7	3.3	3.5	3.6	3.4	3.9	3.4
11.1.2 Alcoholic drinks (away from home)	1.0	0.9	1.0	1.3	1.2	1.3	1.4	1.7	1.6	1.6	1.4
11.1.3 Take away meals eaten at home	0.9	1.0	0.8	0.8	1.1	1.0	1.0	1.0	1.0	0.9	1.0
11.1.4 Other take-away and snack food	0.5	0.6	0.7	0.7	0.8	0.9	0.9	1.0	1.1	1.1	0.9
11.1.5 Contract catering (food) and canteens	[0.0]	0.2	0.2	0.2	0.4	0.3	0.4	0.3	0.3	0.5	0.3
11.2 Accommodation services	1.0	1.4	1.4	1.5	1.8	1.5	1.9	1.9	2.3	2.8	2.0
11.2.1 Holiday in the UK	0.6	0.8	0.9	1.0	1.2	1.0	1.2	1.2	1.2	1.1	1.1
11.2.2 Holiday abroad	[0.3]	0.6	0.4	0.5	0.5	0.6	0.7	0.7	1.2	1.7	0.9
11.2.3 Room hire	:	..	..	:	..	..	..	..	:	..	0.0~

Note: The commodity and service categories are not comparable to those in publications before 2001-02.

The numbering system is sequential, it does not use actual COICOP codes.

Please see background notes for symbols and conventions used in this report.

5 For FYE 2019 onwards, excludes payments made as part of a combined bill.

Table 3.2

Detailed household expenditure as a percentage of total expenditure by disposable income decile group (cont.)
UK, financial year ending 2020

Commodity or service	Lowest ten per cent	Second decile group	Third decile group	Fourth decile group	Fifth decile group	Sixth decile group	Seventh decile group	Eighth decile group	Ninth decile group	Highest ten per cent	All house-holds
					Percentage of total expenditure						
12 Miscellaneous goods & services	**7.8**	**6.9**	**7.5**	**8.2**	**7.9**	**7.9**	**7.6**	**8.1**	**7.5**	**7.9**	**7.8**
12.1 Personal care	2.4	2.2	2.2	2.5	2.3	2.5	2.2	2.4	2.2	2.2	2.3
12.1.1 Hairdressing, beauty treatment	0.8	0.8	0.7	0.9	0.7	0.9	0.7	0.9	0.7	0.6	0.7
12.1.2 Toilet paper	0.3	0.2	0.2	0.2	0.2	0.2	0.2	0.2	0.1	0.1	0.2
12.1.3 Toiletries and soap	0.5	0.4	0.5	0.5	0.5	0.4	0.5	0.4	0.4	0.4	0.5
12.1.4 Baby toiletries and accessories (disposable)	0.1	0.1	0.1	0.1	0.1	0.1	0.1	0.1	0.1	0.1	0.1
12.1.5 Hair products, cosmetics and related electrical appliances	0.8	0.6	0.7	0.9	0.8	0.9	0.7	0.8	0.9	0.9	0.8
12.2 Personal effects	0.5	0.4	0.4	1.1	0.6	0.8	0.7	0.6	0.7	0.8	0.7
12.3 Social protection	..	..	[0.3]	[0.8]	0.8	0.6	0.5	0.7	0.4	1.1	0.6
12.4 Insurance	3.0	3.6	3.9	3.3	3.3	3.4	3.3	3.3	3.2	3.0	3.3
12.4.1 Household insurances - structural, contents and appliances	1.1	1.1	1.1	0.9	1.0	0.9	0.8	0.7	0.7	0.7	0.8
12.4.2 Medical insurance premiums[6]	0.3	0.4	0.2	0.2	0.3	0.3	0.3	0.5	0.5	0.6	0.4
12.4.3 Vehicle insurance including boat insurance	1.5	1.9	2.4	1.9	2.0	2.1	2.0	1.9	1.8	1.6	1.9
12.4.4 Non-package holiday, other travel insurance[7]	0.1	0.2	0.2	0.2	0.2	0.2	0.1	0.1	0.1	0.2	0.2
12.5 Other services	1.8	0.7	0.7	0.4	0.8	0.6	0.9	1.1	1.0	0.8	0.9
12.5.1 Moving house	[0.2]	[0.4]	0.3	0.3	0.5	0.3	0.4	0.6	0.5	0.4	0.4
12.5.2 Bank, building society, post office, credit card charges	0.1	0.1	0.1	0.1	0.1	0.1	0.1	0.1	0.1	0.1	0.1
12.5.3 Other services and professional fees	[1.5]	[0.3]	0.3	0.1	0.3	0.2	0.4	0.4	0.4	0.3	0.4
1-12 All expenditure groups	**90.2**	**89.2**	**89.7**	**89.9**	**87.3**	**87.5**	**86.2**	**86.0**	**84.8**	**83.7**	**86.5**
13 Other expenditure items	**9.8**	**10.8**	**10.3**	**10.1**	**12.7**	**12.5**	**13.8**	**14.0**	**15.2**	**16.3**	**13.5**
13.1 Housing: mortgage interest payments, council tax etc.	7.1	6.6	7.1	6.7	8.1	8.4	8.9	9.5	9.3	9.5	8.6
13.2 Licences, fines and transfers	0.5	0.6	0.6	0.6	0.7	0.8	0.7	0.6	0.6	0.7	0.6
13.3 Holiday spending	[0.6]	..	[0.6]	[0.8]	1.6	1.4	1.8	1.3	3.1	3.9	2.1
13.4 Money transfers and credit	1.6	3.0	2.0	1.9	2.3	1.9	2.4	2.5	2.1	2.2	2.2
13.4.1 Money, cash gifts given to children	..	..	..	..	..	[0.0]	[0.2]	..	[0.1]	[0.0]	0.1
13.4.2 Cash gifts and donations	1.5	2.8	1.7	1.6	2.1	1.7	2.0	2.3	1.9	2.0	2.0
13.4.3 Club instalment payments (child) and interest on credit cards	[0.1]	0.2	0.3	0.2	0.1	0.2	0.2	0.2	0.1	0.2	0.2
Total expenditure	**100.0**	**100.0**	**100.0**	**100.0**	**100.0**	**100.0**	**100.0**	**100.0**	**100.0**	**100.0**	**100.0**

Note: The commodity and service categories are not comparable to those in publications before 2001-02.

The numbering system is sequential, it does not use actual COICOP codes.

Please see background notes for symbols and conventions used in this report.

6 For FYE 2019, critical illness cover, personal accident insurance and other medical insurance are included here. They were not included in previous years.

7 For FYE 2019, information about insurance for non-package holiday and other travel insurance was collected in the questionnaire in addition to the diary. In previous years, this was based on diary data only.

Source: Office for National Statistics

Table 3.2E

Detailed household expenditure as a percentage of total expenditure by equivalised disposable income decile group (OECD-modified scale)

UK, financial year ending 2020

	Lowest ten per cent	Second decile group	Third decile group	Fourth decile group	Fifth decile group	Sixth decile group	Seventh decile group	Eighth decile group	Ninth decile group	Highest ten per cent	All house-holds
Lower boundary of group (£ per week)		182	240	296	342	398	462	529	629	781	
Weighted number of households (thousands)	2,780	2,780	2,780	2,790	2,780	2,780	2,780	2,780	2,790	2,770	27,820
Total number of households in sample	550	560	580	560	570	540	530	520	520	510	5,440
Total number of persons in sample	1,090	1,260	1,320	1,310	1,360	1,290	1,350	1,260	1,250	1,200	12,670
Total number of adults in sample	770	890	970	1,010	1,030	1,030	1,110	1,050	1,020	1,010	9,880
Weighted average number of persons per household	2.0	2.3	2.2	2.4	2.4	2.4	2.5	2.5	2.5	2.4	2.4

Commodity or service					Percentage of total expenditure						

	Lowest ten per cent	Second decile group	Third decile group	Fourth decile group	Fifth decile group	Sixth decile group	Seventh decile group	Eighth decile group	Ninth decile group	Highest ten per cent	All house-holds
1 Food & non-alcoholic drinks	**15.0**	**14.3**	**13.6**	**13.1**	**12.3**	**11.0**	**11.3**	**9.5**	**9.3**	**7.4**	**10.8**
1.1 Food	13.7	13.1	12.4	11.9	11.3	10.1	10.4	8.7	8.5	6.8	9.9
1.1.1 Bread, rice and cereals	1.4	1.4	1.3	1.2	1.1	1.0	1.1	0.9	0.8	0.6	1.0
1.1.2 Pasta products	0.1	0.1	0.1	0.1	0.1	0.1	0.1	0.1	0.1	0.1	0.1
1.1.3 Buns, cakes, biscuits etc.	1.0	1.0	1.0	0.9	0.9	0.7	0.7	0.6	0.5	0.4	0.7
1.1.4 Pastry (savoury)	0.2	0.2	0.2	0.2	0.2	0.2	0.2	0.2	0.1	0.1	0.2
1.1.5 Beef (fresh, chilled or frozen)	0.5	0.4	0.4	0.4	0.3	0.4	0.3	0.3	0.3	0.2	0.3
1.1.6 Pork (fresh, chilled or frozen)	0.1	0.1	0.1	0.1	0.1	0.1	0.1	0.1	0.1	0.0~	0.1
1.1.7 Lamb (fresh, chilled or frozen)	0.1	0.2	0.1	0.1	0.2	0.1	0.1	0.1	0.1	0.1	0.1
1.1.8 Poultry (fresh, chilled or frozen)	0.6	0.5	0.5	0.5	0.4	0.5	0.5	0.4	0.4	0.3	0.4
1.1.9 Bacon and ham	0.2	0.2	0.2	0.2	0.2	0.2	0.1	0.1	0.1	0.1	0.1
1.1.10 Other meat and meat preparations	1.5	1.6	1.6	1.5	1.3	1.1	1.2	1.0	0.9	0.7	1.1
1.1.11 Fish and fish products	0.6	0.6	0.5	0.6	0.6	0.5	0.6	0.5	0.5	0.5	0.5
1.1.12 Milk	0.6	0.6	0.6	0.5	0.4	0.4	0.4	0.3	0.2	0.2	0.4
1.1.13 Cheese and curd	0.5	0.5	0.5	0.4	0.4	0.4	0.4	0.3	0.4	0.3	0.4
1.1.14 Eggs	0.2	0.2	0.2	0.2	0.1	0.1	0.1	0.1	0.1	0.1	0.1
1.1.15 Other milk products	0.6	0.5	0.5	0.5	0.5	0.4	0.4	0.4	0.3	0.3	0.4
1.1.16 Butter	0.1	0.1	0.1	0.1	0.1	0.1	0.1	0.1	0.1	0.1	0.1
1.1.17 Margarine, other vegetable fats and peanut butter	0.2	0.2	0.2	0.2	0.1	0.1	0.1	0.1	0.1	0.1	0.1
1.1.18 Cooking oils and fats	0.1	0.1	0.1	0.1	0.1	0.1	0.1	0.0~	0.1	0.0~	0.1
1.1.19 Fresh fruit	0.9	0.8	0.8	0.8	0.7	0.7	0.7	0.6	0.6	0.5	0.7
1.1.20 Other fresh, chilled or frozen fruits	0.1	0.1	0.1	0.1	0.1	0.1	0.1	0.1	0.1	0.1	0.1
1.1.21 Dried fruit and nuts	0.1	0.2	0.2	0.2	0.3	0.1	0.2	0.1	0.1	0.1	0.2
1.1.22 Preserved fruit and fruit based products	0.0~	0.0~	0.0~	0.0~	0.0~	0.0~	0.0~	0.0~	0.0~	0.0~	0.0~
1.1.23 Fresh vegetables	1.0	0.9	0.8	0.8	0.8	0.8	0.9	0.7	0.8	0.6	0.8
1.1.24 Dried vegetables	0.0~	[0.0]	0.0~	0.0~	0.0~	0.0~	0.0~	0.0~	0.0~	0.0~	0.0~
1.1.25 Other preserved or processed vegetables	0.4	0.3	0.4	0.3	0.4	0.3	0.3	0.3	0.3	0.3	0.3
1.1.26 Potatoes	0.2	0.2	0.2	0.2	0.1	0.1	0.1	0.1	0.1	0.1	0.1
1.1.27 Other tubers and products of tuber vegetables	0.5	0.5	0.5	0.4	0.4	0.3	0.3	0.2	0.2	0.2	0.3
1.1.28 Sugar and sugar products	0.1	0.1	0.1	0.1	0.1	0.1	0.1	0.1	0.0~	0.0~	0.1
1.1.29 Jams, marmalades	0.1	0.1	0.1	0.1	0.1	0.0~	0.1	0.0~	0.0~	0.0~	0.1
1.1.30 Chocolate	0.5	0.5	0.5	0.5	0.5	0.4	0.4	0.3	0.4	0.3	0.4
1.1.31 Confectionery products	0.2	0.2	0.2	0.2	0.2	0.1	0.1	0.1	0.1	0.1	0.1
1.1.32 Edible ices and ice cream	0.2	0.2	0.2	0.2	0.1	0.1	0.1	0.1	0.1	0.1	0.1
1.1.33 Other food products	0.7	0.7	0.5	0.5	0.5	0.5	0.5	0.4	0.4	0.3	0.5
1.2 Non-alcoholic drinks	1.3	1.2	1.2	1.1	1.0	1.0	0.9	0.8	0.7	0.6	0.9
1.2.1 Coffee	0.2	0.2	0.2	0.2	0.2	0.2	0.2	0.2	0.1	0.2	0.2
1.2.2 Tea	0.1	0.1	0.1	0.1	0.1	0.1	0.1	0.1	0.1	0.1	0.1
1.2.3 Cocoa and powdered chocolate	0.0~	0.0~	0.0~	0.0~	0.0~	0.0~	0.0~	0.0~	0.0~	0.0~	0.0~
1.2.4 Fruit and vegetable juices (inc. fruit squash)	0.3	0.2	0.2	0.2	0.2	0.2	0.2	0.2	0.2	0.1	0.2
1.2.5 Mineral or spring waters	0.1	0.1	0.1	0.1	0.1	0.1	0.1	0.0~	0.0~	0.0~	0.1
1.2.6 Soft drinks (inc. fizzy and ready to drink fruit drinks)	0.6	0.5	0.5	0.5	0.5	0.4	0.4	0.3	0.3	0.2	0.4

Note: The commodity and service categories are not comparable to those in publications before 2001-02.
The numbering system is sequential, it does not use actual COICOP codes.
Please see background notes for symbols and conventions used in this report.

Table 3.2E

Detailed household expenditure as a percentage of total expenditure by equivalised disposable income decile group (OECD-modified scale) (cont)

UK, financial year ending 2020

Commodity or service	Lowest ten per cent	Second decile group	Third decile group	Fourth decile group	Fifth decile group	Sixth decile group	Seventh decile group	Eighth decile group	Ninth decile group	Highest ten per cent	All house-holds
					Percentage of total expenditure						
2 Alcoholic drink, tobacco & narcotics	**3.2**	**2.5**	**2.6**	**2.6**	**2.4**	**2.0**	**2.3**	**2.1**	**2.0**	**1.7**	**2.2**
2.1 Alcoholic drinks	1.7	1.4	1.7	1.6	1.5	1.5	1.6	1.6	1.6	1.5	1.6
2.1.1 Spirits and liqueurs (brought home)	0.4	0.4	0.5	0.5	0.4	0.4	0.4	0.4	0.4	0.3	0.4
2.1.2 Wines, fortified wines (brought home)	0.6	0.6	0.7	0.8	0.7	0.7	0.7	0.8	0.8	1.0	0.8
2.1.3 Beer, lager, ciders and perry (brought home)	0.7	0.4	0.5	0.3	0.4	0.4	0.5	0.4	0.4	0.3	0.4
2.1.4 Alcopops (brought home)	..	[0.0]	..	..	..	..	..	..	..	..	0.0~
2.2 Tobacco and narcotics	1.5	1.1	0.9	1.0	0.9	0.5	0.7	0.4	0.4	0.2	0.6
2.2.1 Cigarettes	1.0	0.8	0.6	0.7	0.6	0.2	0.5	0.3	0.3	0.1	0.4
2.2.2 Cigars, other tobacco products and narcotics	0.4	0.3	0.3	0.3	0.3	0.2	0.2	0.1	0.1	[0.0]	0.2
3 Clothing & footwear	**4.2**	**4.0**	**3.4**	**3.4**	**4.3**	**4.4**	**4.1**	**4.2**	**3.9**	**3.9**	**4.0**
3.1 Clothing	3.2	3.2	2.7	2.6	3.4	3.6	3.4	3.3	3.1	3.0	3.2
3.1.1 Men's outer garments	0.7	0.6	0.7	0.5	0.9	0.9	1.0	0.8	0.7	0.9	0.8
3.1.2 Men's under garments	0.1	0.1	0.1	0.1	0.1	0.1	0.1	0.1	0.1	0.1	0.1
3.1.3 Women's outer garments	1.3	1.4	1.0	1.1	1.4	1.7	1.3	1.5	1.5	1.3	1.4
3.1.4 Women's under garments	0.2	0.3	0.2	0.2	0.2	0.2	0.2	0.2	0.2	0.2	0.2
3.1.5 Boys' outer garments (5-15)	0.1	0.2	0.2	0.1	0.2	0.1	0.1	0.1	0.1	0.1	0.1
3.1.6 Girls' outer garments (5-15)	0.3	0.3	0.2	0.1	0.2	0.2	0.2	0.2	0.1	0.1	0.2
3.1.7 Infants' outer garments (under 5)	0.1	0.1	0.1	0.2	0.1	0.1	0.1	0.1	0.1	0.1	0.1
3.1.8 Children's under garments (under 16)	0.1	0.1	0.1	0.1	0.1	0.1	0.1	0.1	0.0~	0.0~	0.1
3.1.9 Accessories	0.1	0.1	0.1	0.1	0.2	0.1	0.2	0.2	0.2	0.1	0.1
3.1.10 Haberdashery and clothing hire	0.1	0.0~	0.1	0.1	0.1	0.1	0.0~	0.0~	0.0~	0.0~	0.1
3.1.11 Dry cleaners, laundry and dyeing	[0.1]	[0.0]	[0.0]	..	[0.0]	..	[0.1]	[0.0]	0.1	0.1	0.0~
3.2 Footwear	0.9	0.8	0.7	0.7	0.9	0.8	0.7	0.9	0.8	0.8	0.8
4 Housing (net)[1], fuel & power	**21.7**	**21.0**	**17.4**	**17.8**	**16.1**	**14.0**	**13.5**	**12.0**	**10.6**	**10.4**	**14.1**
4.1 Actual rentals for housing	27.9	20.1	13.0	11.5	9.5	6.6	7.0	6.0	4.9	4.5	8.9
4.1.1 Gross rent	27.9	20.1	13.0	11.5	9.5	6.6	7.0	6.0	4.9	4.5	8.9
4.1.2 *less housing benefit, rebates & allowances rec'd*	17.5	8.9	4.9	2.1	0.8	0.1	0.6	0.1	0.1	[0.0]	2.1
4.1.3 Net rent[2]	10.4	11.2	8.1	9.4	8.6	6.5	6.4	6.0	4.8	4.5	6.8
4.1.4 Second dwelling rent	:	:	:	:	:	:	:	..	:	:	..
4.2 Maintenance and repair of dwelling	0.9	0.9	1.3	1.2	1.1	1.8	1.4	1.2	1.2	1.9	1.4
4.3 Water supply and miscellaneous services relating to the dwelling	2.9	2.8	2.1	2.0	1.8	1.7	1.8	1.5	1.4	1.4	1.8
4.4 Electricity, gas and other fuels	7.6	6.2	5.8	5.3	4.6	4.0	3.8	3.4	3.3	2.7	4.2
4.4.1 Electricity	4.0	3.3	3.0	2.7	2.4	2.1	1.9	1.7	1.6	1.3	2.1
4.4.2 Gas	3.3	2.7	2.5	2.2	2.0	1.7	1.7	1.5	1.4	1.1	1.8
4.4.3 Other fuels	0.3	0.3	0.3	0.4	0.2	0.2	0.2	0.2	0.3	0.2	0.3

Note: The commodity and service categories are not comparable to those in publications before 2001-02.

The numbering system is sequential, it does not use actual COICOP codes.

Please see background notes for symbols and conventions used in this report.

1 Excluding mortgage interest payments, council tax and Northern Ireland rates.

2 The figure included in total expenditure is net rent as opposed to gross rent.

Table 3.2E
Detailed household expenditure as a percentage of total expenditure by
equivalised disposable income decile group (OECD-modified scale) (cont)
UK, financial year ending 2020

Commodity or service	Lowest ten per cent	Second decile group	Third decile group	Fourth decile group	Fifth decile group	Sixth decile group	Seventh decile group	Eighth decile group	Ninth decile group	Highest ten per cent	All house-holds
					Percentage of total expenditure						
5 Household goods & services	**5.4**	**5.5**	**6.5**	**7.0**	**5.6**	**6.3**	**6.6**	**5.8**	**6.2**	**6.5**	**6.2**
5.1 Furniture and furnishings, carpets and other floor coverings	2.8	2.6	3.6	3.9	2.9	3.2	3.8	3.2	3.3	4.0	3.4
5.1.1 Furniture and furnishings	2.1	2.2	2.6	2.9	2.5	2.7	3.2	2.8	2.7	3.3	2.8
5.1.2 Floor coverings	0.7	0.4	0.9	1.0	0.4	0.5	0.6	0.4	0.6	0.7	0.6
5.2 Household textiles	0.3	0.3	0.3	0.4	0.2	0.4	0.4	0.4	0.3	0.4	0.3
5.3 Household appliances	0.5	0.6	0.5	0.6	0.4	0.7	0.5	0.3	0.6	0.4	0.5
5.4 Glassware, tableware and household utensils	0.2	0.3	0.3	0.4	0.3	0.3	0.4	0.3	0.4	0.3	0.3
5.5 Tools and equipment for house and garden	0.3	0.5	0.5	0.5	0.6	0.6	0.5	0.6	0.6	0.3	0.5
5.6 Goods and services for routine household maintenance	1.3	1.3	1.4	1.2	1.1	1.2	1.0	1.0	1.1	1.2	1.2
5.6.1 Cleaning materials	0.6	0.6	0.6	0.5	0.5	0.5	0.5	0.4	0.4	0.3	0.5
5.6.2 Household goods and hardware	0.4	0.4	0.4	0.3	0.3	0.4	0.4	0.3	0.3	0.2	0.3
5.6.3 Domestic services, carpet cleaning, hire/repair of furniture/furnishings	0.3	0.3	0.3	0.3	0.3	0.3	0.1	0.3	0.5	0.7	0.4
6 Health	**0.9**	**1.5**	**1.6**	**1.4**	**1.1**	**1.5**	**1.1**	**1.4**	**1.5**	**1.6**	**1.4**
6.1 Medical products, appliances and equipment	0.6	0.9	0.9	0.8	0.6	0.8	0.7	0.8	0.8	0.7	0.8
6.1.1 Medicines, prescriptions, healthcare products etc.	0.5	0.5	0.5	0.5	0.4	0.4	0.5	0.4	0.6	0.3	0.4
6.1.2 Spectacles, lenses, accessories and repairs	[0.1]	0.5	0.3	0.2	0.2	0.4	0.2	0.4	0.3	0.4	0.3
6.2 Hospital services	[0.3]	0.6	0.8	0.6	0.5	0.8	0.4	0.6	0.6	0.9	0.6
7 Transport	**10.1**	**11.0**	**12.9**	**12.7**	**12.8**	**13.9**	**14.5**	**15.1**	**16.1**	**14.5**	**13.9**
7.1 Purchase of vehicles	2.6	2.7	4.7	4.0	3.7	5.0	4.4	5.1	4.9	5.0	4.5
7.1.1 Purchase of new cars and vans	..	[0.7]	[0.7]	1.1	0.7	2.2	1.2	1.4	1.3	2.0	1.3
7.1.2 Purchase of second hand cars or vans	2.0	1.9	2.6	2.9	2.9	2.7	3.2	3.6	3.5	2.8	2.9
7.1.3 Purchase of motorcycles and other vehicles	..	..	..	..	..	..	..	..	..	[0.1]	0.2
7.2 Operation of personal transport	4.9	5.3	5.8	5.8	6.4	6.3	6.2	5.9	6.5	4.4	5.7
7.2.1 Spares and accessories	0.4	0.5	0.4	0.4	0.4	0.5	0.4	0.3	0.6	0.3	0.4
7.2.2 Petrol, diesel and other motor oils	3.4	3.5	3.8	3.9	4.1	4.4	4.2	4.1	4.2	2.7	3.8
7.2.3 Repairs and servicing	0.8	0.8	1.2	1.2	1.3	1.0	1.0	1.1	1.2	1.0	1.1
7.2.4 Other motoring costs	0.3	0.4	0.4	0.3	0.6	0.5	0.6	0.4	0.5	0.4	0.5
7.3 Transport services	2.5	3.1	2.4	2.9	2.7	2.6	3.8	4.1	4.6	5.1	3.7
7.3.1 Rail and tube fares	0.4	0.4	0.3	0.4	0.5	0.5	0.8	1.0	1.3	1.2	0.8
7.3.2 Bus and coach fares	0.6	0.4	0.3	0.4	0.4	0.3	0.3	0.2	0.2	0.1	0.3
7.3.3 Combined fares	..	..	..	..	..	..	..	[0.1]	[0.1]	[0.1]	0.1
7.3.4 Other travel and transport	1.4	2.3	1.8	2.0	1.8	1.7	2.6	2.9	3.0	3.7	2.5
8 Communication	**4.5**	**4.5**	**4.4**	**4.4**	**3.9**	**3.9**	**3.8**	**3.4**	**3.2**	**2.6**	**3.6**
8.1 Postal services	0.2	0.1	0.1	0.1	0.1	0.1	0.1	0.1	0.1	0.1	0.1
8.2 Telephone and telefax equipment	0.2	[0.2]	0.2	[0.4]	0.1	0.3	0.3	0.3	0.1	0.4	0.3
8.3 Telephone and telefax services[3]	1.7	1.8	1.8	1.6	1.6	1.6	1.5	1.3	1.3	0.9	1.4
8.4 Internet subscription fees (ex. combined packages)	0.2	0.2	0.1	0.1	0.1	0.1	0.1	0.1	0.1	0.1	0.1
8.5 Combined telecom services[4]	2.3	2.2	2.2	2.1	2.0	1.9	1.8	1.6	1.4	1.1	1.7

Note: The commodity and service categories are not comparable to those in publications before 2001-02.

The numbering system is sequential, it does not use actual COICOP codes.

Please see background notes for symbols and conventions used in this report.

3 For FYE 2019 onwards, excludes payments made as part of a combined bill.

4 New for FYE 2019. This encompasses all telecoms bills that include more than one service. Due to the nature of combined packages, this also includes packages that includes television services.

Table 3.2E
Detailed household expenditure as a percentage of total expenditure by equivalised disposable income decile group (OECD-modified scale) (cont)
UK, financial year ending 2020

	Lowest ten per cent	Second decile group	Third decile group	Fourth decile group	Fifth decile group	Sixth decile group	Seventh decile group	Eighth decile group	Ninth decile group	Highest ten per cent	All house-holds
Commodity or service					Percentage of total expenditure						
9 Recreation & culture	**10.7**	**11.2**	**11.7**	**11.1**	**11.7**	**12.4**	**12.4**	**13.4**	**14.4**	**14.0**	**12.7**
9.1 Audio-visual, photographic and information processing equipment	0.6	0.6	0.7	0.6	0.7	1.1	0.7	0.9	1.0	0.5	0.8
9.1.1 Audio equipment and accessories, CD players	0.3	0.3	0.1	0.2	0.2	0.2	0.2	0.2	0.3	0.2	0.2
9.1.2 TV, video and computers	0.3	0.3	0.6	0.5	0.4	0.9	0.5	0.6	0.4	0.3	0.5
9.1.3 Photographic, cine and optical equipment	..	..	..	:	..	..	..	..	..	..	0.1
9.2 Other major durables for recreation and culture	..	..	..	..	[0.5]	[0.5]	[0.1]	[0.3]	[0.4]	[0.4]	0.3
9.3 Other recreational items and equipment, gardens and pets	2.5	2.8	2.9	2.7	2.4	2.5	2.7	2.5	2.7	2.7	2.6
9.3.1 Games, toys and hobbies	0.5	0.5	0.7	0.7	0.6	0.6	0.6	0.5	0.6	0.4	0.5
9.3.2 Computer software and games	[0.2]	0.4	0.2	0.1	0.2	0.2	0.1	0.2	0.1	0.1	0.2
9.3.3 Equipment for sport, camping and open-air recreation	0.2	0.2	0.2	0.1	0.3	0.1	0.1	0.3	0.3	0.6	0.3
9.3.4 Horticultural goods, garden equipment and plants	0.4	0.4	0.6	0.6	0.5	0.5	0.4	0.5	0.6	0.4	0.5
9.3.5 Pets and pet food	1.2	1.2	1.2	1.2	0.9	1.0	1.4	1.1	1.2	1.2	1.2
9.4 Recreational and cultural services	3.4	3.2	3.1	3.0	3.1	3.1	3.8	3.3	3.4	3.8	3.4
9.4.1 Sports admissions, subscriptions, leisure class fees and equipment hire	1.0	0.9	1.0	1.0	1.0	1.1	1.4	1.5	1.4	2.0	1.3
9.4.2 Cinema, theatre and museums etc.	0.6	0.4	0.4	0.4	0.4	0.4	0.8	0.5	0.7	0.7	0.6
9.4.3 TV, video, satellite rental, cable subscriptions and TV licences[5]	1.1	0.9	0.9	0.9	0.9	0.8	0.8	0.7	0.8	0.6	0.8
9.4.4 Miscellaneous entertainments	0.1	0.2	0.1	0.2	0.4	0.3	0.2	0.3	0.2	0.2	0.2
9.4.5 Development of film, deposit for film development, passport photos, holiday and school photos	..	..	..	[0.0]	[0.0]	[0.0]	[0.0]	[0.0]	0.0~	0.0~	0.0~
9.4.6 Gambling payments	0.6	0.8	0.7	0.5	0.5	0.4	0.4	0.4	0.3	0.2	0.4
9.5 Newspapers, books and stationery	1.0	1.0	1.1	0.9	1.0	0.9	0.9	0.9	0.9	0.9	0.9
9.5.1 Books	0.3	0.2	0.2	0.2	0.2	0.2	0.2	0.2	0.3	0.2	0.2
9.5.2 Diaries, address books, cards etc.	0.3	0.3	0.5	0.4	0.5	0.3	0.4	0.3	0.4	0.5	0.4
9.5.3 Newspapers	0.3	0.3	0.3	0.2	0.3	0.2	0.2	0.1	0.1	0.2	0.2
9.5.4 Magazines and periodicals	0.2	0.2	0.1	0.1	0.1	0.1	0.1	0.1	0.1	0.1	0.1
9.6 Package holidays[4]	3.2	3.1	3.7	3.6	4.0	4.4	4.2	5.5	6.0	5.6	4.7
9.6.1 Package holidays - UK	[0.3]	[0.3]	0.3	[0.4]	0.3	0.3	[0.2]	[0.3]	0.4	0.4	0.3
9.6.2 Package holidays - abroad	2.9	2.8	3.4	3.2	3.7	4.1	4.0	5.2	5.7	5.3	4.4
10 Education	**[0.3]**	**0.5**	**[0.2]**	**0.8**	**0.8**	**0.5**	**0.6**	**1.0**	**0.6**	**1.4**	**0.8**
10.1 Education fees	..	[0.4]	..	[0.8]	[0.5]	[0.4]	0.5	0.9	0.5	1.3	0.7
10.2 Payments for school trips, other ad-hoc expenditure	..	[0.1]	..	..	[0.3]	..	[0.1]	[0.1]	[0.0]	..	0.1
11 Restaurants & hotels	**7.4**	**6.8**	**7.6**	**7.0**	**8.7**	**8.3**	**9.9**	**10.1**	**10.1**	**10.0**	**9.0**
11.1 Catering services	6.2	5.8	6.1	5.7	7.1	6.9	8.0	7.7	7.9	6.9	7.0
11.1.1 Restaurant and café meals	2.8	2.8	2.9	2.7	3.5	3.4	3.9	3.7	3.9	3.5	3.4
11.1.2 Alcoholic drinks (away from home)	1.0	0.8	1.0	1.0	1.2	1.3	1.8	1.6	1.8	1.5	1.4
11.1.3 Take away meals eaten at home	1.3	1.2	1.1	0.9	1.1	1.0	1.0	1.1	0.9	0.7	1.0
11.1.4 Other take-away and snack food	0.9	0.8	0.8	0.8	0.9	0.8	1.0	1.0	1.0	0.8	0.9
11.1.5 Contract catering (food) and canteens	0.2	0.3	0.3	0.2	0.4	0.4	0.3	0.4	0.3	0.3	0.3
11.2 Accommodation services	1.1	1.0	1.6	1.3	1.6	1.3	2.0	2.4	2.2	3.1	2.0
11.2.1 Holiday in the UK	0.7	0.7	0.9	0.9	1.3	0.9	1.2	1.2	1.2	1.1	1.1
11.2.2 Holiday abroad	[0.4]	0.3	0.6	0.4	0.3	0.4	0.7	1.1	1.0	1.9	0.9
11.2.3 Room hire	..	..	..	:	..	..	..	..	..	..	0.0~

Note: The commodity and service categories are not comparable to those in publications before 2001-02.
The numbering system is sequential, it does not use actual COICOP codes.
Please see background notes for symbols and conventions used in this report.
5 For FYE 2019 onwards, excludes payments made as part of a combined bill.

Table 3.2E

Detailed household expenditure as a percentage of total expenditure by equivalised disposable income decile group (OECD-modified scale) (cont)

UK, financial year ending 2020

Commodity or service	Lowest ten per cent	Second decile group	Third decile group	Fourth decile group	Fifth decile group	Sixth decile group	Seventh decile group	Eighth decile group	Ninth decile group	Highest ten per cent	All house-holds
					Percentage of total expenditure						
12 Miscellaneous goods & services	**6.6**	**7.6**	**6.9**	**7.2**	**8.1**	**8.4**	**7.7**	**8.4**	**7.6**	**7.9**	**7.8**
12.1 Personal care	2.3	2.6	2.2	2.4	2.4	2.4	2.4	2.3	2.4	1.9	2.3
12.1.1 Hairdressing, beauty treatment	0.6	0.8	0.6	0.8	0.7	0.8	0.8	0.8	0.9	0.7	0.7
12.1.2 Toilet paper	0.2	0.3	0.3	0.2	0.2	0.2	0.2	0.1	0.1	0.1	0.2
12.1.3 Toiletries and soap	0.5	0.5	0.5	0.5	0.5	0.5	0.5	0.4	0.4	0.4	0.5
12.1.4 Baby toiletries and accessories (disposable)	0.2	0.2	0.1	0.1	0.1	0.1	0.1	0.1	0.1	0.0~	0.1
12.1.5 Hair products, cosmetics and related electrical appliances	0.8	0.9	0.7	0.8	0.9	0.8	0.9	0.8	0.9	0.8	0.8
12.2 Personal effects	0.4	0.6	0.4	0.4	0.6	0.8	0.8	1.0	0.6	0.9	0.7
12.3 Social protection	..	[0.1]	0.5	0.6	0.6	1.3	0.6	0.6	[0.2]	1.1	0.6
12.4 Insurance	3.4	2.9	3.4	3.4	3.8	3.1	3.2	3.3	3.5	2.9	3.3
12.4.1 Household insurances - structural, contents and appliances	0.9	0.8	1.1	0.9	0.8	0.8	0.8	0.9	0.8	0.8	0.8
12.4.2 Medical insurance premiums[6]	0.4	0.2	0.2	0.3	0.3	0.3	0.2	0.4	0.6	0.7	0.4
12.4.3 Vehicle insurance including boat insurance	2.0	1.8	2.0	2.1	2.6	1.9	2.0	2.0	1.9	1.3	1.9
12.4.4 Non-package holiday, other travel insurance[7]	0.1	0.1	0.2	0.1	0.1	0.1	0.2	0.1	0.2	0.2	0.2
12.5 Other services	0.4	1.3	0.5	0.5	0.8	0.8	0.7	1.2	0.9	1.0	0.9
12.5.1 Moving house	0.3	[0.2]	[0.1]	0.3	0.5	0.4	0.3	0.6	0.4	0.6	0.4
12.5.2 Bank, building society, post office, credit card charges	0.1	0.1	0.1	0.1	0.1	0.1	0.1	0.1	0.1	0.1	0.1
12.5.3 Other services and professional fees	[0.0]	1.1	0.3	0.1	0.2	0.3	0.4	0.6	0.3	0.3	0.4
1-12 All expenditure groups	**89.8**	**90.6**	**88.9**	**88.5**	**87.9**	**86.7**	**87.7**	**86.5**	**85.3**	**81.8**	**86.5**
13 Other expenditure items	**10.2**	**9.4**	**11.1**	**11.5**	**12.1**	**13.3**	**12.3**	**13.5**	**14.7**	**18.2**	**13.5**
13.1 Housing: mortgage interest payments, council tax etc.	6.8	6.5	7.0	7.6	8.1	8.3	8.8	9.0	9.9	9.7	8.6
13.2 Licences, fines and transfers	0.6	0.6	0.7	0.6	0.7	0.7	0.7	0.6	0.6	0.7	0.6
13.3 Holiday spending	..	[0.9]	[1.5]	..	[1.2]	2.4	1.2	1.9	1.8	4.7	2.1
13.4 Money transfers and credit	2.4	1.4	1.9	2.3	2.1	1.9	1.6	2.0	2.3	3.1	2.2
13.4.1 Money, cash gifts given to children	..	..	..	..	..	..	..	..	..	[0.1]	0.1
13.4.2 Cash gifts and donations	2.3	1.1	1.7	2.0	1.9	1.7	1.4	1.7	2.1	2.9	2.0
13.4.3 Club instalment payments (child) and interest on credit cards	0.1	0.3	0.2	0.2	0.2	0.2	0.3	0.2	0.1	0.1	0.2
Total expenditure	**100.0**	**100.0**	**100.0**	**100.0**	**100.0**	**100.0**	**100.0**	**100.0**	**100.0**	**100.0**	**100.0**

Note: The commodity and service categories are not comparable to those in publications before 2001-02.

The numbering system is sequential, it does not use actual COICOP codes.

Please see background notes for symbols and conventions used in this report.

6 For FYE 2019, critical illness cover, personal accident insurance and other medical insurance are included here. They were not included in previous years.

7 For FYE 2019, information about insurance for non-package holiday and other travel insurance was collected in the questionnaire in addition to the diary. In previous years, this was based on diary data only.

Source: Office for National Statistics

Table 3.3

Expenditure of one adult non-retired households by disposable income quintile group
UK, financial year ending 2020

	Lowest twenty per cent	Second quintile group	Third quintile group	Fourth quintile group	Highest twenty per cent	All house-holds
Lower boundary of group (£ per week)[1]		384	617	851	1179	
Weighted number of households (thousands)	2,290	1,180	540	180	170	4,370
Total number of households in sample	460	220	100	30	30	840
Total number of persons in sample	460	220	100	30	30	840
Total number of adults in sample	460	220	100	30	30	840
Weighted average number of persons per household	1.0	1.0	1.0	1.0	1.0	1.0

Commodity or service	Average weekly household expenditure (£)					
1 Food & non-alcoholic drinks	29.40	33.80	37.60	41.80	38.80	32.50
2 Alcoholic drinks, tobacco & narcotics	9.80	8.00	9.60	[9.60]	[8.70]	9.20
3 Clothing & footwear	6.40	12.10	22.60	[22.00]	[15.10]	11.00
4 Housing (net)[2], fuel & power	71.90	72.90	80.90	64.30	97.30	74.00
5 Household goods & services	14.20	20.30	30.00	19.30	42.40	19.10
6 Health	3.40	4.90	8.80	[18.70]	[6.60]	5.30
7 Transport	25.50	50.80	70.90	76.40	157.80	45.20
8 Communication	11.10	16.40	16.30	17.80	15.60	13.60
9 Recreation & culture	24.30	39.90	53.50	40.10	46.40	33.70
10 Education	..	..	..	..	:	[1.40]
11 Restaurants & hotels	16.50	30.50	43.10	50.40	69.10	27.10
12 Miscellaneous goods & services	15.20	37.90	45.80	44.00	43.50	27.40
1-12 All expenditure groups	229.50	328.00	422.20	404.90	541.20	299.40
13 Other expenditure items	27.30	54.20	86.00	182.40	255.60	57.20
Total expenditure	**256.90**	**382.20**	**508.10**	**587.40**	**796.80**	**356.60**
Average weekly expenditure per person (£)						
Total expenditure	**256.90**	**382.20**	**508.10**	**587.40**	**796.80**	**356.60**

Note: The commodity and service categories are not comparable to those in publications before 2001-02.

Please see background notes for symbols and conventions used in this report.

1 Quintile groups have been calculated separately for retired and non-retired households.

2 Excluding mortgage interest payments, council tax and Northern Ireland rates.

Source: Office for National Statistics

Table 3.3E

Expenditure of one adult non-retired households by disposable equivalised income quintile group (OECD-modified scale)

UK, financial year ending 2020

	Lowest twenty per cent	Second quintile group	Third quintile group	Fourth quintile group	Highest twenty per cent	All house- holds
Lower boundary of group (£ per week)[1]		257	378	495	673	
Weighted number of households (thousands)	1,340	900	760	640	730	4,370
Total number of households in sample	270	180	140	120	130	840
Total number of persons in sample	270	180	140	120	130	840
Total number of adults in sample	270	180	140	120	130	840
Weighted average number of persons per household	1.0	1.0	1.0	1.0	1.0	1.0
Commodity or service	Average weekly household expenditure (£)					
1 Food & non-alcoholic drinks	28.40	31.10	34.80	33.60	38.10	32.50
2 Alcoholic drinks, tobacco & narcotics	10.40	9.20	7.80	9.60	8.40	9.20
3 Clothing & footwear	6.60	6.00	13.80	13.40	20.10	11.00
4 Housing (net)[2], fuel & power	63.20	85.70	75.40	79.20	73.40	74.00
5 Household goods & services	12.50	17.00	18.00	23.30	31.40	19.10
6 Health	4.40	2.30	5.10	5.00	11.10	5.30
7 Transport	21.50	32.30	49.50	54.50	92.10	45.20
8 Communication	9.40	13.60	16.20	16.00	16.50	13.60
9 Recreation & culture	22.30	27.40	34.50	46.20	50.40	33.70
10 Education	..	..	..	..	..	[1.40]
11 Restaurants & hotels	16.20	16.60	27.90	37.70	49.90	27.10
12 Miscellaneous goods & services	12.70	19.00	45.20	29.60	44.50	27.40
1-12 All expenditure groups	209.10	262.00	328.80	348.60	438.30	299.40
13 Other expenditure items	23.50	30.70	50.00	66.00	151.60	57.20
Total expenditure	**232.50**	**292.70**	**378.80**	**414.60**	**589.90**	**356.60**
Average weekly expenditure per person (£)						
Total expenditure	**232.50**	**292.70**	**378.80**	**414.60**	**589.90**	**356.60**

Note: The commodity and service categories are not comparable to those in publications before 2001-02.

Please see background notes for symbols and conventions used in this report.

1 Quintile groups have been calculated separately for retired and non-retired households.

2 Excluding mortgage interest payments, council tax and Northern Ireland rates.

Source: Office for National Statistics

Table 3.7
Expenditure of two adult non-retired households
by disposable income quintile group
UK, financial year ending 2020

	Lowest twenty per cent	Second quintile group	Third quintile group	Fourth quintile group	Highest twenty per cent	All house-holds
Lower boundary of group (£ per week)[1]		384	617	851	1179	
Weighted number of households (thousands)	720	1,240	1,580	1,620	1,050	6,220
Total number of households in sample	140	250	300	290	200	1,190
Total number of persons in sample	290	500	610	590	410	2,390
Total number of adults in sample	290	500	610	590	410	2,390
Weighted average number of persons per household	2.0	2.0	2.0	2.0	2.0	2.0

Commodity or service	Average weekly household expenditure (£)					
1 Food & non-alcoholic drinks	56.50	60.60	61.10	65.80	72.00	63.50
2 Alcoholic drinks, tobacco & narcotics	12.00	17.60	14.00	17.20	17.30	15.90
3 Clothing & footwear	13.70	15.40	21.60	27.30	39.60	24.00
4 Housing (net)[2], fuel & power	74.60	90.70	98.40	95.00	93.20	92.30
5 Household goods & services	28.90	37.70	33.30	45.30	66.80	42.50
6 Health	7.10	4.50	7.90	13.10	19.90	10.50
7 Transport	56.30	67.00	94.20	120.10	152.20	101.00
8 Communication	17.70	20.10	23.70	24.20	31.70	23.80
9 Recreation & culture	57.10	63.50	77.10	95.00	140.30	87.40
10 Education	..	..	..	..	..	2.70
11 Restaurants & hotels	35.80	46.70	59.10	72.40	94.00	63.30
12 Miscellaneous goods & services	29.80	37.30	44.90	54.00	65.80	47.50
1-12 All expenditure groups	391.70	463.80	537.80	632.10	796.10	574.40
13 Other expenditure items	37.40	53.10	75.30	100.20	176.70	90.10
Total expenditure	**429.10**	**517.00**	**613.20**	**732.30**	**972.80**	**664.50**
Average weekly expenditure per person (£) **Total expenditure**	**214.60**	**258.50**	**306.60**	**366.20**	**486.40**	**332.30**

Note: The commodity and service categories are not comparable to those in publications before 2001-02.

Please see background notes for symbols and conventions used in this report.

1 Quintile groups have been calculated separately for retired and non-retired households.

2 Excluding mortgage interest payments, council tax and Northern Ireland rates.

Source: Office for National Statistics

Table 3.7E

Expenditure of two adult non-retired households by disposable equivalised income quintile group (OECD-modified scale)

UK, financial year ending 2020

	Lowest twenty per cent	Second quintile group	Third quintile group	Fourth quintile group	Highest twenty per cent	All house-holds
Lower boundary of group (£ per week)[1]		257	378	495	673	
Weighted number of households (thousands)	730	900	1,260	1,540	1,790	6,220
Total number of households in sample	150	180	240	290	330	1,190
Total number of persons in sample	290	370	480	590	670	2,390
Total number of adults in sample	290	370	480	590	670	2,390
Weighted average number of persons per household	2.0	2.0	2.0	2.0	2.0	2.0
Commodity or service			Average weekly household expenditure (£)			
1 Food & non-alcoholic drinks	56.50	58.40	61.30	64.60	69.50	63.50
2 Alcoholic drinks, tobacco & narcotics	12.10	17.00	14.70	15.10	18.40	15.90
3 Clothing & footwear	13.70	15.00	18.60	27.50	33.40	24.00
4 Housing (net)[2], fuel & power	75.70	88.00	97.40	97.50	93.30	92.30
5 Household goods & services	29.50	40.70	30.40	39.00	60.20	42.50
6 Health	7.20	4.50	5.60	11.40	17.70	10.50
7 Transport	57.40	66.30	93.30	99.70	142.60	101.00
8 Communication	17.70	19.90	22.70	24.80	28.10	23.80
9 Recreation & culture	56.90	62.80	73.00	84.00	125.40	87.40
10 Education	..	..	..	..	[2.90]	2.70
11 Restaurants & hotels	36.20	41.60	55.50	66.50	87.80	63.30
12 Miscellaneous goods & services	30.30	36.40	41.20	51.20	61.40	47.50
1-12 All expenditure groups	395.30	454.00	515.40	584.60	740.60	574.40
13 Other expenditure items	37.60	50.60	66.60	92.10	146.30	90.10
Total expenditure	**432.90**	**504.70**	**582.00**	**676.80**	**886.90**	**664.50**
Average weekly expenditure per person (£)						
Total expenditure	**216.40**	**252.30**	**291.00**	**338.40**	**443.50**	**332.30**

Note: The commodity and service categories are not comparable to those in publications before 2001-02.

Please see background notes for symbols and conventions used in this report.

1 Quintile groups have been calculated separately for retired and non-retired households.

2 Excluding mortgage interest payments, council tax and Northern Ireland rates.

Source: Office for National Statistics

Table 3.12
Percentage of households by composition in each disposable and equivalised income decile group
(OECD-modified scale)
UK, financial year ending 2020

Percentages

	Lowest ten per cent		Second		Third		Fourth		Fifth	
	Disposable	Equivalised	Disposable	Equivalised	Disposable	Equivalised	Disposable	Equivalised	Disposable	Equivalised
Lower boundary of group (£ per week)			224	182	321	240	413	296	510	342
Average size of household	**1.3**	**2.0**	**1.6**	**2.3**	**1.8**	**2.2**	**2.1**	**2.4**	**2.4**	**2.4**
One adult retired mainly dependent on state pensions[1]	17.0	9.0	7.0	10.0	[2.00]	4.0	..	..	:	..
One adult, other retired	24.0	12.0	32.0	16.0	19.0	18.0	12.0	16.0	6.0	13.0
One adult, non-retired	39.0	31.0	25.0	13.0	26.0	14.0	20.0	12.0	16.0	17.0
One adult, one child	4.0	4.0	4.0	4.0	6.0	5.0	[2.00]	[2.00]	[3.00]	[2.00]
One adult, two or more children	[3.00]	7.0	5.0	5.0	3.0	3.0	3.0	[1.00]	[2.00]	[2.00]
Two adults, retired mainly dependent on state pensions[1]	..	[2.00]	4.0	5.0	8.0	6.0	3.0	[2.00]	..	..
Two adults, other retired	..	[3.00]	7.0	9.0	10.0	11.0	20.0	15.0	17.0	14.0
Two adults, non-retired	8.0	11.0	9.0	11.0	13.0	12.0	20.0	16.0	23.0	15.0
Two adults, one child	..	5.0	[3.00]	7.0	4.0	6.0	6.0	7.0	10.0	9.0
Two adults, two children	..	[5.00]	..	7.0	[2.00]	9.0	5.0	8.0	9.0	14.0
Two adults, three children	..	4.0	..	6.0	[2.00]	[3.00]	[3.00]	[4.00]	5.0	[3.00]
Two adults, four or more children	:	..	..	..	..	[2.00]	..	..	..	..
Three adults	..	[2.00]	..	[3.00]	..	[3.00]	[3.00]	6.0	4.0	5.0
Three adults, one or more children	..	[2.00]	..	..	..	[2.00]	..	[4.00]	..	[3.00]
All other households without children	:	..	:	..	..	..	..	..	..	[1.00]
All other households with children	:	..	:	..	:	..	..	..	..	..

	Sixth		Seventh		Eighth		Ninth		Highest ten per cent	
	Disposable	Equivalised	Disposable	Equivalised	Disposable	Equivalised	Disposable	Equivalised	Disposable	Equivalised
Lower boundary of group (£ per week)	624	398	750	462	892	529	1,064	629	1,386	781
Average size of household	**2.5**	**2.4**	**2.8**	**2.5**	**2.9**	**2.5**	**3.0**	**2.5**	**3.4**	**2.4**
One adult retired mainly dependent on state pensions[1]	:	..	..	..	:	:	:	:	:	..
One adult, other retired	[3.00]	8.0	..	8.0	..	4.0	..	[4.00]	..	[2.00]
One adult, non-retired	11.0	17.0	7.0	10.0	4.0	14.0	5.0	13.0	[3.00]	17.0
One adult, one child	..	..	..	..	..	..	..	..	..	..
One adult, two or more children	[1.00]	..	..	..	..	..	..	..	..	..
Two adults, retired mainly dependent on state pensions[1]	..	..	:	:	:	:	:	:	:	:
Two adults, other retired	14.0	11.0	11.0	12.0	9.0	10.0	7.0	8.0	[3.00]	8.0
Two adults, non-retired	34.0	24.0	31.0	25.0	32.0	33.0	31.0	37.0	23.0	39.0
Two adults, one child	9.0	8.0	11.0	10.0	12.0	9.0	11.0	9.0	10.0	9.0
Two adults, two children	12.0	12.0	14.0	9.0	14.0	9.0	14.0	10.0	18.0	9.0
Two adults, three children	[3.00]	[2.00]	5.0	..	[3.00]	[2.00]	[2.00]	..	5.0	[2.00]
Two adults, four or more children	[2.00]	..	..	..	..	..	..	..	..	..
Three adults	6.0	8.0	9.0	10.0	13.0	9.0	12.0	8.0	11.0	7.0
Three adults, one or more children	[2.00]	4.0	4.0	[4.00]	5.0	[3.00]	6.0	[3.00]	7.0	..
All other households without children	..	[4.00]	..	7.0	[2.00]	[4.00]	8.0	[3.00]	14.0	[5.00]
All other households with children	..	..	..	..	..	..	[2.00]	..	[3.00]	..

Please see background notes for symbols and conventions used in this report.

1 Mainly dependent on state pension and not economically active.

Source: Office for National Statistics

Trends in household expenditure over time tables

Table 4.1

Household expenditure based on COICOP classification, 2001-02 to 2019-20 at 2019-20 prices[1]

United Kingdom

Commodity or service	2001-02	2002-03	2003-04	2004-05	2005-06	2006[2]	2006[3]	2007	2008	2009	2010	2011	2012	2013	2014	2014-15	2015-16	2016-17	2017-18	2018-19	2019-20
Weighted number of households (thousands)	24,450	24,350	24,670	24,430	24,800	24,790	25,440	25,350	25,690	25,980	26,320	26,110	26,410	26,840	26,600	26,760	27,220	27,210	27,150	27,480	27,820
Total number of households in sample	7,470	6,930	7,050	6,800	6,790	6,650	6,650	6,140	5,850	5,830	5,260	5,690	5,600	5,140	5,130	5,170	4,920	5,040	5,410	5,480	5,440
Total number of persons in sample	18,120	16,590	16,970	16,260	16,090	15,850	15,850	14,650	13,830	13,740	12,180	13,430	13,180	12,120	12,120	12,160	11,620	11,960	12,780	12,790	12,670
Total number of adults in sample	13,450	12,450	12,620	12,260	12,170	12,000	12,000	11,220	10,640	10,650	9,430	10,330	10,200	9,350	9,440	9,510	8,950	9,260	9,940	9,980	9,880
Weighted average number of persons per household	2.4	2.4	2.4	2.4	2.4	2.4	2.3	2.4	2.4	2.3	2.3	2.4	2.3	2.4	2.4	2.4	2.4	2.4	2.4	2.4	2.4
Average weekly household expenditure (£)																					
1 Food & non-alcoholic drinks	62.50	64.10	64.10	65.60	65.50	66.20	65.40	65.10	62.90	61.30	60.50	59.10	59.30	59.20	59.30	59.20	59.20	61.40	62.80	62.80	63.70
2 Alcoholic drinks, tobacco & narcotics	22.30	21.90	22.20	21.00	19.60	19.80	19.70	19.20	17.80	17.70	17.70	16.60	16.30	14.70	14.40	13.90	13.00	13.40	13.50	13.30	12.90
3 Clothing & footwear	15.90	16.60	17.60	19.50	19.50	20.50	20.30	20.20	21.20	22.30	25.10	22.80	24.40	23.30	24.40	24.30	24.00	25.70	24.50	24.30	23.40
4 Housing (net)[4], fuel & power	68.10	68.40	70.80	70.30	72.20	72.30	72.20	75.00	70.60	73.20	76.90	76.40	78.10	82.10	77.90	77.90	77.20	77.10	79.20	80.90	83.00
5 Household goods & services	38.20	37.90	39.40	39.90	38.00	38.50	38.10	38.40	36.90	33.10	36.10	30.00	30.50	35.20	37.30	38.60	37.30	41.30	41.60	41.30	36.50
6 Health	7.30	7.60	7.70	7.40	8.00	8.40	8.30	7.90	6.90	6.90	6.40	8.10	7.60	7.20	8.00	7.90	8.00	7.90	7.30	8.20	8.20
7 Transport	97.10	97.80	97.40	92.40	91.80	90.60	88.90	87.50	85.20	77.90	79.70	75.00	71.50	77.70	82.30	81.20	81.90	88.00	86.20	86.50	81.60
8 Communication[5]	12.90	13.10	13.80	14.60	15.10	14.90	14.70	15.60	16.10	15.50	16.50	16.20	16.20	16.50	17.40	17.40	17.60	18.40	19.00	22.20	21.40
9 Recreation & culture	58.20	59.80	61.70	64.20	63.50	65.10	64.10	64.50	67.90	64.60	63.60	69.90	67.20	69.10	73.80	74.30	73.30	78.60	78.40	78.30	74.80
10 Education	19.70	17.30	16.30	19.40	18.60	19.30	18.70	16.00	13.00	13.70	18.60	12.40	11.00	12.20	12.30	11.10	8.10	6.30	9.20	5.80	4.50
11 Restaurants & hotels	56.70	58.20	55.60	55.90	54.90	55.40	54.90	52.60	51.30	51.00	50.70	49.00	48.60	47.20	48.40	48.20	50.30	54.30	52.90	52.70	52.90
12 Miscellaneous goods & services	43.50	45.80	45.30	45.40	43.30	43.70	43.30	41.90	41.30	39.80	39.80	41.80	40.60	41.00	41.80	42.40	41.30	43.00	44.50	46.50	45.70
1-12 All expenditure groups	502.40	508.50	511.90	515.60	509.90	514.60	508.50	503.70	491.10	476.90	491.80	477.30	471.30	485.50	497.30	496.40	491.20	515.50	519.20	523.00	508.50
13 Other expenditure items[6]	84.50	81.70	82.80	83.40	86.90	85.00	82.90	78.20	81.90	84.30	77.80	78.40	75.60	79.50	75.60	72.30	79.10	77.80	81.40	80.00	79.30
Total expenditure	586.90	590.20	594.70	599.10	596.80	599.60	591.30	581.90	572.90	561.20	569.50	555.70	546.90	565.00	572.90	568.60	570.30	593.20	600.60	603.10	587.90
Average weekly expenditure per person (£)																					
Total expenditure	247.00	247.80	252.30	251.00	253.10	253.60	252.90	247.00	243.00	239.80	244.30	236.00	233.50	239.60	239.20	238.50	242.10	250.30	250.60	253.40	248.70

Note: The commodity and service categories are not comparable to those in publications before 2001-02.

1 Figures have been deflated to 2020 prices using deflators specific to the COICOP category.

2 From 2001-02 to this version of 2006, figures shown are based on weighted data using non-response weights based on the 1991 Census and population figures from the 1991 and 2001 Censuses.

3 From this version of 2006, figures shown are based on weighted data using updated weights, with non-response weights and population figures based on the 2001 Census.

4 Excluding mortgage interest payments, council tax and Northern Ireland rates.

5 Changes to the questionnaire in FYE 2019 has resulted in the COICOP division "Communication" not being directly comparable with previous years. Please see the technical report for more information.

6 An improvement to the imputation of mortgage interest payments has been implemented for 2006 data onwards. This means there is a slight discontinuity between 2006 data and earlier years.

Source: Office for National Statistics

Table 4.2

Household expenditure as a percentage of total expenditure based on COICOP classification, 2001-02 to 2019-20 at 2019-20 prices[1]

United Kingdom

	2001-02	2002-03	2003-04	2004-05	2005-06	2006[2]	2006[3]	2007	2008	2009	2010	2011	2012	2013	2014	2014-15	2015-16	2016-17	2017-18	2018-19	2019-20
Weighted number of households (thousands)	24,450	24,350	24,670	24,430	24,800	24,790	25,440	25,350	25,690	25,980	26,320	26,110	26,410	26,840	26,600	26,760	27,220	27,210	27,150	27,480	27,820
Total number of households in sample	7,470	6,930	7,050	6,800	6,790	6,650	6,650	6,140	5,850	5,830	5,260	5,690	5,600	5,140	5,130	5,170	4,920	5,040	5,410	5,480	5,440
Total number of persons in sample	18,120	16,590	16,970	16,260	16,090	15,850	15,850	14,650	13,830	13,740	12,180	13,430	13,180	12,120	12,120	12,160	11,620	11,960	12,780	12,790	12,670
Total number of adults in sample	13,450	12,450	12,620	12,260	12,170	12,000	12,000	11,220	10,640	10,650	9,430	10,330	10,200	9,350	9,440	9,510	8,950	9,260	9,940	9,980	9,880
Weighted average number of persons per household	2.4	2.4	2.4	2.4	2.4	2.4	2.3	2.4	2.4	2.3	2.3	2.4	2.3	2.4	2.4	2.4	2.4	2.4	2.4	2.4	2.4
Commodity or service						Percentage of total expenditure															
1 Food & non-alcoholic drinks	11	11	11	11	11	11	11	11	11	11	11	11	11	10	10	10	10	10	10	10	11
2 Alcoholic drinks, tobacco & narcotics	4	4	4	4	3	3	3	3	3	3	3	3	3	3	3	2	2	2	2	2	2
3 Clothing & footwear	3	3	3	3	3	3	3	3	4	4	4	4	4	4	4	4	4	4	4	4	4
4 Housing (net)[4], fuel & power	12	12	12	12	12	12	12	13	12	13	13	14	14	15	14	14	14	13	13	13	14
5 Household goods & services	7	6	7	7	6	6	6	7	6	6	6	5	6	6	7	7	7	7	7	7	6
6 Health	1	1	1	1	1	1	1	1	1	1	1	1	1	1	1	1	1	1	1	1	1
7 Transport	17	17	16	15	15	15	15	15	15	14	14	13	13	14	14	14	14	15	14	14	14
8 Communication[5]	2	2	2	2	3	2	2	3	3	3	3	3	3	3	3	3	3	3	3	4	4
9 Recreation & culture	10	10	10	11	11	11	11	11	12	12	11	13	12	12	13	13	13	13	13	13	13
10 Education	3	3	3	3	3	3	3	3	2	2	3	2	2	2	2	2	1	1	2	1	1
11 Restaurants & hotels	10	10	9	9	9	9	9	9	9	9	9	9	9	8	8	8	9	9	9	9	9
12 Miscellaneous goods & services	7	8	8	8	7	7	7	7	7	7	7	8	7	7	7	7	7	7	7	8	8
1-12 All expenditure groups	86	86	86	86	85	86	86	87	86	85	86	86	86	86	87	87	86	87	86	87	87
13 Other expenditure items[6]	14	14	14	14	15	14	14	13	14	15	14	14	14	14	13	13	14	13	14	13	13
Total expenditure	100	100	100	100	100	100	100	100	100	100	100	100	100	100	100	100	100	100	100	100	100

Note: The commodity and service categories are not comparable to those in publications before 2001-02.

1 Figures have been deflated to 2020 prices using deflators specific to the COICOP category.

2 From 2001-02 to this version of 2006, figures shown are based on weighted data using non-response weights based on the 1991 Census and population figures from the 1991 and 2001 Censuses.

3 From this version of 2006, figures shown are based on weighted data using updated weights, with non-response weights and population figures based on the 2001 Census.

4 Excluding mortgage interest payments, council tax and Northern Ireland rates.

5 Changes to the questionnaire in FYE 2019 has resulted in the COICOP division "Communication" not being directly comparable with previous years. Please see the technical report for more information.

6 An improvement to the imputation of mortgage interest payments has been implemented for 2006 data onwards. This means there is a slight discontinuity between 2006 and earlier years.

Source: Office for National Statistics

Table 4.3

Household expenditure at current[1] prices

UK, financial year ending March 2002 to financial year ending March 2020

	2001-02	2002-03	2003-04	2004-05	2005-06	2006[2]	2006[3]	2007	2008	2009	2010	2011	2012	2013	2014	2014-15	2015-16	2016-17	2017-18	2018-19	2019-20
Weighted number of households (thousands)	24,450	24,350	24,670	24,430	24,800	24,790	25,440	25,350	25,690	25,980	26,320	26,110	26,410	26,840	26,600	26,760	27,220	27,210	27,150	27,480	27,820
Total number of households in sample	7,470	6,930	7,050	6,800	6,790	6,650	6,650	6,140	5,850	5,830	5,260	5,690	5,600	5,140	5,130	5,170	4,920	5,040	5,410	5,480	5,440
Total number of persons in sample	18,120	16,590	16,970	16,260	16,090	15,850	15,850	14,650	13,830	13,740	12,180	13,430	13,180	12,120	12,120	12,160	11,620	11,960	12,780	12,790	12,670
Total number of adults in sample	13,450	12,450	12,620	12,260	12,170	12,000	12,000	11,220	10,640	10,650	9,430	10,330	10,200	9,350	9,440	9,510	8,950	9,260	9,940	9,980	9,880
Weighted average number of persons per household	2.4	2.4	2.4	2.4	2.4	2.4	2.3	2.4	2.4	2.3	2.3	2.4	2.3	2.4	2.4	2.4	2.4	2.4	2.4	2.4	2.4
Commodity or service						**Average weekly household expenditure (£)**															
1 Food & non-alcoholic drinks	41.80	42.70	43.50	44.70	45.30	46.90	46.30	48.10	50.70	52.20	53.20	54.80	56.80	58.80	58.80	58.30	56.80	58.00	61.00	61.90	63.70
2 Alcoholic drinks, tobacco & narcotics	11.40	11.40	11.70	11.30	10.80	11.10	11.10	11.20	10.80	11.20	11.80	12.00	12.60	12.00	12.30	12.00	11.40	11.90	12.60	13.00	12.90
3 Clothing & footwear	22.90	22.30	22.70	23.90	22.70	23.20	23.00	22.00	21.60	20.90	23.40	21.70	23.40	22.60	23.70	23.70	23.50	25.10	24.70	24.50	23.40
4 Housing(net)[4], fuel & power	35.90	36.90	39.00	40.40	44.20	47.60	47.50	51.80	53.00	57.30	60.40	63.30	68.00	74.40	72.70	72.80	72.50	72.60	76.20	79.40	83.00
5 Household goods & services	30.50	30.20	31.30	31.60	30.00	30.30	29.90	30.70	30.10	27.90	31.40	27.30	28.50	33.10	35.40	36.70	35.50	39.30	40.90	41.00	36.50
6 Health	4.50	4.80	5.00	4.90	5.50	5.90	5.80	5.70	5.10	5.30	5.00	6.60	6.40	6.20	7.10	7.00	7.20	7.30	7.00	8.00	8.20
7 Transport	57.80	59.20	60.70	59.60	61.70	62.00	60.80	61.70	63.40	58.40	64.90	65.70	64.10	70.40	74.80	73.30	72.70	79.70	81.20	85.00	81.60
8 Communication[5]	10.40	10.60	11.20	11.70	11.90	11.70	11.60	11.90	12.00	11.70	13.00	13.30	13.80	14.50	15.50	15.50	16.00	17.20	17.90	21.30	21.40
9 Recreation & culture	54.10	56.40	57.30	59.00	57.50	58.50	57.60	57.40	60.10	57.90	58.10	63.90	61.50	63.90	68.80	69.30	68.00	73.50	75.00	77.20	74.80
10 Education	5.60	5.20	5.20	6.50	6.60	7.20	7.00	6.80	6.20	7.00	10.00	7.00	6.80	8.80	9.80	9.00	7.00	5.70	8.70	5.70	4.50
11 Restaurants & hotels	33.40	35.40	34.90	36.10	36.70	37.90	37.60	37.20	37.70	38.40	39.20	39.70	40.50	40.40	42.50	42.50	45.10	50.10	50.30	51.40	52.90
12 Miscellaneous goods & services	30.70	33.10	33.60	34.90	34.60	36.00	35.70	35.30	35.60	35.00	35.90	38.60	38.40	39.10	40.00	40.40	39.70	41.80	43.80	45.70	45.70
1-12 All expenditure groups	338.80	348.30	356.20	364.70	367.60	378.30	373.80	379.80	386.30	383.10	406.30	413.90	420.70	444.30	461.20	460.50	455.30	482.20	499.20	514.10	508.50
13 Other expenditure items[6]	59.50	57.90	61.90	69.70	75.80	77.60	75.10	79.30	84.60	71.80	67.30	69.70	68.30	73.00	70.10	66.90	73.60	72.00	76.50	77.90	79.30
Total expenditure	**398.30**	**406.20**	**418.10**	**434.40**	**443.40**	**455.90**	**449.00**	**459.20**	**471.00**	**455.00**	**473.60**	**483.60**	**489.00**	**517.30**	**531.30**	**527.30**	**528.90**	**554.20**	**575.70**	**592.00**	**587.90**
Average weekly expenditure per person (£)																					
Total expenditure	**167.60**	**170.50**	**177.40**	**182.00**	**188.00**	**192.80**	**192.00**	**194.80**	**199.80**	**194.40**	**203.10**	**205.40**	**208.70**	**219.40**	**221.80**	**221.20**	**224.50**	**233.80**	**240.20**	**248.80**	**248.70**

Note: The commodity and service categories are not comparable to those in publications before 2001-02

1 Data in Table 4.3 have not been deflated to 2012 prices and therefore show the actual expenditure for the year they were collected.
Because inflation is not taken into account, comparisons between the years should be made with caution.
2 From 2002-03 to this version of 2006, figures shown are based on weighted data using non-response weights based on the 1991 Census and population figures from the 1991 and 2001 Censuses.
3 From this version of 2006, figures shown are based on weighted data using updated weights, with non-response weights and population figures based on the 2001 Census.
4 Excluding mortgage interest payments, council tax and Northern Ireland rates.
5 Changes to the questionnaire in FYE 2019 has resulted in the COICOP division "Communication" not being directly comparable with previous years. Please see the technical report for more information.
6 An error was discovered in the derivation of mortgage capital repayments which was leading to double counting. This has been amended for the 2006 data onwards.

Source: Office for National Statistics

Appendix A

Table A1

Components of household expenditure

UK, financial year ending 2020

	Average weekly expenditure all house-holds (£)	Total weekly expenditure (£ million)	Recording house-holds in sample	Percentage standard error (full method)
Total number of households			5,440	
Commodity or service				
1 Food & non-alcoholic drinks	**63.70**	**1,772**	**5,400**	*1.0*
1.1 Food	58.40	1,624	5,400	*1.0*
1.1.1 Bread, rice and cereals	5.80	163	5,280	*1.3*
1.1.1.1 Rice	0.50	15	1,740	*5.2*
1.1.1.2 Bread	2.70	74	5,070	*1.5*
1.1.1.3 Other breads and cereals	2.60	73	4,470	*1.5*
1.1.2 Pasta products	0.50	13	2,360	*2.9*
1.1.3 Buns, cakes, biscuits etc.	4.10	114	4,900	*1.6*
1.1.3.1 Buns, crispbread and biscuits	2.50	69	4,600	*1.6*
1.1.3.2 Cakes and puddings	1.60	45	3,520	*2.6*
1.1.4 Pastry (savoury)	1.00	27	2,290	*2.6*
1.1.5 Beef (fresh, chilled or frozen)	1.90	52	2,450	*2.7*
1.1.6 Pork (fresh, chilled or frozen)	0.50	15	1,080	*4.3*
1.1.7 Lamb (fresh, chilled or frozen)	0.70	19	650	*7.7*
1.1.8 Poultry (fresh, chilled or frozen)	2.40	68	3,010	*2.6*
1.1.9 Bacon and ham	0.80	23	2,300	*2.7*
1.1.10 Other meats and meat preparations	6.60	184	4,770	*1.6*
1.1.10.1 Sausages	0.90	25	2,400	*2.7*
1.1.10.2 Offal, pate etc.	0.10	3	610	*7.4*
1.1.10.3 Other preserved or processed meat and meat preparations	5.60	156	4,600	*1.7*
1.1.10.4 Other fresh, chilled or frozen edible meat	[0.00~]	[0~]	20	*32.6*
1.1.11 Fish and fish products	3.20	88	3,530	*2.4*
1.1.11.1 Fish (fresh, chilled or frozen)	1.00	28	1,310	*5.3*
1.1.11.2 Seafood, dried, smoked or salted fish	0.70	19	1,200	*4.0*
1.1.11.3 Other preserved or processed fish and seafood	1.50	41	2,810	*2.4*
1.1.12 Milk	2.10	59	4,840	*1.7*
1.1.12.1 Whole milk	0.40	12	1,450	*3.8*
1.1.12.2 Low fat milk	1.50	41	4,050	*1.7*
1.1.12.3 Preserved milk	0.20	6	310	*9.3*
1.1.13 Cheese and curd	2.20	61	4,070	*1.7*
1.1.14 Eggs	0.80	21	3,300	*2.0*
1.1.15 Other milk products	2.30	65	4,320	*1.7*
1.1.15.1 Other milk products	1.10	32	3,250	*2.5*
1.1.15.2 Yoghurt	1.20	34	3,230	*2.1*
1.1.16 Butter	0.50	13	1,590	*3.2*
1.1.17 Margarine, other vegetable fats and peanut butter	0.60	17	2,410	*2.3*
1.1.18 Cooking oils and fats	0.40	10	1,240	*5.2*
1.1.18.1 Olive oil	0.20	5	450	*8.7*
1.1.18.2 Edible oils and other edible animal fats	0.20	6	890	*5.3*
1.1.19 Fresh fruit	4.00	111	4,670	*1.6*
1.1.19.1 Citrus fruits (fresh)	0.60	17	2,610	*2.4*
1.1.19.2 Bananas (fresh)	0.50	15	3,410	*1.8*
1.1.19.3 Apples (fresh)	0.60	16	2,350	*2.5*
1.1.19.4 Pears (fresh)	0.10	4	840	*4.3*
1.1.19.5 Stone fruits (fresh)	0.60	17	1,980	*3.7*
1.1.19.6 Berries (fresh)	1.50	43	3,130	*2.1*
1.1.20 Other fresh, chilled or frozen fruits	0.50	13	1,690	*3.7*
1.1.21 Dried fruit and nuts	0.90	25	1,940	*5.9*
1.1.22 Preserved fruit and fruit based products	0.20	5	910	*4.7*
1.1.23 Fresh vegetables	4.50	124	4,890	*1.5*
1.1.23.1 Leaf and stem vegetables (fresh or chilled)	1.00	27	3,480	*2.0*
1.1.23.2 Cabbages (fresh or chilled)	0.40	12	2,430	*2.7*
1.1.23.3 Vegetables grown for their fruit (fresh, chilled or frozen)	1.60	44	4,100	*1.8*
1.1.23.4 Root crops, non-starchy bulbs and mushrooms (fresh, chilled or frozen)	1.50	41	4,350	*2.0*

Note: The commodity and service categories are not comparable with those in publications before 2001-02.

The numbering is sequential, it does not use actual COICOP codes.

Please see background notes for symbols and conventions used in this report.

Components of household expenditure (cont.)

UK, financial year ending 2020

Commodity or service	Average weekly expenditure all house- holds (£)	Total weekly expenditure (£ million)	Recording house- holds in sample	Percentage standard error (full method)
1 Food & non-alcoholic drinks (continued)				
1.1.24 Dried vegetables	0.10	2	310	8.6
1.1.25 Other preserved or processed vegetables	2.00	54	4,140	2.3
1.1.26 Potatoes	0.70	20	3,330	1.8
1.1.27 Other tubers and products of tuber vegetables	1.80	50	4,070	1.6
1.1.28 Sugar and sugar products	0.40	11	1,720	3.5
1.1.28.1 Sugar	0.20	6	1,310	4.6
1.1.28.2 Other sugar products	0.20	5	650	4.8
1.1.29 Jams, marmalades	0.30	9	1,480	4.6
1.1.30 Chocolate	2.30	65	3,660	2.7
1.1.31 Confectionery products	0.80	22	2,690	2.6
1.1.32 Edible ices and ice cream	0.70	21	1,990	2.8
1.1.33 Other food products	2.80	77	4,490	2.2
1.1.33.1 Sauces, condiments	1.30	37	3,650	1.8
1.1.33.2 Baker's yeast, dessert preparations, soups	1.10	31	2,850	4.4
1.1.33.3 Salt, spices, culinary herbs and other food products	0.30	10	1,440	4.8
1.2 Non-alcoholic drinks	5.30	148	4,910	1.5
1.2.1 Coffee	1.10	30	1,930	3.8
1.2.2 Tea	0.50	14	1,560	3.3
1.2.3 Cocoa and powdered chocolate	0.10	3	390	8.2
1.2.4 Fruit and vegetable juices	1.10	30	3,000	2.2
1.2.5 Mineral or spring waters	0.40	10	1,440	3.8
1.2.6 Soft drinks (inc. fizzy and ready to drink fruit drinks)	2.20	62	3,510	2.1
2 Alcoholic drink, tobacco & narcotics	**12.90**	**360**	**3,300**	**2.7**
2.1 Alcoholic drinks	9.30	259	2,970	2.6
2.1.1 Spirits and liqueurs (brought home)	2.30	63	1,030	4.3
2.1.2 Wines, fortified wines (brought home)	4.60	127	1,980	3.5
2.1.2.1 Wine from grape or other fruit (brought home)	3.90	108	1,800	3.8
2.1.2.2 Fortified wine (brought home)	0.10	4	130	12.7
2.1.2.3 Champagne and sparkling wines (brought home)	0.50	15	380	7.7
2.1.3 Beer, lager, ciders and perry (brought home)	2.50	68	1,630	3.6
2.1.3.1 Beer and lager (brought home)	2.10	58	1,400	3.9
2.1.3.2 Ciders and perry (brought home)	0.40	10	460	7.0
2.1.4 Alcopops (brought home)	0.00~	1	50	18.4
2.2 Tobacco and narcotics	3.60	101	850	5.6
2.2.1 Cigarettes	2.60	72	620	7.0
2.2.2 Cigars, other tobacco products and narcotics	1.10	29	400	7.0
2.2.2.1 Cigars	[0.10]	[2]	20	39.8
2.2.2.2 Other tobacco	1.00	27	390	6.7
2.2.2.3 Narcotics	..	..	..	..
3 Clothing & footwear	**23.40**	**650**	**3,550**	**2.5**
3.1 Clothing	18.70	519	3,360	2.6
3.1.1 Men's outer garments	4.60	128	1,020	4.9
3.1.2 Men's under garments	0.60	15	420	6.2
3.1.3 Women's outer garments	8.00	223	1,920	3.7
3.1.4 Women's under garments	1.20	34	880	5.6
3.1.5 Boys' outer garments (5-15)	0.80	22	350	8.4
3.1.6 Girls' outer garments (5-15)	1.00	28	430	7.2
3.1.7 Infants' outer garments (under 5)	0.70	19	350	8.6
3.1.8 Children's under garments (under 16)	0.40	12	430	7.2

Note: The commodity and service categories are not comparable with those in publications before 2001-02.

The numbering is sequential, it does not use actual COICOP codes.

Please see background notes for symbols and conventions used in this report.

Table A1

Components of household expenditure (cont.)

UK, financial year ending 2020

Commodity or service	Average weekly expenditure all house-holds (£)	Total weekly expenditure (£ million)	Recording house-holds in sample	Percentage standard error (full method)
3 Clothing & footwear (continued)				
3.1.9 Accessories	0.80	23	720	7.6
3.1.9.1 Men's accessories	0.30	7	240	9.7
3.1.9.2 Women's accessories	0.30	10	340	10.4
3.1.9.3 Children's accessories	0.10	3	170	11.1
3.1.9.4 Protective head gear (crash helmets)	0.10	3	20	44.1
3.1.10 Haberdashery, clothing materials and clothing hire	0.30	8	290	16.3
3.1.11 Dry cleaners, laundry and dyeing	0.20	7	130	14.7
3.1.11.1 Dry cleaners and dyeing	0.20	6	100	16.5
3.1.11.2 Laundry, launderettes	0.00~	1	40	26.6
3.2 Footwear	4.70	132	1,300	4.3
3.2.1 Footwear for men	1.60	44	380	7.2
3.2.2 Footwear for women	2.20	62	760	5.8
3.2.3 Footwear for children (5 to 15 years) and infants (under 5)	0.90	25	360	8.3
3.2.4 Repair and hire of footwear	0.00~	1	30	29.8
4 Housing(net)[1], fuel & power	**83.00**	**2,308**	**5,430**	**1.7**
4.1 Actual rentals for housing	52.50	1,461	1,740	2.6
4.1.1 Gross rent	52.50	1,461	1,740	2.6
4.1.2 *less* housing benefit, rebates and allowances received	12.40	345	1,000	4.6
4.1.3 Net rent[2]	40.10	1,117	1,550	3.2
4.1.4 Second dwelling - rent	..	..	..	..
4.2 Maintenance and repair of dwelling	8.00	222	1,860	6.5
4.2.1 Central heating repairs	1.20	34	880	13.0
4.2.2 House maintenance etc.	4.70	131	870	7.7
4.2.3 Paint, wallpaper, timber	1.20	34	410	9.3
4.2.4 Equipment hire, small materials	0.80	24	320	23.3
4.3 Water supply and miscellaneous services relating to the dwelling	10.40	289	5,100	2.3
4.3.1 Water charges	8.20	227	4,990	1.0
4.3.2 Other regular housing payments including service charge for rent	2.10	60	610	10.7
4.3.3 Refuse collection, including skip hire	0.10	2	30	31.5
4.4 Electricity, gas and other fuels	24.50	680	5,400	0.9
4.4.1 Electricity	12.50	347	5,390	1.0
4.4.2 Gas	10.50	292	4,470	1.4
4.4.3 Other fuels	1.50	42	440	9.5
4.4.3.1 Coal and coke	0.20	5	100	16.2
4.4.3.2 Oil for central heating	1.10	29	280	8.7
4.4.3.3 Paraffin, wood, peat, hot water etc.	0.30	7	100	36.9
5 Household goods & services	**36.50**	**1,016**	**5,120**	**3.1**
5.1 Furniture and furnishings, carpets and other floor coverings	20.10	560	2,250	5.1
5.1.1 Furniture and furnishings	16.60	461	2,020	5.3
5.1.1.1 Furniture	15.00	418	1,470	5.6
5.1.1.2 Fancy, decorative goods	1.00	27	780	7.7
5.1.1.3 Garden furniture	0.60	17	60	42.1
5.1.2 Floor coverings	3.50	98	620	8.8
5.1.2.1 Soft floor coverings	3.20	88	590	9.0
5.1.2.2 Hard floor coverings	0.40	10	40	29.9
5.2 Household textiles	2.00	54	1,070	7.6
5.2.1 Bedroom textiles, including duvets and pillows	0.80	23	420	7.9
5.2.2 Other household textiles, including cushions, towels, curtains	1.10	31	1,070	11.3

Note: The commodity and service categories are not comparable with those in publications before 2001-02.

The numbering is sequential, it does not use actual COICOP codes.

Please see background notes for symbols and conventions used in this report.

1 Excluding mortgage interest payments, council tax and NI rates.

2 The figure included in total expenditure is net rent as opposed to gross rent.

Table A1

Components of household expenditure (cont.)

UK, financial year ending 2020

	Average weekly expenditure all house-holds (£)	Total weekly expenditure (£ million)	Recording house-holds in sample	Percentage standard error (full method)
Commodity or service				
5 Household goods & services (continued)				
5.3 Household appliances	2.90	79	430	9.1
5.3.1 Gas cookers	..	..	..	..
5.3.2 Electric cookers, combined gas/electric cookers	[0.10]	[41]	20	61.9
5.3.3 Clothes washing machines and drying machines	0.50	14	40	27.4
5.3.4 Refrigerators, freezers and fridge-freezers	0.30	8	30	38.2
5.3.5 Other major electrical appliances, dishwashers, micro-waves vacuum cleaners, heaters etc.	1.10	30	170	12.0
5.3.6 Fire extinguisher, water softener, safes etc	[0.10]	[3]	10	81.0
5.3.7 Small electric household appliances, excluding hairdryers	0.50	13	150	13.8
5.3.8 Repairs to gas and electrical appliances and spare parts	0.30	7	40	23.6
5.3.9 Rental/hire of major household appliances	..	..	..	..
5.4 Glassware, tableware and household utensils	1.80	51	1,680	5.0
5.4.1 Glassware, china, pottery, cutlery and silverware	0.50	14	590	8.0
5.4.2 Kitchen and domestic utensils	0.70	20	1,000	6.2
5.4.3 Repair of glassware, tableware and household utensils	..	..	..	..
5.4.4 Storage and other durable household articles	0.60	17	600	8.3
5.5 Tools and equipment for house and garden	3.00	83	1,660	5.8
5.5.1 Electrical tools	0.50	14	90	15.6
5.5.2 Garden tools, equipment and accessories e.g. lawn mowers etc.	0.50	13	250	12.9
5.5.3 Small tools	0.50	13	360	10.6
5.5.4 Door, electrical and other fittings	0.80	23	390	14.9
5.5.5 Electrical consumables	0.70	20	1,030	5.1
5.6 Goods and services for routine household maintenance	6.80	189	4,830	2.7
5.6.1 Cleaning materials	2.70	75	3,700	2.2
5.6.1.1 Detergents, washing-up liquid, washing powder	1.10	31	2,190	3.2
5.6.1.2 Disinfectants, polishes, other cleaning materials etc.	1.60	44	3,180	2.6
5.6.2 Household goods and hardware	1.90	52	4,110	2.4
5.6.2.1 Kitchen disposables	1.10	30	3,790	2.4
5.6.2.2 Household hardware and appliances, matches	0.30	10	650	7.0
5.6.2.3 Kitchen gloves, cloths etc.	0.20	5	880	5.5
5.6.2.4 Pins, needles, tape measures, nails, nuts and bolts etc.	0.20	7	380	8.7
5.6.3 Domestic services, carpet cleaning, hire/repair of furniture/furnishings	2.20	62	810	7.2
5.6.3.1 Domestic services, including cleaners, gardeners, au pairs	1.60	46	380	9.0
5.6.3.2 Carpet cleaning, ironing service, window cleaner	0.60	16	520	8.1
5.6.3.3 Hire/repair of household furniture and furnishings	..	..	..	..
6 Health	**8.20**	**228**	**3,060**	**5.5**
6.1 Medical products, appliances and equipment	4.50	125	2,890	6.3
6.1.1 Medicines, prescriptions and healthcare products	2.60	73	2,700	6.6
6.1.1.1 NHS prescription charges and payments	0.30	8	210	8.6
6.1.1.2 Medicines and medical goods (not NHS)	1.80	50	2,430	4.0
6.1.1.3 Other medical products (e.g. plasters, condoms, hot water bottle etc.)	0.20	6	370	9.7
6.1.1.4 Non-optical appliances and equipment (e.g. wheelchairs, batteries for hearing aids, shoe build-up)	0.30	10	60	46.5
6.1.2 Spectacles, lenses, accessories and repairs	1.80	51	430	11.7
6.1.2.1 Purchase of spectacles, lenses, prescription sunglasses	1.80	50	380	11.9
6.1.2.2 Accessories/repairs to spectacles/lenses	0.00~	1	70	19.8
6.2 Hospital services	3.70	103	510	8.8
6.2.1 Out patient services	3.60	100	500	8.9
6.2.1.1 NHS medical, optical, dental and medical auxiliary services	0.80	23	220	10.3
6.2.1.2 Private medical, optical, dental and medical auxiliary services	2.70	76	300	11.5
6.2.1.3 Other services	..	..	..	..
6.2.2 In-patient hospital services	..	..	..	..

Note: The commodity and service categories are not comparable with those in publications before 2001-02.
The numbering is sequential, it does not use actual COICOP codes.
Please see background notes for symbols and conventions used in this report.

		Average weekly expenditure all house-holds (£)	Total weekly expenditure (£ million)	Recording house-holds in sample	Percentage standard error (full method)
Commodity or service					
7	**Transport**	**81.60**	**2,270**	**4,850**	*2.0*
7.1	Purchase of vehicles	26.30	731	1,340	*4.9*
	7.1.1 Purchase of new cars and vans	7.90	219	340	*10.9*
	7.1.1.1 Outright purchases	3.00	83	60	*18.5*
	7.1.1.2 Loan/Hire Purchase of new car/van	4.90	136	290	*13.1*
	7.1.2 Purchase of second hand cars or vans	17.20	479	1,000	*5.0*
	7.1.2.1 Outright purchases	10.20	284	450	*7.0*
	7.1.2.2 Loan/Hire Purchase of second hand car/van	7.00	195	600	*6.2*
	7.1.3 Purchase of motorcycles	1.20	33	70	*41.9*
	7.1.3.1 Outright purchases of new or second hand motorcycles	0.20	6	20	*26.9*
	7.1.3.2 Loan/Hire Purchase of new or second hand motorcycles	..	..	..	*..*
	7.1.3.3 Purchase of bicycles and other vehicles	0.90	24	40	*56.1*
7.2	Operation of personal transport	33.60	935	4,280	*1.7*
	7.2.1 Spares and accessories	2.40	67	450	*9.3*
	7.2.1.1 Car/van accessories and fittings	0.20	5	100	*17.5*
	7.2.1.2 Car/van spare parts	1.90	53	260	*10.9*
	7.2.1.3 Motorcycle accessories and spare parts	[0.10]	[2]	20	*47.8*
	7.2.1.4 Bicycle accessories, repairs and other costs	0.20	6	90	*22.5*
	7.2.2 Petrol, diesel and other motor oils	22.30	619	3,490	*1.7*
	7.2.2.1 Petrol	13.60	377	2,550	*2.2*
	7.2.2.2 Diesel oil	8.60	239	1,460	*2.9*
	7.2.2.3 Other motor oils	0.10	3	60	*21.5*
	7.2.3 Repairs and servicing	6.20	173	2,960	*3.7*
	7.2.3.1 Car or van repairs, servicing and other work	6.20	171	2,950	*3.7*
	7.2.3.2 Motorcycle repairs and servicing	0.00~	1	40	*21.8*
	7.2.4 Other motoring costs	2.80	77	2,010	*6.1*
	7.2.4.1 Motoring organisation subscription (e.g. AA and RAC)	0.40	12	670	*8.1*
	7.2.4.2 Garage rent, other costs (excluding fines), car washing etc.	0.70	20	330	*9.4*
	7.2.4.3 Parking fees, tolls, and permits (excluding motoring fines)	1.00	29	1,200	*7.0*
	7.2.4.4 Driving lessons	0.30	9	30	*25.0*
	7.2.4.5 Anti-freeze, battery water, cleaning materials	0.20	6	290	*35.6*
7.3	Transport services	21.70	604	2,640	*3.3*
	7.3.1 Rail and tube fares	4.60	129	900	*6.1*
	7.3.1.1 Season tickets	1.80	49	220	*11.0*
	7.3.1.2 Other than season tickets	2.90	80	760	*6.8*
	7.3.2 Bus and coach fares	1.50	43	790	*6.1*
	7.3.2.1 Season tickets	0.60	18	200	*9.7*
	7.3.2.2 Other than season tickets	0.90	25	670	*6.1*
	7.3.3 Combined fares	0.60	16	80	*13.5*
	7.3.3.1 Combined fares other than season tickets	0.20	5	40	*19.5*
	7.3.3.2 Combined fares season tickets	0.40	11	40	*17.6*
	7.3.4 Other travel and transport	15.00	417	1,850	*4.1*
	7.3.4.1 Air fares (within UK)	0.30	9	120	*14.1*
	7.3.4.2 Air fares (international)	6.80	189	670	*6.3*
	7.3.4.3 School travel	[0.00~]	[1]	20	*47.9*
	7.3.4.4 Taxis and hired cars with drivers	1.40	39	630	*6.3*
	7.3.4.5 Other personal travel and transport services	0.20	5	310	*15.1*
	7.3.4.6 Hire of self-drive cars, vans, bicycles	0.30	8	30	*28.2*
	7.3.4.7 Car leasing	5.70	159	460	*6.0*
	7.3.4.8 Water travel, ferries and season tickets	0.20	6	60	*26.2*

Note: The commodity and service categories are not comparable with those in publications before 2001-02.

The numbering is sequential, it does not use actual COICOP codes.

Please see background notes for symbols and conventions used in this report.

Table A1

Components of household expenditure (cont.)

UK, financial year ending 2020

	Average weekly expenditure all house-holds (£)	Total weekly expenditure (£ million)	Recording house-holds in sample	Percentage standard error (full method)
Commodity or service				
8 **Communication**[3]	**21.40**	**594**	**5,300**	*1.5*
8.1 Postal services	0.70	18	830	*8.0*
8.2 Telephone and telefax equipment	1.50	42	230	*17.0*
8.2.1 Telephone purchase	[0.00~]	[1]	20	*27.2*
8.2.2 Mobile phone purchase	1.50	41	210	*17.6*
8.2.3 Answering machine, fax machine, modem purchase	:	:	:	*..*
8.3 Telephone and telefax services	8.40	232	4,070	*1.5*
8.3.1 Telephone account (excluding combined payments)[4]	0.60	17	520	*5.9*
8.3.2 Telephone coin and other payments	..	..	..	*..*
8.3.3 Mobile phone account (excluding combined payments)[5]	7.50	208	3,690	*1.6*
8.3.4 Mobile phone - other payments	0.20	7	180	*10.6*
8.4 Internet subscription fees (ex. combined packages)[6]	0.70	19	540	*5.4*
8.5 Combined telecom services[7]	10.10	282	4,340	*1.0*
9 **Recreation & culture**[3]	**74.80**	**2,080**	**5,370**	*2.6*
9.1 Audio-visual, photographic and information processing equipment	4.50	125	960	*9.6*
9.1.1 Audio equipment and accessories, CD players	1.10	30	430	*9.7*
9.1.1.1 Audio equipment, CD players including in car	0.30	9	70	*21.8*
9.1.1.2 Audio accessories e.g. tapes, headphones etc.	0.80	21	380	*10.9*
9.1.2 TV, video and computers	2.90	80	600	*11.0*
9.1.2.1 Purchase of TV and digital decoder	0.70	19	50	*26.3*
9.1.2.2 Satellite dish purchase and installation	:	:	:	*..*
9.1.2.3 Cable TV connection	:	:	:	*..*
9.1.2.4 Video recorder	..	..	..	*..*
9.1.2.5 DVD player/recorder	..	..	..	*..*
9.1.2.6 Blank, pre-recorded video cassettes, DVDs	0.20	7	220	*10.3*
9.1.2.7 Personal computers, printers and calculators	1.80	50	300	*13.9*
9.1.2.8 Spare parts for TV, video, audio	0.10	2	40	*29.4*
9.1.2.9 Repair of audio-visual, photographic and information processing	[0.10]	[3]	20	*38.8*
9.1.3 Photographic, cine and optical equipment	0.50	14	50	*48.9*
9.1.3.1 Photographic and cine equipment	0.40	12	30	*55.2*
9.1.3.2 Camera films	..	..	..	*..*
9.1.3.3 Optical instruments, binoculars, telescopes, microscopes	..	..	..	*..*
9.2 Other major durables for recreation and culture	2.00	54	110	*19.7*
9.2.1 Purchase of boats, trailers and horses	[0.40]	[10]	10	*42.4*
9.2.2 Purchase of caravans, mobile homes (including decoration)	0.50	13	20	*31.4*
9.2.3 Accessories for boats, horses, caravans and motor caravans	..	..	..	*..*
9.2.4 Musical instruments (purchase and hire)	0.30	7	40	*29.4*
9.2.5 Major durables for indoor recreation	..	..	..	*..*
9.2.6 Maintenance and repair of other major durables	0.30	7	30	*44.0*
9.2.7 Purchase of motor caravan (new and second-hand) - outright purchase	..	..	..	*..*
9.2.8 Purchase of motor caravan (new and second-hand) - loan/HP	..	..	..	*..*
9.3 Other recreational items and equipment, gardens and pets	15.50	432	3,780	*4.3*
9.3.1 Games, toys and hobbies	3.20	89	1,440	*6.1*
9.3.2 Computer software and games	1.00	28	280	*11.8*
9.3.2.1 Computer software and game cartridges	0.70	18	250	*11.0*
9.3.2.2 Computer games consoles	0.30	9	50	*24.5*
9.3.3 Equipment for sport, camping and open-air recreation	1.70	47	400	*19.1*
9.3.4 Horticultural goods, garden equipment and plants etc.	2.80	78	1,890	*3.6*
9.3.4.1 BBQ and swings	0.10	2	40	*29.2*
9.3.4.2 Plants, flowers, seeds, fertilisers, insecticides	2.50	71	1,800	*3.9*
9.3.4.3 Garden decorative	0.10	4	130	*12.3*
9.3.4.4 Artificial flowers, pot pourri	0.00~	1	60	*17.7*
9.3.5 Pets and pet food	6.80	190	2,200	*7.2*
9.3.5.1 Pet food	2.90	82	2,030	*3.8*
9.3.5.2 Pet purchase and accessories	1.20	35	740	*10.2*
9.3.5.3 Veterinary and other services for pets identified separately	2.70	74	290	*17.3*

Note: The commodity and service categories are not comparable with those in publications before 2001-02.

The numbering is sequential, it does not use actual COICOP codes.

Please see background notes for symbols and conventions used in this report.

3 Changes to the questionnaire in FYE 2019 has resulted in the COICOP division "Communication" not being directly comparable with previous years. Please see the technical report for more information.

4 For FYE 2019 onwards, telephone payments made as part of a combined bill are excluded from this category and included in 8.5 instead.

5 For FYE 2019 onwards, mobile phone payments made as part of a combined bill are excluded from this category and included in 8.5 instead.

6 For FYE 2019 onwards, internet subscription fee payments made as part of a combined bill are excluded from this category and included in 8.5 instead.

7 New for FYE 2019. This encompasses all telecoms bills that include more than one service. Due to the nature of combined packages, this also includes packages that include television services. Television services reported as single bills are included in 9.4.3.

Table A1

Components of household expenditure (cont.)

UK, financial year ending 2020

	Average weekly expenditure all house-holds (£)	Total weekly expenditure (£ million)	Recording house-holds in sample	Percentage standard error (full method)
Commodity or service				
9 Recreation & culture (continued)				
9.4 Recreational and cultural services	19.80	550	5,030	3.5
9.4.1 Sports admissions, subscriptions, leisure class fees and equipment hire	7.80	217	2,070	7.9
9.4.1.1 Spectator sports: admission charges	0.80	22	170	19.8
9.4.1.2 Participant sports (excluding subscriptions)	1.80	49	790	14.3
9.4.1.3 Subscriptions to sports and social clubs	2.80	78	1,010	16.3
9.4.1.4 Leisure class fees	2.40	67	760	6.6
9.4.1.5 Hire of equipment for sport and open air recreation	0.00~	1	30	26.4
9.4.2 Cinema, theatre and museums etc.	3.30	93	940	5.6
9.4.2.1 Cinemas	0.80	23	470	7.2
9.4.2.2 Live entertainment: theatre, concerts, shows	1.70	48	330	8.3
9.4.2.3 Museums, zoological gardens, theme parks, houses and gardens	0.80	22	260	12.4
9.4.3 TV, video, satellite rental, cable subscriptions and TV licences	4.70	129	4,580	1.6
9.4.3.1 TV licences	2.20	60	4,280	0.6
9.4.3.2 Satellite subscriptions (excluding combined packages)[8]	1.40	39	700	4.6
9.4.3.3 Rent for TV/Satellite/VCR (excluding combined packages)[9]	..	..	..	..
9.4.3.4 Cable subscriptions (excluding combined packages)[10]	0.10	4	170	13.1
9.4.3.5 TV slot meter payments	..	..	..	..
9.4.3.6 Video, cassette and CD hire, including online entertainment packages	0.90	26	1,400	3.7
9.4.4 Miscellaneous entertainments	1.40	40	1,080	6.4
9.4.4.1 Admissions to clubs, dances, discos, bingo	0.80	21	420	8.9
9.4.4.2 Social events and gatherings	0.20	7	160	22.1
9.4.4.3 Subscriptions for leisure activities and other subscriptions	0.40	12	620	8.8
9.4.5 Development of film, deposit for film development, passport photos, holiday and school photos	0.20	4	130	14.3
9.4.6 Gambling payments	2.40	67	1,820	4.8
9.4.6.1 Football pools stakes	[0.00~]	[1]	20	35.2
9.4.6.2 Bingo stakes excluding admission	0.20	5	80	22.7
9.4.6.3 Lottery	1.70	46	1,570	4.1
9.4.6.4 Bookmaker, tote, other betting stakes	0.50	14	430	13.1
9.5 Newspapers, books and stationery	5.50	152	3,910	4.4
9.5.1 Books	1.20	34	1,000	5.5
9.5.2 Stationery, diaries, address books, art materials	1.10	30	1,300	19.7
9.5.3 Cards, calendars, posters and other printed matter	1.30	35	2,170	4.2
9.5.4 Newspapers	1.20	34	1,710	3.8
9.5.5 Magazines and periodicals	0.70	19	1,290	6.3
9.6 Package holidays[11]	27.50	766	1,140	4.8
9.6.1 Package holidays - UK	1.90	53	200	10.3
9.6.2 Package holidays - abroad	25.60	713	1,000	5.0
10 Education	**4.50**	**126**	**260**	**17.3**
10.1 Education fees	4.10	113	170	19.3
10.1.1 Nursery and primary education	0.60	17	30	35.3
10.1.2 Secondary education	1.10	31	20	41.2
10.1.3 Sixth form college/college education	0.70	19	40	26.7
10.1.4 University education	1.30	35	40	39.3
10.1.5 Other education	0.40	11	40	41.7
10.2 Payments for school trips, other ad-hoc expenditure	0.50	13	110	26.8
10.2.1 Nursery and primary education	0.10	3	60	19.0
10.2.2 Secondary education	0.20	6	50	20.8
10.2.3 Sixth form college/college education	..	..	..	..
10.2.4 University education	..	..	..	..
10.2.5 Other education	..	..	..	..

Note: The commodity and service categories are not comparable with those in publications before 2001-02.

The numbering is sequential, it does not use actual COICOP codes.

Please see background notes for symbols and conventions used in this report.

8 For FYE 2019 onwards, satellite payments made as part of a combined bill are excluded from this category and included in 8.5 instead.

9 For FYE 2019 onwards, rent for TV/satellite/VCR payments made as part of a combined bill are excluded from this category and included in 8.5 instead.

10 For FYE 2019 onwards, cable subscription payments made as part of a combined bill are excluded from this category and included in 8.5 instead.

11 Recording of expenditure on package holidays was changed from 2011.

Table A1

Components of household expenditure (cont.)

UK, financial year ending 2020

	Average weekly expenditure all house- holds (£)	Total weekly expenditure (£ million)	Recording house- holds in sample	Percentage standard error (full method)
Commodity or service				
11 Restaurants & hotels	**52.90**	**1,470**	**4,790**	*1.7*
11.1 Catering services	41.30	1,148	4,700	*1.6*
11.1.1 Restaurant and café meals	20.20	561	3,910	*1.9*
11.1.2 Alcoholic drinks (away from home)	8.30	231	2,270	*3.2*
11.1.3 Take away meals eaten at home	5.60	156	2,270	*2.3*
11.1.4 Other take-away and snack food	5.30	147	2,910	*2.4*
11.1.4.1 Hot and cold food	4.00	111	2,610	*2.7*
11.1.4.2 Confectionery	0.30	8	1,070	*4.2*
11.1.4.3 Ice cream	0.20	4	400	*7.3*
11.1.4.4 Soft drinks	0.80	23	1,840	*3.1*
11.1.5 Contract catering (food)	0.20	6	30	*27.1*
11.1.6 Canteens	1.70	48	1,110	*4.1*
11.1.6.1 School meals	0.70	20	420	*6.0*
11.1.6.2 Meals bought and eaten at the workplace	1.00	28	820	*5.2*
11.2 Accommodation services	11.60	322	1,720	*4.3*
11.2.1 Holiday in the UK	6.30	174	1,350	*4.1*
11.2.2 Holiday abroad	5.20	145	480	*7.8*
11.2.3 Room hire	0.10	3	30	*33.8*
12 Miscellaneous goods and services	**45.70**	**1,270**	**5,340**	*2.4*
12.1 Personal care	13.40	373	4,760	*2.2*
12.1.1 Hairdressing, beauty treatment	4.40	122	1,300	*4.3*
12.1.2 Toilet paper	1.00	27	2,230	*2.6*
12.1.3 Toiletries and soap	2.60	74	3,880	*2.2*
12.1.3.1 Toiletries (disposable including tampons, lipsyl, toothpaste etc.)	1.60	45	3,340	*2.7*
12.1.3.2 Bar of soap, liquid soap, shower gel etc.	0.50	14	1,840	*4.1*
12.1.3.3 Toilet requisites (durable including razors, hairbrushes, toothbrushes etc.)	0.50	14	1,130	*4.9*
12.1.4 Baby toiletries and accessories (disposable)	0.60	16	1,050	*4.7*
12.1.5 Hair products, cosmetics and electrical appliances for personal care	4.80	135	2,950	*3.4*
12.1.5.1 Hair products	1.00	28	1,620	*4.1*
12.1.5.2 Cosmetics and related accessories	3.50	99	2,300	*4.0*
12.1.5.3 Electrical appliances for personal care, including hairdryers, shavers etc.	0.30	8	120	*15.8*
12.2 Personal effects	4.20	118	1,180	*10.1*
12.2.1 Jewellery, clocks and watches and other personal effects	2.70	75	820	*15.1*
12.2.2 Leather and travel goods (excluding baby items)	1.10	30	390	*14.6*
12.2.3 Sunglasses (non-prescription)	0.10	3	70	*23.4*
12.2.4 Baby equipment (excluding prams and pushchairs)	0.10	3	40	*30.2*
12.2.5 Prams, pram accessories and pushchairs	[0.10]	[3]	20	*40.4*
12.2.6 Repairs to personal goods	0.10	4	30	*30.7*
12.3 Social protection	3.70	104	230	*15.0*
12.3.1 Residential homes	..	..	..	*..*
12.3.2 Home help	[0.50]	[14]	10	*58.6*
12.3.3 Nursery, crèche, playschools	1.10	30	80	*23.5*
12.3.4 Child care payments	2.00	56	150	*18.8*

Note: The commodity and service categories are not comparable with those in publications before 2001-02.

The numbering is sequential, it does not use actual COICOP codes.

Please see background notes for symbols and conventions used in this report.

Components of household expenditure (cont.)

UK, financial year ending 2020

	Average weekly expenditure all house- holds (£)	Total weekly expenditure (£ million)	Recording house- holds in sample	Percentage standard error (full method)
Commodity or service				
12 Miscellaneous goods and services (continued)				
12.4 Insurance	19.30	536	4,910	2.0
12.4.1 Household insurances	4.90	137	4,220	2.5
12.4.1.1 Structure insurance	2.30	63	3,460	2.2
12.4.1.2 Contents insurance	2.10	59	4,030	1.8
12.4.1.3 Insurance for household appliances[12]	0.50	15	540	15.9
12.4.2 Medical insurance premiums[13]	2.40	66	860	6.9
12.4.3 Vehicle insurance including boat insurance	11.10	309	4,280	2.5
12.4.3.1 Vehicle insurance	11.00	305	4,280	2.4
12.4.3.2 Boat insurance (not home)	..	..	..	..
12.4.4 Non-package holiday, other travel insurance[14]	0.90	25	1,480	6.8
12.5 Other services	5.00	140	1,870	9.7
12.5.1 Moving house	2.40	67	340	9.9
12.5.1.1 Moving and storage of furniture	0.40	11	150	15.9
12.5.1.2 Property transaction - purchase and sale	0.90	26	90	13.3
12.5.1.3 Property transaction - sale only	0.40	11	40	23.5
12.5.1.4 Property transaction - purchase only	0.40	12	60	22.9
12.5.1.5 Property transaction - other payments	0.20	7	100	16.8
12.5.2 Bank, building society, post office, credit card charges	0.50	15	1,240	4.1
12.5.2.1 Bank and building society charges	0.40	12	1,120	4.1
12.5.2.2 Bank and Post Office counter charges	..	..	..	..
12.5.2.3 Annual standing charge for credit cards	0.10	2	220	12.9
12.5.2.4 Commission travellers' cheques and currency	..	..	..	..
12.5.3 Other services and professional fees	2.10	58	630	21.8
12.5.3.1 Other professional fees including court fines	0.40	10	30	36.7
12.5.3.2 Legal fees	0.40	12	30	43.2
12.5.3.3 Funeral expenses	[0.60]	[16]	20	66.1
12.5.3.4 TU and professional organisations	0.60	17	510	13.2
12.5.3.5 Other payments for services e.g. photocopying	0.10	3	80	37.2
1-12 All expenditure groups	**508.50**	**14,146**	**5,440**	*1.1*
13 Other expenditure items	**79.30**	**2,206**	**5,250**	**2.2**
13.1 Housing: mortgage interest payments, council tax etc.	50.40	1,403	5,000	1.6
13.1.1 Mortgage interest payments	22.30	619	1,620	2.8
13.1.2 Mortgage protection premiums	1.00	29	580	5.6
13.1.3 Council tax, domestic rates	26.00	724	4,990	0.9
13.1.4 Council tax, mortgage (second dwelling)	1.10	30	50	20.0
13.2 Licences, fines and transfers	3.80	105	4,030	4.8
13.2.1 Stamp duty, licences and fines (excluding motoring fines)	0.50	13	70	36.4
13.2.2 Motoring fines	[0.10]	[3]	20	25.1
13.2.3 Motor vehicle road taxation payments less refunds	3.20	89	4,020	1.6
13.3 Holiday spending	12.10	337	280	10.3
13.3.1 Money spent abroad	12.10	337	280	10.3
13.3.2 Duty free goods bought in UK	:	:	:	..

Note: The commodity and service categories are not comparable with those in publications before 2001-02.

The numbering is sequential, it does not use actual COICOP codes.

Please see background notes for symbols and conventions used in this report.

12 For FYE 2019, information about insurance for household appliances was collected in the questionnaire in addition to the diary. In previous years, this was based on diary data only.

13 For FYE 2019, critical illness cover, personal accident insurance and other medical insurance are included here. In previous years, these were included in other insurance.

14 For FYE 2019, information about insurance for non-package holiday and other travel insurance was collected in the questionnaire in addition to the diary. In previous years, this was based on diary data only.

Components of household expenditure (cont.)

UK, financial year ending 2020

Commodity or service	Average weekly expenditure all house- holds (£)	Total weekly expenditure (£ million)	Recording house- holds in sample	Percentage standard error (full method)
13 Other expenditure items (continued)				
13.4 Money transfers and credit	13.00	361	2,490	5.6
13.4.1 Money, cash gifts given to children	0.30	8	70	34.6
13.4.1.1 Money given to children for specific purposes	0.10	3	60	28.1
13.4.1.2 Cash gifts to children (no specific purpose)	..	..	..	..
13.4.2 Cash gifts and donations	11.70	324	2,170	6.1
13.4.2.1 Money/presents given to those outside the household	5.40	149	850	10.4
13.4.2.2 Charitable donations and subscriptions	2.70	76	1,440	7.9
13.4.2.3 Money sent abroad	1.30	37	240	20.3
13.4.2.4 Maintenance allowance expenditure	2.20	62	150	13.4
13.4.3 Club instalment payments (child) and interest on credit cards	1.00	29	540	8.3
13.4.3.1 Club instalment payment	:	:	:	..
13.4.3.2 Interest on credit cards	1.00	29	540	8.3
Total expenditure	**587.90**	**16,352**	**5,440**	*1.1*
14 Other items recorded				
14.1 Life assurance, contributions to pension funds	34.70	965	3,290	3.5
14.1.1 Life assurance premiums	2.90	81	1,620	4.3
14.1.2 Contributions to pension and superannuation funds etc.	26.90	748	2,590	4.2
14.1.3 Personal pensions	4.90	136	390	12.9
14.2 Other insurance including friendly societies	2.40	66	1,640	3.3
14.3 Income tax, payments less refunds	105.20	2,927	4,060	3.5
14.3.1 Income tax paid by employees under PAYE	81.90	2,279	2,880	3.5
14.3.2 Income tax paid direct e.g. by retired or unoccupied persons	3.00	83	160	19.8
14.3.3 Income tax paid direct by self-employed	4.90	137	230	13.6
14.3.4 Income tax deducted at source from income under covenant from investments or from annuities and pensions	14.10	392	1,300	8.6
14.3.5 Income tax on bonus earnings	3.30	93	560	16.7
14.3.6 Income tax refunds under PAYE	0.30	9	30	43.5
14.3.7 Income tax refunds other than PAYE	1.70	48	250	36.0
14.4 National insurance contribution	40.50	1,125	2,990	2.0
14.4.1 NI contributions paid by employees	40.30	1,122	2,970	2.0
14.4.2 NI contributions paid by non-employees	0.10	4	40	26.3
14.5 Purchase or alteration of dwellings (contracted out), mortgages	60.60	1,684	2,080	4.7
14.5.1 Outright purchase of houses, flats etc. including deposits	..	..	..	..
14.5.2 Capital repayment of mortgage	28.20	783	1,490	3.0
14.5.3 Central heating installation	1.40	39	130	10.9
14.5.4 DIY improvements: Double glazing, kitchen units, sheds etc.	1.40	39	80	31.3
14.5.5 Home improvements - contracted out	24.50	681	720	8.2
14.5.6 Bathroom fittings	0.40	12	90	32.1
14.5.7 Purchase of materials for Capital Improvements	0.40	11	30	33.9
14.5.8 Purchase of second dwelling	3.40	95	80	41.5
14.6 Savings and investments	9.20	255	630	14.9
14.6.1 Savings, investments (excluding AVCs)	8.40	233	470	16.2
14.6.2 Additional Voluntary Contributions	0.60	16	60	19.5
14.6.3 Food stamps, other food related expenditure	0.20	6	130	16.8
14.7 Pay off loan to clear other debt	2.20	61	240	9.5
14.8 Windfall receipts from gambling etc.[15]	1.30	37	430	19.7

Note: The commodity and service categories are not comparable with those in publications before 2001-02.

The numbering is sequential, it does not use actual COICOP codes.

Please see background notes for symbols and conventions used in this report.

15 Expressed as an income figure as opposed to an expenditure figure.

Source: Office for National Statistics

Table A2

Expenditure on food and non-alcoholic drinks by place of purchase

UK, financial year ending 2020

			Large supermarket chains[1]			Other outlets			Internet expenditure[2]		
			Average weekly expenditure all households (£)	Total weekly expenditure (£ million)	Recording households in sample	Average weekly expenditure all households (£)	Total weekly expenditure (£ million)	Recording households in sample	Average weekly expenditure all households (£)	Total weekly expenditure (£ million)	Recording households in sample
1		Food and non-alcoholic drinks	48.70	1,353	5,300	10.40	289	4,680	4.70	130	610
1.1		Food	44.80	1,246	5,300	9.40	261	4,590	4.20	117	580
	1.1.1	Bread, rice and cereals	4.60	129	5,070	0.80	22	1,990	0.40	11	440
	1.1.2	Pasta products	0.40	10	2,070	0.10	2	270	0.00~	1	210
	1.1.3	Buns, cakes, biscuits etc.	3.20	90	4,620	0.70	18	1,730	0.20	6	350
	1.1.4	Pastry (savoury)	0.90	24	2,110	0.00~	1	150	0.10	2	150
	1.1.5	Beef (fresh, chilled or frozen)	1.30	37	2,040	0.50	13	410	0.10	3	170
	1.1.6	Pork (fresh, chilled or frozen)	0.40	11	880	0.10	4	190	0.00~	1	60
	1.1.7	Lamb (fresh, chilled or frozen)	0.40	10	460	0.30	9	160	0.00~	1	40
	1.1.8	Poultry (fresh, chilled or frozen)	1.80	50	2,610	0.50	13	410	0.20	5	220
	1.1.9	Bacon and ham	0.70	19	2,000	0.10	3	310	0.10	1	140
	1.1.10	Other meats and meat preparations	5.20	146	4,480	0.90	26	1,410	0.40	12	390
	1.1.11	Fish and fish products	2.50	69	3,200	0.50	13	490	0.20	6	270
	1.1.12	Milk	1.60	44	4,360	0.40	12	1,360	0.10	3	340
	1.1.13	Cheese and curd	1.80	51	3,730	0.20	5	510	0.20	5	330
	1.1.14	Eggs	0.60	17	2,790	0.10	3	530	0.10	2	240
	1.1.15	Other milk products	2.00	56	4,060	0.10	4	540	0.20	6	340
	1.1.16	Butter	0.40	11	1,370	0.00~	1	170	0.00~	1	110
	1.1.17	Margarine, other vegetable fats and peanut butter	0.50	15	2,140	0.00~	1	230	0.00~	1	170
	1.1.18	Cooking oils and fats	0.30	8	1,070	0.10	2	130	0.00~	1	80
	1.1.19	Fresh fruit	3.40	93	4,430	0.40	10	830	0.30	8	370
	1.1.20	Other fresh, chilled or frozen fruits	0.40	11	1,500	0.10	1	170	0.00~	1	130
	1.1.21	Dried fruit and nuts	0.60	18	1,680	0.20	4	350	0.10	3	110
	1.1.22	Preserved fruit and fruit based products	0.10	4	800	0.00~	0~	70	0.00~	0~	60
	1.1.23	Fresh vegetables	3.60	100	4,660	0.50	15	960	0.30	10	400
	1.1.24	Dried vegetables and other preserved and processed vegetables	0.80	22	3,030	1.10	31	2,870	0.10	3	290
	1.1.25	Potatoes	0.60	16	2,940	0.10	2	410	0.00~	1	230
	1.1.26	Other tubers and products of tuber vegetables	1.50	41	3,690	0.20	6	920	0.10	4	290
	1.1.27	Sugar and sugar products	0.30	8	1,390	0.10	2	310	0.00~	1	120
	1.1.28	Jams, marmalades	0.20	6	1,260	0.10	2	210	0.00~	1	100
	1.1.29	Chocolate	1.70	46	3,160	0.50	15	1,340	0.10	4	200
	1.1.30	Confectionery products	0.50	13	2,060	0.30	8	1,180	0.00~	1	90
	1.1.31	Edible ices and ice cream	0.60	17	1,760	0.10	2	240	0.10	1	140
	1.1.32	Other food products	2.00	57	4,120	0.40	12	1,080	0.30	9	390
1.2		Non-alcoholic drinks	3.90	107	4,530	1.00	28	1,960	0.50	13	430
	1.2.1	Coffee	0.70	20	1,570	0.20	6	380	0.20	4	130
	1.2.2	Tea	0.40	10	1,260	0.10	3	270	0.00~	1	100
	1.2.3	Cocoa and powdered chocolate	0.10	2	310	0.00~	1	70	[0.00~]	[0~]	20
	1.2.4	Fruit and vegetable juices (inc fruit squash)	0.90	24	2,690	0.10	3	370	0.10	3	240
	1.2.5	Mineral or spring waters	0.30	7	1,200	0.10	2	300	0.00~	1	70
	1.2.6	Soft drinks	1.60	44	3,020	0.50	14	1,400	0.10	4	240

Note: The commodity and service categories are not comparable with those in publications before 2001-02.

The numbering is sequential, it does not use actual COICOP codes.

Please see background notes for symbols and conventions used in this report.

1 In 2011 the list of large supermarket chains was updated.

2 Includes internet expenditure from large supermarket chains.

Source: Office for National Statistics

Table A3

Expenditure on clothing and footwear by place of purchase

UK, financial year ending 2020

		Large supermarket chains[1]			Clothing chains			Other outlets[2]		
		Average weekly expenditure all house-holds (£)	Total weekly expenditure (£ million)	Recording house-holds in sample	Average weekly expenditure all house-holds (£)	Total weekly expenditure (£ million)	Recording house-holds in sample	Average weekly expenditure all house-holds (£)	Total weekly expenditure (£ million)	Recording house-holds in sample
3	**Clothing and footwear**	**2.10**	**57**	**1,270**	**6.50**	**181**	**1,620**	**14.40**	**401**	**2,480**
3.1	Clothing	1.90	52	1,200	5.80	162	1,540	10.60	295	2,200
3.1.1	Men's outer garments	0.20	6	170	1.40	38	390	3.00	84	620
3.1.2	Men's under garments	0.10	3	110	0.20	7	170	0.20	6	170
3.1.3	Women's outer garments	0.70	18	450	2.60	73	880	4.70	132	1,090
3.1.4	Women's under garments	0.20	6	280	0.50	15	400	0.50	13	280
3.1.5	Boys' outer garments	0.10	4	130	0.20	5	100	0.50	13	170
3.1.6	Girls' outer garments	0.20	4	140	0.30	8	150	0.60	16	230
3.1.7	Infants' outer garments	0.10	4	140	0.20	7	130	0.30	8	140
3.1.8	Children's under garments	0.20	4	200	0.20	4	140	0.10	3	140
3.1.9	Accessories	0.10	1	100	0.20	5	200	0.50	13	440
3.1.9	Men's accessories	0.00~	0~	30	0.10	2	70	0.20	5	150
3.1.9	Women's accessories	0.00~	1	40	0.10	3	110	0.20	6	210
3.1.9	Children's accessories	0.00~	0~	40	0.00~	0~	40	0.10	2	100
3.1.10	Haberdashery and clothing hire	0.00~	1	50	..	..	..	0.30	7	240
3.2	Footwear	0.20	5	210	0.70	19	330	3.80	106	880
3.2.1	Men's	0.00~	1	40	0.20	4	60	1.40	38	290
3.2.2	Women's	0.10	2	100	0.40	12	220	1.70	48	490
3.2.3	Children's	0.10	2	90	0.10	3	80	0.70	20	220

Note: The commodity and service categories are not comparable with those in publications before 2001-02.
The numbering system is sequential, it does not use actual COICOP codes.
Please see background notes for symbols and conventions used in this report.

1 In 2011 the list of large supermarket chains was updated.
2 Includes internet expenditure from large supermarket chains.

Source: Office for National Statistics

Table A4

Household expenditure by gross income decile group

UK, financial year ending 2020

	Lowest ten per cent	Second decile group	Third decile group	Fourth decile group	Fifth decile group	Sixth decile group	Seventh decile group	Eighth decile group	Ninth decile group	Highest ten per cent	All house-holds
Lower boundary of group (£ per week)		228	335	446	568	708	873	1,051	1,296	1,733	
Weighted number of households (thousands)	2,780	2,780	2,780	2,780	2,780	2,780	2,780	2,780	2,780	2,780	27,820
Total number of households in sample	550	550	570	580	570	560	530	530	520	480	5,440
Total number of persons in sample	710	870	1,090	1,220	1,300	1,420	1,460	1,510	1,530	1,560	12,670
Total number of adults in sample	620	720	880	980	1,030	1,080	1,100	1,150	1,190	1,140	9,880
Weighted average number of persons per household	1.3	1.6	1.9	2.1	2.3	2.5	2.8	2.8	3.0	3.3	2.4
Commodity or service					Average weekly household expenditure (£)						
1 Food & non-alcoholic drinks	34.40	41.30	48.50	54.30	61.90	64.40	74.00	76.90	82.60	98.70	63.70
2 Alcoholic drinks, tobacco & narcotics	8.80	8.40	9.00	10.80	12.10	13.20	13.00	16.80	17.20	20.20	12.90
3 Clothing & footwear	8.50	9.30	12.00	16.80	18.30	20.80	28.50	34.30	33.70	51.50	23.40
4 Housing(net)[1], fuel & power	57.90	58.90	75.50	76.30	79.90	91.10	90.30	90.90	90.70	118.30	83.00
5 Household goods & services	12.30	18.80	23.40	30.40	32.50	30.70	38.70	47.60	52.90	77.80	36.50
6 Health	4.20	5.40	5.00	5.80	8.10	7.70	9.00	12.20	9.20	15.30	8.20
7 Transport	21.30	27.00	44.60	51.10	65.70	91.10	90.80	114.60	125.90	184.20	81.60
8 Communication	10.30	14.30	16.00	18.70	20.80	22.20	24.50	25.40	28.10	33.40	21.40
9 Recreation & culture	28.60	34.30	41.40	53.40	65.70	67.70	81.20	100.80	117.30	157.60	74.80
10 Education	..	..	[1.20]	[2.60]	[1.90]	3.40	6.20	2.60	6.50	19.60	4.50
11 Restaurants & hotels	15.30	20.40	23.70	32.80	45.80	51.80	57.10	71.00	84.20	126.50	52.90
12 Miscellaneous goods & services	19.20	19.70	26.90	35.00	41.10	45.50	50.30	64.40	61.10	93.70	45.70
1-12 All expenditure groups	221.60	258.50	327.20	387.90	453.90	509.60	563.50	657.40	709.60	996.80	508.50
13 Other expenditure items	23.30	28.60	36.00	48.10	61.20	74.50	87.00	104.50	127.60	202.70	79.30
Total expenditure	**244.90**	**287.10**	**363.20**	**436.00**	**515.10**	**584.20**	**650.50**	**761.90**	**837.20**	**1199.50**	**587.90**
Average weekly expenditure per person (£)											
Total expenditure	**190.80**	**180.50**	**191.70**	**208.30**	**225.70**	**230.90**	**231.30**	**269.40**	**281.20**	**358.40**	**248.70**

Note: The commodity and service categories are not comparable to those in publications before 2001-02.

Please see background notes for symbols and conventions used in this report.

1 Excluding mortgage interest payments, council tax and Northern Ireland rates.

Source: Office for National Statistics

Table A5

Household expenditure as a percentage of total expenditure by gross income decile group

UK, financial year ending 2020

	Lowest ten per cent	Second decile group	Third decile group	Fourth decile group	Fifth decile group	Sixth decile group	Seventh decile group	Eighth decile group	Ninth decile group	Highest ten per cent	All house-holds
Lower boundary of group (£ per week)		228	335	446	568	708	873	1,051	1,296	1,733	
Weighted number of households (thousands)	2,780	2,780	2,780	2,780	2,780	2,780	2,780	2,780	2,780	2,780	27,820
Total number of households in sample	550	550	570	580	570	560	530	530	520	480	5,440
Total number of persons in sample	710	870	1,090	1,220	1,300	1,420	1,460	1,510	1,530	1,560	12,670
Total number of adults in sample	620	720	880	980	1,030	1,080	1,100	1,150	1,190	1,140	9,880
Weighted average number of persons per household	1.3	1.6	1.9	2.1	2.3	2.5	2.8	2.8	3.0	3.3	2.4
Commodity or service	Percentage of total expenditure										
1 Food & non-alcoholic drinks	14	14	13	12	12	11	11	10	10	8	11
2 Alcoholic drinks, tobacco & narcotics	4	3	2	2	2	2	2	2	2	2	2
3 Clothing & footwear	3	3	3	4	4	4	4	5	4	4	4
4 Housing(net)[1], fuel & power	24	21	21	18	16	16	14	12	11	10	14
5 Household goods & services	5	7	6	7	6	5	6	6	6	6	6
6 Health	2	2	1	1	2	1	1	2	1	1	1
7 Transport	9	9	12	12	13	16	14	15	15	15	14
8 Communication	4	5	4	4	4	4	4	3	3	3	4
9 Recreation & culture	12	12	11	12	13	12	12	13	14	13	13
10 Education	..	..	[0]	[1]	[0]	1	1	0~	1	2	1
11 Restaurants & hotels	6	7	7	8	9	9	9	9	10	11	9
12 Miscellaneous goods & services	8	7	7	8	8	8	8	8	7	8	8
1-12 All expenditure groups	91	90	90	89	88	87	87	86	85	83	87
13 Other expenditure items	9	10	10	11	12	13	13	14	15	17	13
Total expenditure	100	100	100	100	100	100	100	100	100	100	100

Note: The commodity and service categories are not comparable to those in publications before 2001-02.

Please see background notes for symbols and conventions used in this report.

1 Excluding mortgage interest payments, council tax and Northern Ireland rates.

Source: Office for National Statistics

Table A6

Detailed household expenditure by gross income decile group

UK, financial year ending 2020

Commodity or service		Lowest ten per cent	Second decile group	Third decile group	Fourth decile group	Fifth decile group	Sixth decile group	Seventh decile group	Eighth decile group	Ninth decile group	Highest ten per cent	All house-holds
Lower boundary of group (£ per week)			228	335	446	568	708	873	1,051	1,296	1,733	
Weighted number of households (thousands)		2,780	2,780	2,780	2,780	2,780	2,780	2,780	2,780	2,780	2,780	27,820
Total number of households in sample		550	550	570	580	570	560	530	530	520	480	5,440
Total number of persons in sample		710	870	1,090	1,220	1,300	1,420	1,460	1,510	1,530	1,560	12,670
Total number of adults in sample		620	720	880	980	1,030	1,080	1,100	1,150	1,190	1,140	9,880
Weighted average number of persons per household		1	2	2	2	2	3	3	3	3	3	2
						Average weekly household expenditure (£)						
1	**Food & non-alcoholic drinks**	**34.40**	**41.30**	**48.50**	**54.30**	**61.90**	**64.40**	**74.00**	**76.90**	**82.60**	**98.70**	**63.70**
1.1	Food	31.60	37.90	44.50	49.80	56.60	59.00	67.70	70.30	75.50	90.80	58.40
1.1.1	Bread, rice and cereals	3.10	3.60	4.30	5.00	5.70	6.10	6.80	7.20	7.50	9.10	5.80
1.1.2	Pasta products	0.20	0.30	0.30	0.40	0.40	0.50	0.50	0.60	0.70	0.80	0.50
1.1.3	Buns, cakes, biscuits etc.	2.40	2.80	3.40	3.80	4.10	4.20	4.60	4.90	5.00	6.00	4.10
1.1.4	Pastry (savoury)	0.40	0.50	0.70	0.60	0.90	1.10	1.10	1.30	1.40	1.60	1.00
1.1.5	Beef (fresh, chilled or frozen)	1.00	1.30	1.30	1.60	1.90	2.10	1.90	2.30	2.30	3.00	1.90
1.1.6	Pork (fresh, chilled or frozen)	0.30	0.40	0.40	0.50	0.50	0.60	0.60	0.70	0.60	0.70	0.50
1.1.7	Lamb (fresh, chilled or frozen)	0.20	0.40	0.50	0.50	0.70	0.70	1.30	0.70	0.90	1.00	0.70
1.1.8	Poultry (fresh, chilled or frozen)	1.00	1.40	1.80	1.90	2.10	2.40	3.00	3.50	3.30	4.20	2.40
1.1.9	Bacon and ham	0.40	0.70	0.70	0.70	0.80	0.80	0.90	0.90	1.00	1.30	0.80
1.1.10	Other meat and meat preparations	4.30	4.80	5.60	5.70	6.20	6.80	7.30	7.80	8.00	9.40	6.60
1.1.11	Fish and fish products	1.60	2.00	2.20	2.80	3.00	3.10	3.80	3.80	4.20	5.20	3.20
1.1.12	Milk	1.50	1.70	2.00	2.00	2.20	2.30	2.40	2.30	2.50	2.50	2.10
1.1.13	Cheese and curd	1.10	1.20	1.70	1.70	2.10	2.10	2.50	3.00	3.20	3.30	2.20
1.1.14	Eggs	0.40	0.50	0.60	0.70	0.70	0.70	0.90	0.90	1.00	1.30	0.80
1.1.15	Other milk products	1.40	1.60	1.70	2.10	2.40	2.30	2.60	2.80	3.10	3.50	2.30
1.1.16	Butter	0.30	0.30	0.40	0.40	0.40	0.50	0.50	0.50	0.70	0.80	0.60
1.1.17	Margarine, other vegetable fats and peanut butter	0.40	0.50	0.60	0.70	0.60	0.60	0.70	0.70	0.70	0.70	0.60
1.1.18	Cooking oils and fats	0.20	0.20	0.30	0.30	0.40	0.30	0.60	0.40	0.50	0.60	0.40
1.1.19	Fresh fruit	2.30	2.60	2.80	3.60	3.80	4.00	4.50	4.60	5.00	6.90	4.00
1.1.20	Other fresh, chilled or frozen fruits	0.20	0.30	0.30	0.40	0.40	0.50	0.50	0.60	0.60	0.90	0.50
1.1.21	Dried fruit and nuts	0.40	0.40	0.60	0.70	1.10	0.70	1.50	0.90	1.20	1.60	0.90
1.1.22	Preserved fruit and fruit based products	0.10	0.10	0.10	0.20	0.20	0.20	0.20	0.10	0.20	0.20	0.20
1.1.23	Fresh vegetables	2.20	2.50	3.10	3.70	4.10	4.30	5.20	5.60	6.30	7.60	4.50
1.1.24	Dried vegetables	[0.00]	[0.00]	0.00–	0.00–	0.00–	0.00–	0.10	0.10	0.10	0.10	0.10
1.1.25	Other preserved or processed vegetables	0.80	0.50	1.30	1.30	2.00	1.90	2.00	2.40	2.90	3.70	2.00
1.1.26	Potatoes	0.40	0.50	0.60	0.70	0.70	0.80	0.80	0.80	0.90	0.80	0.70
1.1.27	Other tubers and products of tuber vegetables	1.00	1.30	1.50	1.60	1.80	2.10	1.90	2.20	2.30	2.30	1.80
1.1.28	Sugar and sugar products	0.20	0.30	0.30	0.30	0.40	0.40	0.50	0.40	0.40	0.60	0.40
1.1.29	Jams, marmalades	0.20	0.20	0.20	0.40	0.40	0.30	0.30	0.40	0.40	0.50	0.30
1.1.30	Chocolate	1.10	1.40	1.80	1.70	2.30	2.10	2.90	2.70	3.30	3.80	2.30
1.1.31	Confectionery products	0.40	0.50	0.70	0.70	0.80	0.90	1.10	1.00	1.00	1.00	0.80
1.1.32	Edible ices and ice cream	0.40	0.50	0.60	0.70	0.80	0.70	0.90	0.80	0.90	1.20	0.70
1.1.33	Other food products	1.50	1.90	2.00	2.30	2.70	3.00	2.90	3.30	3.60	4.60	2.80
1.2	Non-alcoholic drinks	2.90	3.40	4.00	4.50	5.30	5.40	6.30	6.50	7.10	7.90	5.30
1.2.1	Coffee	0.70	0.60	0.80	0.90	1.10	1.10	1.20	1.30	1.40	1.70	1.10
1.2.2	Tea	0.40	0.40	0.50	0.50	0.40	0.40	0.50	0.60	0.60	0.70	0.50
1.2.3	Cocoa and powdered chocolate	0.10	0.10	0.10	0.10	0.10	0.10	0.10	0.10	0.10	0.10	0.10
1.2.4	Fruit and vegetable juices (inc. fruit squash)	0.50	0.70	0.80	0.90	1.10	1.10	1.10	1.40	1.40	1.80	1.10
1.2.5	Mineral or spring waters	0.20	0.20	0.20	0.30	0.30	0.40	0.60	0.40	0.50	0.50	0.40
1.2.6	Soft drinks (inc. fizzy and ready to drink fruit drinks)	1.20	1.40	1.70	1.80	2.30	2.30	2.80	2.80	3.00	3.00	2.20

Note: The commodity and service categories are not comparable to those in publications before 2001-02.
The numbering system is sequential, it does not use actual COICOP codes.
Please see background notes for symbols and conventions used in this report.

Table A6

Detailed household expenditure by gross income decile group (cont.)

UK, financial year ending 2020

Commodity or service		Lowest ten per cent	Second decile group	Third decile group	Fourth decile group	Fifth decile group	Sixth decile group	Seventh decile group	Eighth decile group	Ninth decile group	Highest ten per cent	All house- holds
						Average weekly household expenditure (£)						
2	**Alcoholic drink, tobacco & narcotics**	**8.80**	**8.40**	**9.00**	**10.80**	**12.10**	**13.20**	**13.00**	**16.80**	**17.20**	**20.20**	**12.90**
2.1	Alcoholic drinks	4.70	4.80	6.10	7.50	8.20	8.40	10.00	12.00	13.50	17.60	9.30
2.1.1	Spirits and liqueurs (brought home)	1.10	1.40	1.70	2.20	2.30	2.50	2.70	2.40	3.20	3.30	2.30
2.1.2	Wines, fortified wines (brought home)	2.10	2.10	2.80	3.50	3.90	3.70	4.80	6.10	6.20	10.20	4.60
2.1.3	Beer, lager, ciders and perry (brought home)	1.50	1.30	1.60	1.70	2.00	2.20	2.50	3.50	4.10	4.10	2.50
2.1.4	Alcopops (brought home)									[0.10]		0.00~
2.2	Tobacco and narcotics	4.10	3.60	2.90	3.30	3.90	4.70	3.00	4.80	3.60	2.50	3.60
2.2.1	Cigarettes	3.10	2.70	1.90	2.40	2.70	3.20	2.00	3.40	2.80	1.80	2.60
2.2.2	Cigars, other tobacco products and narcotics	0.90	0.90	1.00	0.90	1.20	1.60	1.00	1.40	0.80	0.80	1.10
3	**Clothing & footwear**	**8.50**	**9.30**	**12.00**	**16.80**	**18.30**	**20.80**	**28.50**	**34.30**	**33.70**	**51.50**	**23.40**
3.1	Clothing	6.80	7.80	10.00	13.50	14.70	16.40	23.10	27.30	27.20	39.90	18.70
3.1.1	Men's outer garments	1.30	1.50	2.80	2.30	3.10	4.10	6.00	7.70	7.00	10.40	4.60
3.1.2	Men's under garments	0.30	0.20	0.40	0.40	0.60	0.50	0.80	0.40	0.80	1.10	0.60
3.1.3	Women's outer garments	3.00	3.70	3.40	6.60	6.40	7.30	9.20	12.00	11.70	16.90	8.00
3.1.4	Women's under garments	1.00	0.50	0.90	0.90	1.00	1.00	1.10	1.50	1.80	2.30	1.20
3.1.5	Boys' outer garments (5-15)	[0.10]	0.20	0.40	0.70	0.50	0.40	1.40	0.80	1.00	2.20	0.80
3.1.6	Girls' outer garments (5-15)	[0.20]	0.50	0.70	0.80	0.90	0.70	1.30	1.40	1.50	2.00	1.00
3.1.7	Infants' outer garments (under 5)	[0.20]	[0.30]	0.40	0.40	0.70	0.60	0.90	0.90	0.60	1.80	0.70
3.1.8	Children's under garments (under 16)	0.10	0.20	0.30	0.40	0.30	0.40	0.60	0.70	0.60	0.70	0.40
3.1.9	Accessories	0.20	0.30	0.40	0.70	0.60	0.90	0.70	1.50	1.40	1.40	0.80
3.1.10	Haberdashery and clothing hire	0.30	0.10	0.10	0.10	0.40	0.40	0.70	0.30	0.40	0.30	0.30
3.1.11	Dry cleaners, laundry and dyeing		[0.10]		[0.20]	[0.20]	[0.10]	[0.40]	0.20		0.80	0.20
3.2	Footwear	1.80	1.60	2.10	3.30	3.60	4.40	5.40	7.00	6.60	11.70	4.70
4	**Housing (net)[1], fuel & power**	**57.90**	**58.90**	**75.50**	**76.30**	**79.90**	**91.10**	**90.30**	**90.90**	**90.70**	**118.30**	**83.00**
4.1	Actual rentals for housing	74.30	57.50	58.90	49.50	45.80	51.50	45.30	44.10	45.80	52.60	52.50
4.1.1	Gross rent	74.30	57.50	58.90	49.50	45.80	51.50	45.30	44.10	45.80	52.50	52.50
4.1.2	*less housing benefit, rebates & allowances rec'd*	47.10	31.70	19.30	11.50	5.30	1.80	3.50	[0.70]			12.40
4.1.3	Net rent[2]	27.20	25.70	39.70	38.10	40.50	49.70	41.80	43.40	43.10	52.40	40.10
4.1.4	Second dwelling rent											
4.2	Maintenance and repair of dwelling	2.60	3.30	4.70	5.60	6.60	7.10	11.00	10.50	10.20	18.10	8.00
4.3	Water supply and miscellaneous services relating to the dwelling	9.20	8.50	9.00	8.60	9.80	10.80	10.90	11.00	10.40	15.80	10.40
4.4	Electricity, gas and other fuels	18.90	21.40	22.10	24.10	23.00	23.50	26.60	26.00	27.00	32.00	24.50
4.4.1	Electricity	10.10	11.20	11.40	12.50	11.60	12.20	13.00	13.20	13.40	16.10	12.50
4.4.2	Gas	7.80	9.10	9.50	10.10	10.10	10.30	11.70	11.10	11.50	13.70	10.50
4.4.3	Other fuels	0.90	1.10	1.20	1.50	1.30	1.00	1.90	1.80	2.10	2.30	1.50

Note: The commodity and service categories are not comparable to those in publications before 2001-02.
The numbering system is sequential, it does not use actual COICOP codes.
Please see background notes for symbols and conventions used in this report.
1 Excluding mortgage interest payments, council tax and Northern Ireland rates.
2 The figure included in total expenditure is net rent as opposed to gross rent.

Table A6

Detailed household expenditure by gross income decile group (cont.)

UK, financial year ending 2020

Commodity or service	Lowest ten per cent	Second decile group	Third decile group	Fourth decile group	Fifth decile group	Sixth decile group	Seventh decile group	Eighth decile group	Ninth decile group	Highest ten per cent	All house-holds
	Average weekly household expenditure (£)										
5 Household goods & services	**12.30**	**18.80**	**23.40**	**30.40**	**32.50**	**30.70**	**38.70**	**47.60**	**52.90**	**77.80**	**36.50**
5.1 Furniture and furnishings, carpets and other floor coverings	5.90	8.30	13.00	17.30	16.70	14.50	19.80	28.30	30.20	47.20	20.10
5.1.1 Furniture and furnishings	4.80	6.40	9.90	13.80	13.50	12.20	16.60	24.40	25.00	39.30	16.60
5.1.2 Floor coverings	1.10	1.90	3.00	3.60	3.20	2.30	3.20	3.90	5.20	7.90	3.50
5.2 Household textiles	0.80	0.80	0.80	1.30	1.50	2.10	2.00	3.20	2.80	4.30	2.00
5.3 Household appliances	0.90	2.70	1.50	2.60	3.60	3.00	3.70	2.10	4.10	4.30	2.90
5.4 Glassware, tableware and household utensils	0.50	0.60	1.00	1.50	1.40	2.00	2.30	2.30	2.30	4.50	1.80
5.5 Tools and equipment for house and garden	0.50	1.70	1.80	2.30	3.10	3.40	3.70	4.90	4.40	4.00	3.00
5.6 Goods and services for routine household maintenance	3.70	4.60	5.30	5.40	6.30	5.80	7.30	6.80	9.20	13.50	6.80
5.6.1 Cleaning materials	1.50	1.80	2.40	2.30	2.90	2.70	3.00	3.00	3.50	3.90	2.70
5.6.2 Household goods and hardware	0.90	1.20	1.50	1.40	1.80	1.90	2.30	2.10	2.60	2.80	1.90
5.6.3 Domestic services, carpet cleaning, hire/repair of furniture/furnishings	1.30	1.70	1.40	1.70	1.50	1.10	2.00	1.70	3.20	6.80	2.20
6 Health	**4.20**	**5.40**	**5.00**	**5.80**	**8.10**	**7.70**	**9.00**	**12.20**	**9.20**	**15.30**	**8.20**
6.1 Medical products, appliances and equipment	2.30	3.60	2.70	2.80	4.50	3.90	5.50	8.20	5.40	5.90	4.50
6.1.1 Medicines, prescriptions, healthcare products etc.	1.30	2.20	1.80	2.10	2.40	2.80	2.70	4.30	3.50	3.40	2.60
6.1.2 Spectacles, lenses, accessories and repairs	[1.00]	1.40	1.00	0.60	2.10	1.10	2.90	3.90	1.90	2.50	1.80
6.2 Hospital services	[2.00]	1.80	2.30	3.00	3.60	3.80	3.50	4.10	3.70	9.50	3.70
7 Transport	**21.30**	**27.00**	**44.60**	**51.10**	**65.70**	**91.10**	**90.80**	**114.60**	**125.90**	**184.20**	**81.60**
7.1 Purchase of vehicles	5.70	6.90	14.60	12.50	19.90	35.90	27.80	37.30	38.70	63.40	26.30
7.1.1 Purchase of new cars and vans	..	[3.10]	[3.70]	5.10	5.80	9.10	7.20	13.00	10.00	20.90	7.90
7.1.2 Purchase of second hand cars or vans	4.80	3.80	10.00	7.20	13.70	21.60	19.90	23.10	26.40	41.80	17.20
7.1.3 Purchase of motorcycles and other vehicles	..	..	..	..	..	[5.20]	..	..	[2.40]	..	1.20
7.2 Operation of personal transport	10.10	13.10	20.50	26.70	31.90	34.80	41.30	49.90	48.90	59.00	33.60
7.2.1 Spares and accessories	[1.80]	[0.50]	1.90	2.80	2.40	2.30	1.90	3.40	2.50	4.60	2.40
7.2.2 Petrol, diesel and other motor oils	6.20	9.20	12.70	17.60	20.50	23.40	27.00	35.40	33.50	37.00	22.30
7.2.3 Repairs and servicing	1.40	2.50	4.50	4.50	6.40	6.40	8.10	8.00	8.40	12.00	6.20
7.2.4 Other motoring costs	0.70	0.90	1.50	1.80	2.60	2.70	4.30	3.10	4.50	5.40	2.80
7.3 Transport services	5.50	6.90	9.50	11.90	13.90	20.40	21.60	27.40	38.30	61.90	21.70
7.3.1 Rail and tube fares	1.00	1.00	1.10	1.30	2.50	3.80	4.50	6.00	10.20	15.10	4.60
7.3.2 Bus and coach fares	1.00	0.80	1.40	1.00	2.00	2.00	1.60	1.30	1.80	2.50	1.50
7.3.3 Combined fares	..	..	..	..	..	..	..	[1.20]	[0.80]	1.70	0.60
7.3.4 Other travel and transport	3.30	5.00	6.60	9.50	9.30	14.20	15.00	19.00	25.50	42.50	15.00
8 Communication	**10.30**	**14.30**	**16.00**	**18.70**	**20.80**	**22.20**	**24.50**	**25.40**	**28.10**	**33.40**	**21.40**
8.1 Postal services	0.40	0.60	0.60	0.50	0.70	0.60	0.50	0.70	0.80	1.10	0.70
8.2 Telephone and telefax equipment	[0.20]	[0.60]	[0.60]	[1.00]	1.30	1.10	1.90	0.50	3.40	4.50	1.50
8.3 Telephone and telefax services[3]	3.70	4.60	5.50	6.40	7.60	9.00	10.10	11.70	11.30	13.60	8.40
8.4 Internet subscription fees (ex. combined packages)	0.40	0.60	0.60	0.50	0.70	1.00	0.60	1.00	0.80	0.70	0.70
8.5 Combined telecom services[4]	5.40	8.00	8.60	10.30	10.30	10.50	11.30	11.60	11.80	13.50	10.10

Note: The commodity and service categories are not comparable to those in publications before 2001-02.

The numbering system is sequential, it does not use actual COICOP codes.

Please see background notes for symbols and conventions used in this report.

3 For FYE 2019 onwards, excludes payments made as part of a combined bill.

4 New for FYE 2019. This encompasses all telecoms bills that include more than one service. Due to the nature of combined packages, this also includes packages that includes television services.

Table A6

Detailed household expenditure by gross income decile group (cont.)

UK, financial year ending 2020

Commodity or service	Lowest ten per cent	Second decile group	Third decile group	Fourth decile group	Fifth decile group	Sixth decile group	Seventh decile group	Eighth decile group	Ninth decile group	Highest ten per cent	All households
					Average weekly household expenditure (£)						
9 **Recreation & culture**	**28.60**	**34.30**	**41.40**	**53.40**	**65.70**	**67.70**	**81.20**	**100.80**	**117.30**	**157.60**	**74.80**
9.1 Audio-visual, photographic and information processing equipment	1.40	1.50	3.00	5.40	3.90	4.50	5.20	5.20	8.30	6.50	4.50
9.1.1 Audio equipment and accessories, CD players	0.50	0.30	0.60	1.10	1.20	0.80	1.10	1.30	1.60	2.40	1.10
9.1.2 TV, video and computers	0.90	1.10	2.30	3.70	2.50	3.50	3.30	3.80	4.20	3.50	2.90
9.1.3 Photographic, cine and optical equipment	..	..	..	..	..	..	..	..	[2.50]	..	0.50
9.2 Other major durables for recreation and culture	..	..	[1.20]	..	..	[3.10]	[0.50]	[2.60]	3.30	2.80	2.00
9.3 Other recreational items and equipment, gardens and pets	6.20	8.10	9.90	10.80	12.00	13.80	16.40	23.70	20.90	33.70	15.50
9.3.1 Games, toys and hobbies	0.80	1.50	1.90	1.90	3.20	4.00	3.80	4.60	4.30	6.00	3.20
9.3.2 Computer software and games	..	[0.70]	[0.50]	0.60	1.30	0.90	1.10	1.40	1.40	1.50	1.00
9.3.3 Equipment for sport, camping and open-air recreation	[0.60]	[0.30]	[0.90]	0.30	1.00	0.70	1.50	1.50	3.00	7.30	1.70
9.3.4 Horticultural goods, garden equipment and plants	1.30	1.60	2.20	2.70	2.60	2.60	3.30	4.10	2.90	4.60	2.80
9.3.5 Pets and pet food	2.90	3.90	4.40	5.40	3.90	5.60	6.70	12.00	9.40	14.40	6.80
9.4 Recreational and cultural services	8.90	9.00	10.10	13.70	16.00	17.30	21.80	28.20	30.40	42.50	19.80
9.4.1 Sports admissions, subscriptions, leisure class fees and equipment hire	1.70	2.30	2.90	4.70	6.30	5.60	7.30	13.70	12.80	20.90	7.80
9.4.2 Cinema, theatre and museums etc.	1.70	1.30	0.70	1.60	1.90	3.00	4.50	3.60	6.40	8.50	3.30
9.4.3 TV, video, satellite rental, cable subscriptions and TV licences[5]	2.80	2.90	3.20	4.20	4.70	4.90	4.80	5.80	5.90	7.40	4.70
9.4.4 Miscellaneous entertainments	0.50	0.40	0.50	0.60	0.90	1.40	2.30	2.50	2.20	2.90	1.40
9.4.5 Development of film, deposit for film development, passport photos, holiday and school photos	..	..	..	..	[0.20]	[0.20]	[0.30]	[0.10]	0.20	0.30	0.20
9.4.6 Gambling payments	2.10	1.90	2.70	2.60	2.00	2.30	2.50	2.40	2.90	2.50	2.40
9.5 Newspapers, books and stationery	3.10	3.20	4.10	4.50	5.00	5.30	6.20	5.10	6.60	11.60	5.50
9.5.1 Books	0.80	0.40	0.50	0.90	0.90	1.30	1.50	1.30	1.90	2.80	1.20
9.5.2 Diaries, address books, cards etc.	0.80	1.30	1.30	1.70	1.90	2.00	2.90	2.50	2.70	6.60	2.40
9.5.3 Newspapers	1.00	1.00	1.60	1.40	1.50	1.30	1.00	0.80	1.10	1.40	1.20
9.5.4 Magazines and periodicals	0.50	0.50	0.70	0.50	0.70	0.80	0.80	0.50	0.90	0.80	0.70
9.6 Package holidays	9.00	11.80	13.20	17.00	25.60	23.60	31.10	36.00	47.70	60.40	27.50
9.6.1 Package holidays - UK	[0.80]	[1.10]	[1.20]	2.50	1.80	1.50	1.60	1.60	[2.90]	4.20	1.90
9.6.2 Package holidays - abroad	8.20	10.70	11.90	14.50	23.80	22.20	29.40	34.40	44.90	56.20	25.60
10 **Education**	..	..	[1.20]	[2.60]	[1.90]	3.40	6.20	2.60	6.50	19.60	4.50
10.1 Education fees	..	..	..	..	[1.70]	[3.20]	4.50	2.20	5.90	18.50	4.10
10.2 Payments for school trips, other ad-hoc expenditure	..	..	..	..	..	[0.20]	[1.70]	[0.40]	0.60	1.10	0.50
11 **Restaurants & hotels**	**15.30**	**20.40**	**23.70**	**32.80**	**45.80**	**51.80**	**57.10**	**71.00**	**84.20**	**126.50**	**52.90**
11.1 Catering services	12.90	16.70	19.60	26.40	36.00	40.90	46.70	56.60	63.50	93.70	41.30
11.1.1 Restaurant and café meals	6.70	8.70	9.30	14.10	19.70	19.20	23.20	25.90	29.70	45.50	20.20
11.1.2 Alcoholic drinks (away from home)	2.60	2.70	3.70	5.50	5.40	8.50	9.00	12.30	13.60	19.70	8.30
11.1.3 Take away meals eaten at home	2.30	3.00	3.30	3.20	5.10	6.20	6.50	8.10	7.70	10.70	5.60
11.1.4 Other take-away and snack food	1.30	1.80	2.70	2.60	4.00	5.10	6.00	7.70	9.30	12.40	5.30
11.1.5 Contract catering (food) and canteens	[0.10]	0.50	0.60	1.00	1.80	2.00	2.10	2.60	3.20	5.30	1.90
11.2 Accommodation services	2.40	3.70	4.20	6.40	9.80	10.90	10.40	14.40	20.80	32.80	11.60
11.2.1 Holiday in the UK	1.60	2.50	3.10	4.20	6.50	7.20	6.40	9.00	10.00	12.30	6.30
11.2.2 Holiday abroad	[0.90]	1.20	1.00	2.20	3.20	3.70	3.70	5.40	10.70	20.20	5.20
11.2.3 Room hire	..	..	..	..	..	..	..	..	..	..	0.10

Note: The commodity and service categories are not comparable to those in publications before 2001-02.

The numbering system is sequential, it does not use actual COICOP codes.

Please see background notes for symbols and conventions used in this report.

5 For FYE 2019 onwards, excludes payments made as part of a combined bill.

Detailed household expenditure by gross income decile group (cont.)

UK, financial year ending 2020

Commodity or service	Lowest ten per cent	Second decile group	Third decile group	Fourth decile group	Fifth decile group	Sixth decile group	Seventh decile group	Eighth decile group	Ninth decile group	Highest ten per cent	All house-holds
					Average weekly household expenditure (£)						
12 Miscellaneous goods & services	**19.20**	**19.70**	**26.90**	**35.00**	**41.10**	**45.50**	**50.30**	**64.40**	**61.10**	**93.70**	**45.70**
12.1 Personal care	5.90	6.20	8.00	11.30	11.60	13.70	15.40	18.50	18.40	25.40	13.40
12.1.1 Hairdressing, beauty treatment	1.80	2.10	2.50	4.00	3.20	4.90	5.10	6.40	6.50	7.40	4.40
12.1.2 Toilet paper	0.70	0.70	0.80	0.80	1.00	1.00	1.30	1.10	1.10	1.20	1.00
12.1.3 Toiletries and soap	1.20	1.30	1.80	2.10	2.40	2.50	3.30	3.30	3.40	5.10	2.60
12.1.4 Baby toiletries and accessories (disposable)	0.20	0.40	0.40	0.40	0.60	0.70	0.70	0.80	0.80	0.70	0.60
12.1.5 Hair products, cosmetics and related electrical appliances	2.00	1.80	2.40	4.00	4.30	4.60	5.00	6.80	6.60	11.00	4.80
12.2 Personal effects	1.40	1.00	1.40	1.90	5.70	4.30	4.40	6.10	5.40	10.80	4.20
12.3 Social protection	..	..	[3.80]	[1.60]	3.10	3.40	1.40	6.60	4.20	12.70	3.70
12.4 Insurance	7.20	10.10	11.60	17.40	17.40	19.70	22.10	24.40	27.50	35.50	19.30
12.4.1 Household insurances - structural, contents and appliances	2.60	3.30	3.40	4.60	5.00	4.80	5.50	5.30	6.20	8.30	4.90
12.4.2 Medical insurance premiums[6]	0.70	0.70	0.70	1.30	1.50	1.70	2.00	3.80	4.30	6.90	2.40
12.4.3 Vehicle insurance including boat insurance	3.60	5.40	7.00	10.60	10.00	12.20	13.50	14.30	15.80	18.60	11.10
12.4.4 Non-package holiday, other travel insurance[7]	0.30	0.60	0.50	0.90	0.90	1.00	1.00	1.00	1.30	1.60	0.90
12.5 Other services	4.40	2.20	2.20	2.80	3.40	4.40	7.00	8.80	5.60	9.30	5.00
12.5.1 Moving house	[0.50]	[1.10]	1.20	1.60	2.00	1.90	2.90	5.30	2.80	4.90	2.40
12.5.2 Bank, building society, post office, credit card charges	0.20	0.20	0.20	0.40	0.40	0.60	0.70	0.80	0.80	1.20	0.50
12.5.3 Other services and professional fees	..	0.90	0.80	0.90	1.00	1.90	3.50	2.80	2.00	3.20	2.10
1-12 All expenditure groups	**221.60**	**258.50**	**327.20**	**387.90**	**453.90**	**509.60**	**563.50**	**657.40**	**709.60**	**996.80**	**508.50**
13 Other expenditure items	**23.30**	**28.60**	**36.00**	**48.10**	**61.20**	**74.50**	**87.00**	**104.50**	**127.60**	**202.70**	**79.30**
13.1 Housing: mortgage interest payments, council tax etc.	16.50	19.20	25.40	30.70	40.00	46.90	57.50	69.20	82.30	116.60	50.40
13.2 Licences, fines and transfers	1.20	1.70	2.20	2.80	3.60	4.10	4.60	4.30	5.10	8.20	3.80
13.3 Holiday spending	..	..	[2.80]	6.10	[5.20]	8.10	10.10	13.20	20.40	52.40	12.10
13.4 Money transfers and credit	4.10	5.90	5.60	8.40	12.50	15.40	14.80	17.80	19.80	25.50	13.00
13.4.1 Money, cash gifts given to children	..	..	..	..	..	[1.20]	[0.30]	[0.50]	..	[0.20]	0.30
13.4.2 Cash gifts and donations	3.90	5.30	5.00	6.90	11.70	13.00	13.20	15.70	17.80	24.00	11.70
13.4.3 Club instalment payments (child) and interest on credit cards	[0.20]	0.50	0.60	1.00	0.70	1.30	1.20	1.60	1.90	1.30	1.00
Total expenditure	**244.90**	**287.10**	**363.20**	**436.00**	**515.10**	**584.20**	**650.50**	**761.90**	**837.20**	**1199.50**	**587.90**
14 Other items recorded											
14.1 Life assurance and contributions to pension funds	2.50	2.90	6.40	10.20	16.40	23.20	31.40	47.70	64.00	142.50	34.70
14.2 Other insurance inc. friendly societies	0.80	1.10	1.20	2.00	1.80	2.10	2.80	3.20	3.60	5.20	2.40
14.3 Income tax, payments less refunds	3.40	3.90	20.10	24.40	48.80	61.40	87.30	123.90	182.40	497.40	105.20
14.4 National insurance contributions	1.10	1.90	6.00	11.90	21.80	32.20	45.80	66.60	86.90	130.60	40.50
14.5 Purchase or alteration of dwellings, mortgages	14.00	13.40	22.00	27.90	37.00	42.60	81.10	80.60	103.00	184.10	60.60
14.6 Savings and investments	[0.90]	1.40	1.00	3.70	5.20	4.30	11.80	14.40	13.70	35.30	9.20
14.7 Pay off loan to clear other debt	..	..	[0.80]	[0.90]	1.10	3.00	3.60	3.20	2.80	6.10	2.20
14.8 Windfall receipts from gambling etc[8]	1.30	0.90	1.60	0.90	0.50	3.20	1.10	0.90	1.70	1.30	1.30

Note: The commodity and service categories are not comparable to those in publications before 2001-02.

The numbering system is sequential, it does not use actual COICOP codes.

Please see background notes for symbols and conventions used in this report.

6 For FYE 2019, critical illness cover, personal accident insurance and other medical insurance are included here. They were not included in previous years.

7 For FYE 2019, information about insurance for non-package holiday and other travel insurance was collected in the questionnaire in addition to the diary. In previous years, this was based on diary data only.

8 Expressed as an income figure as opposed to an expenditure figure.

Source: Office for National Statistics

Table A7

Household expenditure by disposable income decile group

UK, financial year ending 2020

	Lowest ten per cent	Second decile group	Third decile group	Fourth decile group	Fifth decile group	Sixth decile group	Seventh decile group	Eighth decile group	Ninth decile group	Highest ten per cent	All house-holds
Lower boundary of group (£ per week)		224	321	413	510	624	750	892	1,064	1,386	
Weighted number of households (thousands)	2,780	2,780	2,780	2,790	2,780	2,780	2,780	2,780	2,790	2,780	27,820
Total number of households in sample	560	550	570	560	570	550	540	530	520	480	5,440
Total number of persons in sample	720	860	1,020	1,180	1,350	1,400	1,490	1,540	1,520	1,600	12,670
Total number of adults in sample	630	710	840	960	1,030	1,070	1,110	1,170	1,190	1,190	9,880
Weighted average number of persons per household	1.3	1.6	1.8	2.1	2.4	2.5	2.8	2.9	3.0	3.4	2.4
Commodity or service					Average weekly household expenditure (£)						
1 Food & non-alcoholic drinks	35.00	40.40	47.00	54.40	60.20	64.60	72.60	79.00	83.10	100.80	63.70
2 Alcoholic drinks, tobacco & narcotics	8.80	8.70	8.80	9.80	12.40	13.70	13.10	15.30	18.60	20.10	12.90
3 Clothing & footwear	8.70	9.10	12.00	15.50	18.10	22.40	29.10	31.50	36.60	50.80	23.40
4 Housing(net)[1], fuel & power	58.60	60.00	74.20	74.80	85.10	86.40	88.60	94.20	87.00	121.00	83.00
5 Household goods & services	13.30	18.90	21.50	29.70	30.90	34.10	36.20	48.50	55.70	76.60	36.50
6 Health	4.30	5.30	5.00	5.90	7.30	8.10	8.80	9.00	12.50	15.80	8.20
7 Transport	22.80	27.10	42.50	52.50	63.50	91.30	91.50	106.20	137.60	181.40	81.60
8 Communication	10.40	14.10	15.80	19.20	20.10	23.20	22.90	26.00	27.90	33.90	21.40
9 Recreation & culture	31.00	33.70	42.60	52.70	57.40	68.60	82.30	94.80	126.70	158.00	74.80
10 Education	..	..	[1.10]	[2.70]	[1.70]	1.30	6.10	4.80	7.30	18.90	4.50
11 Restaurants & hotels	16.00	20.20	24.40	32.70	45.20	48.30	59.00	71.00	85.10	126.90	52.90
12 Miscellaneous goods & services	19.90	20.10	26.90	35.10	39.80	46.00	49.10	60.40	65.50	94.10	45.70
1-12 All expenditure groups	229.70	258.30	321.80	384.90	441.70	508.20	559.20	640.70	743.50	998.20	508.50
13 Other expenditure items	25.00	31.10	36.80	43.20	64.00	72.80	89.50	104.30	132.90	193.70	79.30
Total expenditure	**254.70**	**289.40**	**358.60**	**428.20**	**505.70**	**581.00**	**648.70**	**745.00**	**876.40**	**1191.90**	**587.90**
Average weekly expenditure per person (£)											
Total expenditure	**196.00**	**185.20**	**204.60**	**207.20**	**212.50**	**229.50**	**233.20**	**258.10**	**296.10**	**348.80**	**248.70**

Note: The commodity and service categories are not comparable to those in publications before 2001-02.

Please see background notes for symbols and conventions used in this report.

1 Excluding mortgage interest payments, council tax and Northern Ireland rates.

Source: Office for National Statistics

Table A8

Household expenditure as a percentage of total expenditure by disposable income decile group

UK, financial year ending 2020

	Lowest ten per cent	Second decile group	Third decile group	Fourth decile group	Fifth decile group	Sixth decile group	Seventh decile group	Eighth decile group	Ninth decile group	Highest ten per cent	All house-holds
Lower boundary of group (£ per week)		224	321	413	510	624	750	892	1,064	1,386	
Weighted number of households (thousands)	2,780	2,780	2,780	2,790	2,780	2,780	2,780	2,780	2,790	2,780	27,820
Total number of households in sample	560	550	570	560	570	550	540	530	520	480	5,440
Total number of persons in sample	720	860	1,020	1,180	1,350	1,400	1,490	1,540	1,520	1,600	12,670
Total number of adults in sample	630	710	840	960	1,030	1,070	1,110	1,170	1,190	1,190	9,880
Weighted average number of persons per household	1.3	1.6	1.8	2.1	2.4	2.5	2.8	2.9	3.0	3.4	2.4
Commodity or service						*Percentage of total expenditure*					
1 Food & non-alcoholic drinks	14	14	13	13	12	11	11	11	9	8	11
2 Alcoholic drinks, tobacco & narcotics	3	3	2	2	2	2	2	2	2	2	2
3 Clothing & footwear	3	3	3	4	4	4	4	4	4	4	4
4 Housing(net)[1], fuel & power	23	21	21	17	17	15	14	13	10	10	14
5 Household goods & services	5	7	6	7	6	6	6	7	6	6	6
6 Health	2	2	1	1	1	1	1	1	1	1	1
7 Transport	9	9	12	12	13	16	14	14	16	15	14
8 Communication	4	5	4	4	4	4	4	3	3	3	4
9 Recreation & culture	12	12	12	12	11	12	13	13	14	13	13
10 Education	..	..	[0]	[1]	[0]	0~	1	1	1	2	1
11 Restaurants & hotels	6	7	7	8	9	8	9	10	10	11	9
12 Miscellaneous goods & services	8	7	7	8	8	8	8	8	7	8	8
1-12 All expenditure groups	90	89	90	90	87	87	86	86	85	84	87
13 Other expenditure items	10	11	10	10	13	13	14	14	15	16	13
Total expenditure	100	100	100	100	100	100	100	100	100	100	100

Note: The commodity and service categories are not comparable to those in publications before 2001-02.

Please see background notes for symbols and conventions used in this report.

1 Excluding mortgage interest payments, council tax and Northern Ireland rates.

Source: Office for National Statistics

Table A9

Household expenditure by age of household reference person

UK, financial year ending 2020

	Less than 30	30 to 49	50 to 64	65 to 74	75 or over	All house-holds
Weighted number of households (thousands)	2,480	9,280	7,820	4,240	3,990	27,820
Total number of households in sample	390	1,790	1,530	980	750	5,440
Total number of persons in sample	940	5,400	3,460	1,710	1,160	12,670
Total number of adults in sample	700	3,280	3,050	1,690	1,160	9,880
Weighted average number of persons per house	2.4	3.0	2.4	1.8	1.5	2.4
Commodity or service	Average weekly household expenditure (£)					
1 Food & non-alcoholic drinks	50.30	69.30	70.80	61.20	47.70	63.70
2 Alcoholic drinks, tobacco & narcotics	8.60	12.20	17.00	14.10	8.10	12.90
3 Clothing & footwear	21.10	29.10	26.90	17.10	11.30	23.40
4 Housing(net)[1], fuel & power	153.50	95.90	75.40	60.60	47.60	83.00
5 Household goods & services	30.60	41.00	42.50	29.80	25.30	36.50
6 Health	2.90	6.50	10.00	9.70	10.50	8.20
7 Transport	76.50	94.10	103.60	63.50	31.90	81.60
8 Communication	21.50	23.70	23.70	17.90	14.90	21.40
9 Recreation & culture	50.80	76.20	90.60	76.90	53.20	74.80
10 Education	5.00	7.90	4.60	[0.60]	..	4.50
11 Restaurants & hotels	53.90	61.00	60.70	44.30	26.90	52.90
12 Miscellaneous goods & services	43.40	51.20	49.50	38.00	35.10	45.70
1-12 All expenditure groups	518.30	568.10	575.40	433.70	312.80	508.50
13 Other expenditure items	74.50	98.70	86.00	61.40	43.30	79.30
Total expenditure	**592.80**	**666.70**	**661.40**	**495.10**	**356.10**	**587.90**
Average weekly expenditure per person (£)						
Total expenditure	**247.50**	**222.20**	**279.30**	**281.30**	**238.00**	**248.70**

Note: The commodity and service categories are not comparable to those in publications before 2001-02.

Please see background notes for symbols and conventions used in this report.

1 Excluding mortgage interest payments, council tax and Northern Ireland rates.

Source: Office for National Statistics

Table A10

Household expenditure as a percentage of total expenditure by age of household reference person

UK, financial year ending 2020

	Less than 30	30 to 49	50 to 64	65 to 74	75 or over	All house-holds
Weighted number of households (thousands)	2,480	9,280	7,820	4,240	3,990	27,820
Total number of households in sample	390	1,790	1,530	980	750	5,440
Total number of persons in sample	940	5,400	3,460	1,710	1,160	12,670
Total number of adults in sample	700	3,280	3,050	1,690	1,160	9,880
Weighted average number of persons per household	2.4	3.0	2.4	1.8	1.5	2.4
Commodity or service	Percentage of total expenditure					
1 Food & non-alcoholic drinks	8	10	11	12	13	11
2 Alcoholic drinks, tobacco & narcotics	1	2	3	3	2	2
3 Clothing & footwear	4	4	4	3	3	4
4 Housing(net)[1], fuel & power	26	14	11	12	13	14
5 Household goods & services	5	6	6	6	7	6
6 Health	0~	1	2	2	3	1
7 Transport	13	14	16	13	9	14
8 Communication	4	4	4	4	4	4
9 Recreation & culture	9	11	14	16	15	13
10 Education	1	1	1	[0]	..	1
11 Restaurants & hotels	9	9	9	9	8	9
12 Miscellaneous goods & services	7	8	7	8	10	8
1-12 All expenditure groups	87	85	87	88	88	87
13 Other expenditure items	13	15	13	12	12	13
Total expenditure	**100**	**100**	**100**	**100**	**100**	**100**

Note: The commodity and service categories are not comparable to those in publications before 2001-02.

Please see background notes for symbols and conventions used in this report.

1 Excluding mortgage interest payments, council tax and Northern Ireland rates.

Source: Office for National Statistics

Table A11

Detailed household expenditure by age of household reference person

UK, financial year ending 2020

	Less than 30	30 to 49	50 to 64	65 to 74	75 or over	All house-holds
Weighted number of households (thousands)	2,480	9,280	7,820	4,240	3,990	27,820
Total number of households in sample	390	1,790	1,530	980	750	5,440
Total number of persons in sample	940	5,400	3,460	1,710	1,160	12,670
Total number of adults in sample	700	3,280	3,050	1,690	1,160	9,880
Weighted average number of persons per household	2.4	3.0	2.4	1.8	1.5	2.4

Commodity or service	Average weekly household expenditure (£)					
1 Food & non-alcoholic drinks	**50.30**	**69.30**	**70.80**	**61.20**	**47.70**	**63.70**
1.1 Food	45.40	63.30	64.70	56.60	44.50	58.40
1.1.1 Bread, rice and cereals	5.20	6.80	6.40	5.00	3.80	5.80
1.1.2 Pasta products	0.60	0.60	0.50	0.30	0.20	0.50
1.1.3 Buns, cakes, biscuits etc.	2.70	4.50	4.40	4.00	3.80	4.10
1.1.4 Pastry (savoury)	0.90	1.30	1.10	0.70	0.40	1.00
1.1.5 Beef (fresh, chilled or frozen)	1.30	1.70	2.40	2.00	1.50	1.90
1.1.6 Pork (fresh, chilled or frozen)	0.50	0.50	0.60	0.60	0.40	0.50
1.1.7 Lamb (fresh, chilled or frozen)	0.20	0.70	0.80	0.90	0.70	0.70
1.1.8 Poultry (fresh, chilled or frozen)	2.50	2.90	2.90	1.90	1.30	2.40
1.1.9 Bacon and ham	0.60	0.80	1.00	0.90	0.70	0.80
1.1.10 Other meat and meat preparations	4.70	6.90	7.50	6.60	5.50	6.60
1.1.11 Fish and fish products	1.50	2.90	3.70	3.70	3.10	3.20
1.1.12 Milk	1.80	2.30	2.20	2.00	2.00	2.10
1.1.13 Cheese and curd	1.90	2.50	2.40	2.10	1.50	2.20
1.1.14 Eggs	0.60	0.90	0.80	0.80	0.60	0.80
1.1.15 Other milk products	1.80	2.60	2.40	2.40	2.00	2.30
1.1.16 Butter	0.20	0.40	0.50	0.60	0.50	0.50
1.1.17 Margarine, other vegetable fats and peanut butter	0.40	0.60	0.70	0.70	0.60	0.60
1.1.18 Cooking oils and fats	0.20	0.40	0.50	0.40	0.20	0.40
1.1.19 Fresh fruit	2.70	4.30	4.10	4.50	3.50	4.00
1.1.20 Other fresh, chilled or frozen fruits	0.30	0.50	0.50	0.40	0.30	0.50
1.1.21 Dried fruit and nuts	0.50	1.10	0.90	1.00	0.80	0.90
1.1.22 Preserved fruit and fruit based products	0.10	0.10	0.20	0.20	0.20	0.20
1.1.23 Fresh vegetables	3.40	4.90	5.00	4.40	3.10	4.50
1.1.24 Dried vegetables	[0.00]	0.10	0.00~	0.10	0.00~	0.10
1.1.25 Other preserved or processed vegetables	1.70	2.30	2.20	1.80	1.00	2.00
1.1.26 Potatoes	0.40	0.70	0.80	0.80	0.70	0.70
1.1.27 Other tubers and products of tuber vegetables	1.60	2.10	2.10	1.50	1.00	1.80
1.1.28 Sugar and sugar products	0.30	0.50	0.40	0.30	0.30	0.40
1.1.29 Jams, marmalades	0.20	0.30	0.30	0.30	0.40	0.30
1.1.30 Chocolate	1.70	2.60	2.70	2.10	1.60	2.30
1.1.31 Confectionery products	0.70	1.00	0.90	0.60	0.50	0.80
1.1.32 Edible ices and ice cream	0.60	0.80	0.80	0.70	0.60	0.70
1.1.33 Other food products	3.40	3.10	2.90	2.30	1.80	2.80
1.2 Non-alcoholic drinks	4.90	6.00	6.10	4.70	3.20	5.30
1.2.1 Coffee	0.70	1.00	1.20	1.40	0.80	1.10
1.2.2 Tea	0.20	0.40	0.60	0.60	0.60	0.50
1.2.3 Cocoa and powdered chocolate	0.20	0.10	0.10	0.10	0.10	0.10
1.2.4 Fruit and vegetable juices (inc. fruit squash)	1.10	1.30	1.10	0.80	0.60	1.10
1.2.5 Mineral or spring waters	0.30	0.40	0.40	0.30	0.20	0.40
1.2.6 Soft drinks (inc. fizzy and ready to drink fruit drinks)	2.50	2.70	2.60	1.50	0.90	2.20

Note: The commodity and service categories are not comparable to those in publications before 2001-02.

The numbering system is sequential, it does not use actual COICOP codes.

Please see background notes for symbols and conventions used in this report.

Table A11

Detailed household expenditure by age of household reference person (cont.)

UK, financial year ending 2020

Commodity or service		Less than 30	30 to 49	50 to 64	65 to 74	75 or over	All house- holds
		Average weekly household expenditure (£)					
2	**Alcoholic drink, tobacco & narcotics**	**8.60**	**12.20**	**17.00**	**14.10**	**8.10**	**12.90**
2.1	Alcoholic drinks	4.60	8.90	12.10	10.10	6.70	9.30
2.1.1	Spirits and liqueurs (brought home)	1.30	2.10	2.70	2.60	2.00	2.30
2.1.2	Wines, fortified wines (brought home)	1.40	3.90	6.10	5.60	3.90	4.60
2.1.3	Beer, lager, ciders and perry (brought home)	1.90	2.90	3.20	1.90	0.90	2.50
2.1.4	Alcopops (brought home)	..	0.00~	[0.00]	..	..	0.00~
2.2	Tobacco and narcotics	4.00	3.30	4.90	4.00	1.40	3.60
2.2.1	Cigarettes	2.50	2.00	3.80	3.10	1.10	2.60
2.2.2	Cigars, other tobacco products and narcotics	1.50	1.20	1.10	0.90	0.30	1.10
3	**Clothing & footwear**	**21.10**	**29.10**	**26.90**	**17.10**	**11.30**	**23.40**
3.1	Clothing	17.10	22.90	21.00	14.60	9.50	18.70
3.1.1	Men's outer garments	5.20	5.20	5.50	3.80	2.00	4.60
3.1.2	Men's under garments	0.30	0.60	0.70	0.40	0.50	0.60
3.1.3	Women's outer garments	6.90	9.00	9.70	6.60	4.70	8.00
3.1.4	Women's under garments	0.90	1.10	1.50	1.10	1.10	1.20
3.1.5	Boys' outer garments (5-15)	[0.30]	1.50	0.60	0.40	[0.10]	0.80
3.1.6	Girls' outer garments (5-15)	0.60	1.90	0.80	0.40	[0.10]	1.00
3.1.7	Infants' outer garments (under 5)	1.10	1.30	0.30	0.30	[0.10]	0.70
3.1.8	Children's under garments (under 16)	0.40	0.70	0.30	0.20	[0.10]	0.40
3.1.9	Accessories	0.90	1.10	0.80	0.60	0.50	0.80
3.1.10	Haberdashery, clothing materials and clothing hire	[0.30]	0.30	0.30	0.50	0.20	0.30
3.1.11	Dry cleaners, laundry and dyeing	..	0.20	0.30	0.20	0.20	0.20
3.2	Footwear	4.00	6.20	5.90	2.50	1.80	4.70
4	**Housing (net)[1], fuel & power**	**153.50**	**95.90**	**75.40**	**60.60**	**47.60**	**83.00**
4.1	Actual rentals for housing	131.30	65.20	38.50	31.20	24.10	52.50
4.1.1	Gross rent	131.30	65.20	38.50	31.20	24.10	52.50
4.1.2	less housing benefit, rebates & allowances rec'd	8.70	10.80	12.00	15.30	16.00	12.40
4.1.3	Net rent[2]	122.60	54.40	26.50	15.90	8.10	40.10
4.1.4	Second dwelling rent	:	..	:	:	:	..
4.2	Maintenance and repair of dwelling	3.80	6.90	11.40	9.60	4.60	8.00
4.3	Water supply and miscellaneous services relating to the dwelling	9.20	10.50	10.40	10.00	11.30	10.40
4.4	Electricity, gas and other fuels	17.90	24.10	27.10	25.10	23.60	24.50
4.4.1	Electricity	10.20	12.50	13.70	12.20	11.60	12.50
4.4.2	Gas	7.20	10.50	11.60	10.60	10.10	10.50
4.4.3	Other fuels	[0.50]	1.10	1.80	2.30	1.80	1.50

Note: The commodity and service categories are not comparable to those in publications before 2001-02.

The numbering system is sequential, it does not use actual COICOP codes.

Please see background notes for symbols and conventions used in this report.

1 Excluding mortgage interest payments, council tax and Northern Ireland rates.

2 The figure included in total expenditure is net rent as opposed to gross rent.

Detailed household expenditure by age of household reference person (cont.)

UK, financial year ending 2020

Commodity or service		Less than 30	30 to 49	50 to 64	65 to 74	75 or over	All house-holds
		Average weekly household expenditure (£)					
5	**Household goods & services**	**30.60**	**41.00**	**42.50**	**29.80**	**25.30**	**36.50**
5.1	Furniture and furnishings and floor coverings	16.20	24.90	24.10	13.70	10.30	20.10
5.1.1	Furniture and furnishings	13.60	20.70	19.60	11.20	8.80	16.60
5.1.2	Floor coverings	2.60	4.30	4.50	2.60	1.50	3.50
5.2	Household textiles	1.80	1.90	2.50	1.70	1.30	2.00
5.3	Household appliances	4.10	2.50	3.30	2.20	2.90	2.90
5.4	Glassware, tableware and household utensils	1.90	2.00	2.20	1.80	0.80	1.80
5.5	Tools and equipment for house and garden	2.50	3.20	3.20	3.40	1.90	3.00
5.6	Goods and services for routine household maintenance	4.10	6.50	7.20	6.90	8.10	6.80
5.6.1	Cleaning materials	2.10	2.60	3.20	2.60	2.40	2.70
5.6.2	Household goods and hardware	1.70	1.90	2.00	1.90	1.30	1.90
5.6.3	Domestic services, carpet cleaning, hire of furniture/furnishings	[0.30]	2.00	2.00	2.40	4.40	2.20
6	**Health**	**2.90**	**6.50**	**10.00**	**9.70**	**10.50**	**8.20**
6.1	Medical products, appliances and equipment	2.40	3.70	5.00	5.30	5.70	4.50
6.1.1	Medicines, prescriptions and healthcare products	2.00	2.40	3.20	2.40	2.80	2.60
6.1.2	Spectacles, lenses, accessories and repairs	0.40	1.30	1.80	2.90	2.90	1.80
6.2	Hospital services	[0.50]	2.80	5.00	4.30	4.70	3.70
7	**Transport**	**76.50**	**94.10**	**103.60**	**63.50**	**31.90**	**81.60**
7.1	Purchase of vehicles	19.10	30.30	35.70	20.80	8.90	26.30
7.1.1	Purchase of new cars and vans	4.50	5.80	12.50	9.20	4.20	7.90
7.1.2	Purchase of second hand cars or vans	13.60	23.20	21.00	11.00	4.60	17.20
7.1.3	Purchase of motorcycles and other vehicles	..	1.20	[2.20]	..	..	1.20
7.2	Operation of personal transport	29.50	37.00	42.10	29.50	16.20	33.60
7.2.1	Spares and accessories	1.30	2.20	3.60	2.40	1.30	2.40
7.2.2	Petrol, diesel and other motor oils	20.30	25.70	27.70	18.20	9.00	22.30
7.2.3	Repairs and servicing	5.20	6.20	7.50	6.10	4.40	6.20
7.2.4	Other motoring costs	2.60	2.90	3.30	2.80	1.40	2.80
7.3	Transport services	27.90	26.90	25.90	13.20	6.90	21.70
7.3.1	Rail and tube fares	8.30	5.40	5.60	2.30	1.30	4.60
7.3.2	Bus and coach fares	2.30	2.10	2.00	0.30	0.20	1.50
7.3.4	Combined fares	..	1.00	[0.50]	..	..	0.60
7.3.5	Other travel and transport	16.30	18.50	17.70	10.60	5.40	15.00
8	**Communication**	**21.50**	**23.70**	**23.70**	**17.90**	**14.90**	**21.40**
8.1	Postal services	0.20	0.40	0.80	0.90	0.90	0.70
8.2	Telephone and telefax equipment	2.50	1.30	2.00	1.10	[1.00]	1.50
8.3	Telephone and telefax services[3]	10.90	10.70	8.90	5.00	3.80	8.40
8.4	Internet subscription fees (ex. combined packages)	1.60	0.90	0.50	0.40	0.30	0.70
8.5	Combined telecom services[4]	6.30	10.40	11.40	10.50	8.90	10.10

Note: The commodity and service categories are not comparable to those in publications before 2001-02.

The numbering system is sequential, it does not use actual COICOP codes.

Please see background notes for symbols and conventions used in this report.

3 For FYE 2019 onwards, excludes payments made as part of a combined bill.

4 New for FYE 2019. This encompasses all telecoms bills that include more than one service. Due to the nature of combined packages, this also includes packages that includes television services.

Table A11

Detailed household expenditure by age of household reference person (cont.)

UK, financial year ending 2020

Commodity or service		Less than 30	30 to 49	50 to 64	65 to 74	75 or over	All house-holds
		Average weekly household expenditure (£)					
9	**Recreation & culture**	**50.80**	**76.20**	**90.60**	**76.90**	**53.20**	**74.80**
9.1	Audio-visual, photographic and information processing equipment	4.40	4.40	5.50	4.80	2.30	4.50
9.1.1	Audio equipment and accessories, CD players	1.90	1.50	1.00	0.70	0.30	1.10
9.1.2	TV, video and computers	2.30	2.80	3.40	3.50	2.00	2.90
9.1.3	Photographic, cine and optical equipment	..	[0.20]	[1.10]	[0.70]	:	0.50
9.2	Other major durables for recreation and culture	..	1.30	3.40	[2.30]	..	2.00
9.3	Other recreational items and equipment, gardens and pets	10.60	17.00	20.00	13.70	8.40	15.50
9.3.1	Games, toys and hobbies	2.80	4.40	3.50	2.00	1.40	3.20
9.3.2	Computer software and games	[1.10]	1.40	1.20	0.70	..	1.00
9.3.3	Equipment for sport, camping and open-air recreation	1.80	1.70	2.90	0.80	[0.20]	1.70
9.3.4	Horticultural goods, garden equipment and plants	1.70	1.90	3.40	3.80	3.40	2.80
9.3.5	Pets and pet food	3.20	7.60	9.10	6.40	3.40	6.80
9.4	Recreational and cultural services	18.20	22.70	22.50	16.10	12.60	19.80
9.4.1	Sports admissions, subscriptions, leisure class fees and equipment hire	7.30	9.80	8.70	4.20	5.70	7.80
9.4.2	Cinema, theatre and museums etc.	3.30	3.80	3.90	2.70	1.90	3.30
9.4.3	TV, video, satellite rental, cable subscriptions and TV licences[5]	4.60	5.20	5.60	4.80	1.60	4.70
9.4.4	Miscellaneous entertainments	1.70	1.70	1.50	1.00	0.90	1.40
9.4.5	Development of film, deposit for film development, passport photos, holiday and school photos	0.30	0.20	0.10	[0.20]	..	0.20
9.4.6	Gambling payments	1.10	2.00	2.70	3.20	2.50	2.40
9.5	Newspapers, books and stationery	2.50	4.40	6.60	6.70	6.30	5.50
9.5.1	Books	0.70	1.40	1.50	1.20	0.70	1.20
9.5.2	Diaries, address books, cards etc.	1.50	2.20	3.30	2.10	1.50	2.40
9.5.3	Newspapers	0.10	0.20	1.10	2.50	3.10	1.20
9.5.4	Magazines and periodicals	0.20	0.50	0.80	0.90	0.90	0.70
9.6	Package holidays	14.80	26.30	32.50	33.30	22.50	27.50
9.6.1	Package holidays - UK	[0.90]	1.20	2.20	2.10	3.50	1.90
9.6.2	Package holidays - abroad	13.90	25.10	30.30	31.20	19.00	25.60
10	**Education**	**5.00**	**7.90**	**4.60**	**[0.60]**	**..**	**4.50**
10.1	Education fees	[5.00]	6.70	4.40	[0.60]	..	4.10
10.2	Payments for school trips, other ad-hoc expenditure	..	1.20	[0.20]	..	..	0.50
11	**Restaurants & hotels**	**53.90**	**61.00**	**60.70**	**44.30**	**26.90**	**52.90**
11.1	Catering services	44.70	48.30	46.70	33.60	20.50	41.30
11.1.1	Restaurant and café meals	16.90	20.50	23.30	20.40	15.20	20.20
11.1.2	Alcoholic drinks (away from home)	9.40	8.60	10.20	8.20	3.30	8.30
11.1.3	Take away meals eaten at home	8.50	7.80	5.90	2.70	1.30	5.60
11.1.4	Other take-away and snack food	7.30	8.00	5.60	2.00	0.60	5.30
11.1.5	Contract catering (food) and canteens	2.50	3.50	1.70	0.30	[0.10]	1.90
11.2	Accommodation services	9.20	12.70	14.00	10.70	6.50	11.60
11.2.1	Holiday in the UK	4.40	6.10	7.60	6.80	4.60	6.30
11.2.2	Holiday abroad	4.70	6.50	6.40	3.90	1.90	5.20
11.2.3	Room hire	..	[0.20]	..	..	..	0.10

Note: The commodity and service categories are not comparable to those in publications before 2001-02.

The numbering system is sequential, it does not use actual COICOP codes.

Please see background notes for symbols and conventions used in this report.

5 For FYE 2019 onwards, excludes payments made as part of a combined bill.

Table A11

Detailed household expenditure by age of household reference person (cont.)

UK, financial year ending 2020

	Less than 30	30 to 49	50 to 64	65 to 74	75 or over	All house-holds
Commodity or service	Average weekly household expenditure (£)					
12 Miscellaneous goods & services	**43.40**	**51.20**	**49.50**	**38.00**	**35.10**	**45.70**
12.1 Personal care	13.00	14.90	15.40	11.70	8.20	13.40
12.1.1 Hairdressing, beauty treatment	4.10	4.20	5.20	4.40	3.40	4.40
12.1.2 Toilet paper	0.80	1.10	1.00	0.90	0.80	1.00
12.1.3 Toiletries and soap	2.10	2.90	3.10	2.30	1.80	2.60
12.1.4 Baby toiletries and accessories (disposable)	1.10	1.00	0.30	0.20	0.10	0.60
12.1.5 Hair products, cosmetics and related electrical appliances	5.00	5.70	5.70	3.80	2.10	4.80
12.2 Personal effects	3.50	5.40	5.20	2.40	1.80	4.20
12.3 Social protection	4.70	6.80	[1.50]	..	[3.40]	3.70
12.4 Insurance	17.80	19.20	21.60	18.90	16.20	19.30
12.4.1 Household insurances - structural, contents and appliances	2.40	4.40	5.70	5.70	5.30	4.90
12.4.2 Medical insurance premiums[6]	0.90	1.80	3.00	2.80	2.80	2.40
12.4.3 Vehicle insurance including boat insurance	14.00	12.50	11.90	8.80	6.90	11.10
12.4.4 Non-package holiday, other travel insurance[7]	0.50	0.50	1.00	1.50	1.40	0.90
12.5 Other services	4.30	4.80	5.70	4.30	5.40	5.00
12.5.1 Moving house	3.10	2.60	3.00	1.30	[1.60]	2.40
12.5.2 Bank, building society, post office, credit card charges	0.40	0.60	0.70	0.60	0.20	0.50
12.5.3 Other services and professional fees	0.80	1.60	2.10	2.40	3.50	2.10
1-12 All expenditure groups	**518.30**	**568.10**	**575.40**	**433.70**	**312.80**	**508.50**
13 Other expenditure items	**74.50**	**98.70**	**86.00**	**61.40**	**43.30**	**79.30**
13.1 Housing: mortgage interest payments, council tax etc.	42.10	72.50	49.80	31.80	25.40	50.40
13.2 Licences, fines and transfers	3.00	4.50	4.20	3.50	2.10	3.80
13.3 Holiday spending	24.00	10.00	17.40	8.20	[3.50]	12.10
13.4 Money transfers and credit	5.40	11.70	14.60	17.90	12.20	13.00
13.4.1 Money, cash gifts given to children	..	0.20	[0.10]	..	..	0.30
13.4.2 Cash gifts and donations	4.80	10.10	13.20	16.00	11.90	11.70
13.4.3 Club instalment payments (child) and interest on credit cards	0.60	1.40	1.30	0.80	0.10	1.00
Total expenditure	**592.80**	**666.70**	**661.40**	**495.10**	**356.10**	**587.90**
14 Other items recorded						
14.1 Life assurance & contributions to pension funds	31.90	50.10	48.10	8.70	2.00	34.70
14.2 Other insurance inc. friendly societies	1.10	2.30	3.00	2.30	1.90	2.40
14.3 Income tax, payments *less* refunds	81.10	144.80	122.20	60.60	42.50	105.20
14.4 National insurance contributions	53.80	63.70	46.90	6.60	1.40	40.50
14.5 Purchase or alteration of dwellings, mortgages	28.00	89.10	77.10	28.60	15.90	60.60
14.6 Savings and investments	10.90	10.90	11.20	6.90	2.50	9.20
14.7 Pay off loan to clear other debt	1.20	4.00	2.20	[0.80]	..	2.20
14.8 Windfall receipts from gambling etc[8]	[0.90]	1.00	1.90	1.20	1.20	1.30

Note: The commodity and service categories are not comparable to those in publications before 2001-02.

The numbering system is sequential, it does not use actual COICOP codes.

Please see background notes for symbols and conventions used in this report.

6 For FYE 2019, critical illness cover, personal accident insurance and other medical insurance are included here. They were not included in previous years.

7 For FYE 2019, information about insurance for non-package holiday and other travel insurance was collected in the questionnaire in addition to the diary. In previous years, this was based on diary data only.

8 Expressed as an income figure as opposed to an expenditure figure.

Source: Office for National Statistics

Table A12

Household expenditure by gross income quintile group where the household reference person is aged under 30

UK, financial year ending 2018 to financial year ending 2020

	Lowest twenty per cent	Second quintile group	Third quintile group	Fourth quintile group	Highest twenty per cent	All house-holds
Lower boundary of group (£ per week)[1]		335	568	873	1,296	
Average weighted number of households (thousands)	430	470	630	640	330	2,490
Total number of households in sample (over 3 years)	240	250	300	280	130	1,190
Total number of persons in sample (over 3 years)	510	570	740	670	380	2,860
Total number of adults in sample (over 3 years)	300	360	540	580	330	2,120
Weighted average number of persons per household	2.2	2.3	2.4	2.4	3.0	2.4
Commodity or service	Average weekly household expenditure (£)					
1 Food & non-alcoholic drinks	34.50	37.20	50.40	51.40	69.40	47.90
2 Alcoholic drinks, tobacco & narcotics	6.50	8.10	9.90	9.60	14.40	9.40
3 Clothing & footwear	11.90	15.80	18.90	25.20	39.10	21.30
4 Housing(net)[2], fuel & power	87.10	121.00	124.40	152.30	246.20	140.50
5 Household goods & services	13.10	27.80	31.80	34.20	42.80	30.00
6 Health	1.00	1.50	4.30	4.10	6.40	3.40
7 Transport	20.90	43.20	64.80	99.40	118.90	69.50
8 Communication	11.90	16.20	24.10	24.00	22.30	20.20
9 Recreation & culture	21.60	29.50	49.70	66.90	93.60	51.30
10 Education	..	[1.80]	4.30	30.10	[22.30]	12.40
11 Restaurants & hotels	21.20	31.80	46.90	58.20	107.20	50.50
12 Miscellaneous goods & services	16.80	33.60	38.90	48.50	62.70	39.70
1-12 All expenditure groups	247.90	367.50	468.30	603.90	845.30	496.20
13 Other expenditure items	21.00	35.10	64.40	89.40	125.70	66.30
Total expenditure	**268.90**	**402.60**	**532.70**	**693.30**	**971.00**	**562.50**
Average weekly expenditure per person (£)						
Total expenditure	**124.00**	**178.90**	**224.10**	**288.70**	**328.80**	**234.30**

Note: The commodity and service categories are not comparable to those in publications before 2001-02.

Please see background notes for symbols and conventions used in this report.

This table is based on a three year average.

1 Lower boundary of 2019-20 gross income quintile groups (£ per week).

2 Excluding mortgage interest payments, council tax and Northern Ireland rates.

Source: Office for National Statistics

Table A12DE

Household expenditure by equivalised disposable income quintile group (OECD-modified scale) where the household reference person is aged under 30

UK, financial year ending 2018 to financial year ending 2020

	Lowest twenty per cent	Second quintile group	Third quintile group	Fourth quintile group	Highest twenty per cent	All house-holds
Lower boundary of group (£ per week)[1]		240	342	462	629	
Average weighted number of households (thousands)	520	360	570	620	420	2,490
Total number of households in sample (over 3 years)	290	190	260	280	170	1,190
Total number of persons in sample (over 3 years)	780	500	610	620	360	2,860
Total number of adults in sample (over 3 years)	430	310	470	560	350	2,120
Weighted average number of persons per household	2.7	2.6	2.3	2.2	2.2	2.4
Commodity or service	Average weekly household expenditure (£)					
1 Food & non-alcoholic drinks	39.50	45.70	48.10	51.10	55.30	47.90
2 Alcoholic drinks, tobacco & narcotics	7.80	9.50	9.90	8.10	12.40	9.40
3 Clothing & footwear	14.00	15.70	21.20	22.50	33.70	21.30
4 Housing(net)[2]. fuel & power	91.40	129.60	133.60	152.50	202.90	140.50
5 Household goods & services	16.00	25.60	30.10	33.80	45.80	30.00
6 Health	1.00	2.40	2.10	6.30	5.00	3.40
7 Transport	27.70	48.30	70.70	92.20	103.70	69.50
8 Communication	13.30	18.90	23.50	23.40	21.00	20.20
9 Recreation & culture	25.60	31.30	51.10	57.90	90.40	51.30
10 Education	[0.40]	[4.10]	11.90	32.80	[7.40]	12.40
11 Restaurants & hotels	24.40	31.30	47.10	60.00	90.50	50.50
12 Miscellaneous goods & services	20.80	36.50	42.60	45.10	53.90	39.70
1-12 All expenditure groups	282.00	398.80	492.00	585.70	722.00	496.20
13 Other expenditure items	22.10	48.80	62.40	75.60	127.80	66.30
Total expenditure	**304.10**	**447.50**	**554.40**	**661.40**	**849.80**	**562.50**
Average weekly expenditure per person (£) **Total expenditure**	**113.90**	**171.50**	**238.20**	**297.10**	**378.10**	**234.30**

Note: The commodity and service categories are not comparable to those in publications before 2001-02.

Please see background notes for symbols and conventions used in this report.

This table is based on a three year average.

1 Lower boundary of 2019-20 gross income quintile groups (£ per week).

2 Excluding mortgage interest payments, council tax and Northern Ireland rates.

Source: Office for National Statistics

Table A13

Household expenditure by gross income quintile group where the household reference person is aged 30 to 49

UK, financial year ending 2018 to financial year ending 2020

	Lowest twenty per cent	Second quintile group	Third quintile group	Fourth quintile group	Highest twenty per cent	All house-holds
Lower boundary of group (£ per week)[1]		335	568	873	1,296	
Average weighted number of households (thousands)	1,000	1,430	1,800	2,400	2,630	9,260
Total number of households in sample (over 3 years)	610	890	1,080	1,420	1,450	5,450
Total number of persons in sample (over 3 years)	1,250	2,480	3,300	4,640	4,920	16,600
Total number of adults in sample (over 3 years)	760	1,400	1,950	2,880	3,170	10,150
Weighted average number of persons per household	2.0	2.8	3.0	3.3	3.4	3.0
Commodity or service	Average weekly household expenditure (£)					
1 Food & non-alcoholic drinks	40.20	53.20	62.30	73.30	87.70	68.60
2 Alcoholic drinks, tobacco & narcotics	9.40	9.80	11.60	13.00	16.00	12.70
3 Clothing & footwear	13.60	19.50	23.10	29.90	47.60	30.20
4 Housing(net)[2], fuel & power	70.40	98.40	103.30	90.30	98.50	94.30
5 Household goods & services	19.00	23.60	29.00	44.00	72.70	43.40
6 Health	1.60	3.30	4.50	5.70	10.80	6.10
7 Transport	31.00	51.00	74.90	101.60	160.90	97.70
8 Communication	13.20	18.60	21.60	24.50	28.80	23.00
9 Recreation & culture	28.30	38.50	52.00	75.00	130.70	75.60
10 Education	2.50	2.00	4.00	4.80	20.30	8.40
11 Restaurants & hotels	20.30	30.10	44.40	60.30	102.90	60.30
12 Miscellaneous goods & services	18.00	27.70	40.70	52.80	82.50	51.30
1-12 All expenditure groups	267.50	375.80	471.40	575.10	859.40	571.60
13 Other expenditure items	28.50	43.60	71.30	103.30	163.90	97.00
Total expenditure	**296.00**	**419.40**	**542.70**	**678.40**	**1023.40**	**668.60**
Average weekly expenditure per person (£) **Total expenditure**	**144.90**	**151.20**	**180.10**	**207.40**	**301.40**	**219.40**

Note: The commodity and service categories are not comparable to those in publications before 2001-02.

Please see background notes for symbols and conventions used in this report.

This table is based on a three year average.

1 Lower boundary of 2019-20 gross income quintile groups (£ per week).

2 Excluding mortgage interest payments, council tax and Northern Ireland rates.

Source: Office for National Statistics

Table A13DE

Household expenditure by equivalised disposable income quintile group (OECD-modified scale) where the household reference person is aged 30 to 49

UK, financial year ending 2018 to financial year ending 2020

	Lowest twenty per cent	Second quintile group	Third quintile group	Fourth quintile group	Highest twenty per cent	All house-holds
Lower boundary of group (£ per week)[1]		240	342	462	629	
Average weighted number of households (thousands)	1,600	1,660	1,820	1,940	2,240	9,260
Total number of households in sample (over 3 years)	980	1,020	1,100	1,130	1,230	5,450
Total number of persons in sample (over 3 years)	3,110	3,340	3,510	3,370	3,270	16,600
Total number of adults in sample (over 3 years)	1,590	1,840	2,110	2,250	2,370	10,150
Weighted average number of persons per household	3.2	3.3	3.2	3.0	2.7	3.0
Commodity or service	Average weekly household expenditure (£)					
1 Food & non-alcoholic drinks	57.30	65.00	71.10	71.80	74.70	68.60
2 Alcoholic drinks, tobacco & narcotics	9.80	11.10	12.20	14.60	14.70	12.70
3 Clothing & footwear	20.30	22.70	28.00	36.10	39.60	30.20
4 Housing(net)[2], fuel & power	90.70	95.30	91.00	92.40	100.50	94.30
5 Household goods & services	23.00	29.80	36.40	49.70	68.40	43.40
6 Health	2.90	3.60	5.50	6.30	10.70	6.10
7 Transport	45.80	65.80	88.50	112.60	153.30	97.70
8 Communication	17.20	22.20	23.50	24.80	25.80	23.00
9 Recreation & culture	37.00	49.40	62.90	88.60	121.60	75.60
10 Education	3.30	3.30	4.20	4.60	22.50	8.40
11 Restaurants & hotels	28.10	37.40	50.60	69.80	100.30	60.30
12 Miscellaneous goods & services	25.10	33.60	50.20	60.00	76.60	51.30
1-12 All expenditure groups	360.60	439.30	524.00	631.40	808.60	571.60
13 Other expenditure items	37.40	62.40	83.60	109.00	166.10	97.00
Total expenditure	**398.00**	**501.60**	**607.60**	**740.40**	**974.70**	**668.60**
Average weekly expenditure per person (£) **Total expenditure**	**123.80**	**152.10**	**189.50**	**248.20**	**365.50**	**219.40**

Note: The commodity and service categories are not comparable to those in publications before 2001-02.

Please see background notes for symbols and conventions used in this report.

This table is based on a three year average.

1 Lower boundary of 2019-20 gross income quintile groups (£ per week).

2 Excluding mortgage interest payments, council tax and Northern Ireland rates.

Source: Office for National Statistics

Table A14

Household expenditure by gross income quintile group where the household reference person is aged 50 to 64

UK, financial year ending 2018 to financial year ending 2020

		Lowest twenty per cent	Second quintile group	Third quintile group	Fourth quintile group	Highest twenty per cent	All house-holds
Lower boundary of group (£ per week)[1]			335	568	873	1,296	
Average weighted number of households (thousands)		1,410	1,270	1,410	1,580	2,000	7,650
Total number of households in sample (over 3 years)		930	820	880	970	1,090	4,690
Total number of persons in sample (over 3 years)		1,270	1,520	1,920	2,460	3,300	10,480
Total number of adults in sample (over 3 years)		1,200	1,350	1,720	2,200	2,860	9,330
Weighted average number of persons per household		1.4	1.9	2.2	2.6	3.2	2.3
Commodity or service		Average weekly household expenditure (£)					
1	Food & non-alcoholic drinks	38.60	53.20	63.70	76.10	95.90	68.30
2	Alcoholic drinks, tobacco & narcotics	11.30	13.30	14.50	17.20	20.80	15.90
3	Clothing & footwear	9.10	14.50	20.30	32.40	49.60	27.40
4	Housing(net)[2], fuel & power	57.30	69.50	70.70	70.60	80.00	70.40
5	Household goods & services	16.40	26.00	39.20	47.50	75.60	44.00
6	Health	4.70	6.40	5.40	11.70	13.70	8.90
7	Transport	31.70	58.90	94.00	112.80	172.00	101.00
8	Communication	11.80	17.30	20.00	24.20	32.50	22.20
9	Recreation & culture	32.80	49.50	71.40	105.50	160.20	90.90
10	Education	..	[3.50]	1.90	7.70	16.80	7.60
11	Restaurants & hotels	19.40	27.90	50.30	64.30	107.80	58.80
12	Miscellaneous goods & services	18.30	29.00	39.10	53.30	79.30	47.00
1-12	All expenditure groups	254.90	369.10	490.50	623.30	904.30	562.50
13	Other expenditure items	26.80	43.50	67.30	91.60	151.50	82.90
Total expenditure		**281.80**	**412.60**	**557.80**	**714.90**	**1055.80**	**645.40**
Average weekly expenditure per person (£) **Total expenditure**		**202.60**	**212.60**	**251.00**	**274.90**	**334.50**	**275.30**

Note: The commodity and service categories are not comparable to those in publications before 2001-02.

Please see background notes for symbols and conventions used in this report.

This table is based on a three year average.

1 Lower boundary of 2019-20 gross income quintile groups (£ per week).

2 Excluding mortgage interest payments, council tax and Northern Ireland rates.

Source: Office for National Statistics

Table A14DE

Household expenditure by equivalised disposable income quintile group (OECD-modified scale) where the household reference person is aged 50 to 64

UK, financial year ending 2018 to financial year ending 2020

	Lowest twenty per cent	Second quintile group	Third quintile group	Fourth quintile group	Highest twenty per cent	All house-holds
Lower boundary of group (£ per week)[1]		240	342	462	629	
Average weighted number of households (thousands)	1,470	1,260	1,380	1,680	1,870	7,650
Total number of households in sample (over 3 years)	930	800	880	1,010	1,080	4,690
Total number of persons in sample (over 3 years)	1,690	1,750	2,010	2,490	2,550	10,480
Total number of adults in sample (over 3 years)	1,470	1,490	1,780	2,260	2,340	9,330
Weighted average number of persons per household	1.9	2.3	2.4	2.6	2.5	2.3
Commodity or service	Average weekly household expenditure (£)					
1 Food & non-alcoholic drinks	47.60	61.00	67.00	77.30	82.30	68.30
2 Alcoholic drinks, tobacco & narcotics	11.70	13.80	15.60	17.40	19.60	15.90
3 Clothing & footwear	11.60	17.30	25.60	33.60	42.20	27.40
4 Housing(net)[2], fuel & power	61.20	71.10	71.30	70.00	76.90	70.40
5 Household goods & services	18.90	30.00	37.10	48.70	74.00	44.00
6 Health	4.40	7.00	7.80	8.70	14.70	8.90
7 Transport	39.00	74.30	89.20	113.20	165.90	101.00
8 Communication	14.00	20.30	21.50	24.30	28.40	22.20
9 Recreation & culture	38.00	51.10	80.30	103.90	155.80	90.90
10 Education	3.80	[2.00]	5.50	6.70	16.70	7.60
11 Restaurants & hotels	23.20	35.00	50.80	70.60	98.00	58.80
12 Miscellaneous goods & services	21.40	33.20	41.30	54.90	73.60	47.00
1-12 All expenditure groups	294.90	416.20	513.20	629.30	848.30	562.50
13 Other expenditure items	35.50	50.50	66.30	86.20	151.50	82.90
Total expenditure	**330.30**	**466.70**	**579.50**	**715.50**	**999.80**	**645.40**
Average weekly expenditure per person (£)						
Total expenditure	**170.50**	**200.70**	**246.20**	**276.50**	**407.50**	**275.30**

Note: The commodity and service categories are not comparable to those in publications before 2001-02.

Please see background notes for symbols and conventions used in this report.

This table is based on a three year average.

1 Lower boundary of 2019-20 gross income quintile groups (£ per week).

2 Excluding mortgage interest payments, council tax and Northern Ireland rates.

Source: Office for National Statistics

Table A15

Household expenditure by gross income quintile group where the household reference person is aged 65 to 74

UK, financial year ending 2018 to financial year ending 2020

	Lowest twenty per cent	Second quintile group	Third quintile group	Fourth quintile group	Highest twenty per cent	All house-holds
Lower boundary of group (£ per week)[1]		335	568	873	1,296	
Average weighted number of households (thousands)	1,100	1,120	910	620	390	4,140
Total number of households in sample (over 3 years)	760	820	640	410	260	2,890
Total number of persons in sample (over 3 years)	900	1,400	1,260	890	610	5,050
Total number of adults in sample (over 3 years)	890	1,390	1,250	860	590	4,980
Weighted average number of persons per household	1.2	1.7	2.0	2.2	2.4	1.8
Commodity or service	Average weekly household expenditure (£)					
1 Food & non-alcoholic drinks	37.50	53.50	66.10	80.50	93.20	59.80
2 Alcoholic drinks, tobacco & narcotics	9.10	11.00	16.40	21.20	24.00	14.40
3 Clothing & footwear	8.00	13.10	22.20	31.50	32.80	18.30
4 Housing(net)[2], fuel & power	47.60	50.60	55.60	66.10	75.70	55.60
5 Household goods & services	17.60	30.70	43.10	45.20	110.30	39.70
6 Health	3.50	8.10	12.40	16.40	18.90	10.10
7 Transport	23.80	53.80	75.40	119.00	146.00	69.00
8 Communication	10.80	15.40	19.10	22.60	23.70	16.90
9 Recreation & culture	31.50	64.80	110.40	134.60	159.20	85.70
10 Education	..	..	..	..	[2.20]	0.90
11 Restaurants & hotels	16.80	34.10	50.70	66.70	101.50	44.30
12 Miscellaneous goods & services	17.50	31.60	43.50	55.00	85.00	39.00
1-12 All expenditure groups	224.10	367.50	515.90	659.60	872.40	453.80
13 Other expenditure items	24.60	48.30	71.90	86.40	161.20	63.70
Total expenditure	**248.60**	**415.80**	**587.80**	**746.00**	**1033.60**	**517.50**
Average weekly expenditure per person (£)						
Total expenditure	**209.70**	**246.00**	**295.70**	**332.20**	**424.00**	**291.50**

Note: The commodity and service categories are not comparable to those in publications before 2001-02.

Please see background notes for symbols and conventions used in this report.

This table is based on a three year average.

1 Lower boundary of 2019-20 gross income quintile groups (£ per week).

2 Excluding mortgage interest payments, council tax and Northern Ireland rates.

Source: Office for National Statistics

Table A15DE

Household expenditure by equivalised disposable income quintile group (OECD-modified scale) where the household reference person is aged 65 to 74

UK, financial year ending 2018 to financial year ending 2020

	Lowest twenty per cent	Second quintile group	Third quintile group	Fourth quintile group	Highest twenty per cent	All house-holds
Lower boundary of group (£ per week)[1]		240	342	462	629	
Average weighted number of households (thousands)	880	1,000	910	720	640	4,140
Total number of households in sample (over 3 years)	600	720	640	490	440	2,890
Total number of persons in sample (over 3 years)	860	1,240	1,180	940	840	5,050
Total number of adults in sample (over 3 years)	840	1,220	1,160	930	830	4,980
Weighted average number of persons per household	1.4	1.8	1.9	1.9	1.9	1.8
Commodity or service	Average weekly household expenditure (£)					
1 Food & non-alcoholic drinks	42.20	54.50	62.60	68.00	78.60	59.80
2 Alcoholic drinks, tobacco & narcotics	9.70	12.10	15.80	15.10	21.50	14.40
3 Clothing & footwear	8.40	13.80	22.50	23.70	26.60	18.30
4 Housing(net)[2], fuel & power	47.80	50.50	58.30	55.60	70.90	55.60
5 Household goods & services	16.50	31.70	39.10	41.70	81.20	39.70
6 Health	3.20	6.20	11.80	14.40	18.00	10.10
7 Transport	26.50	48.60	74.40	87.20	131.30	69.00
8 Communication	11.40	15.10	18.20	20.20	21.60	16.90
9 Recreation & culture	35.70	54.10	91.10	116.10	160.00	85.70
10 Education	..	..	[0.80]	..	[1.00]	0.90
11 Restaurants & hotels	18.00	32.80	43.90	59.90	81.60	44.30
12 Miscellaneous goods & services	19.50	28.00	40.90	48.80	69.60	39.00
1-12 All expenditure groups	239.90	347.90	479.40	552.10	762.00	453.80
13 Other expenditure items	25.20	42.00	67.20	68.90	139.80	63.70
Total expenditure	**265.10**	**389.90**	**546.60**	**621.00**	**901.80**	**517.50**
Average weekly expenditure per person (£)						
Total expenditure	**185.80**	**220.00**	**292.50**	**320.30**	**464.70**	**291.50**

Note: The commodity and service categories are not comparable to those in publications before 2001-02.

Please see background notes for symbols and conventions used in this report.

This table is based on a three year average.

1 Lower boundary of 2019-20 gross income quintile groups (£ per week).

2 Excluding mortgage interest payments, council tax and Northern Ireland rates.

Source: Office for National Statistics

Table A16

Household expenditure by gross income quintile group where the household reference person is aged 75 or over

UK, financial year ending 2018 to financial year ending 2020

	Lowest twenty per cent	Second quintile group	Third quintile group	Fourth quintile group	Highest twenty per cent	All house-holds
Lower boundary of group (£ per week)[1]		335	568	873	1,296	
Average weighted number of households (thousands)	1,570	1,200	750	270	140	3,930
Total number of households in sample (over 3 years)	790	650	430	160	80	2,110
Total number of persons in sample (over 3 years)	930	1,030	800	320	160	3,240
Total number of adults in sample (over 3 years)	930	1,030	790	310	150	3,220
Weighted average number of persons per household	1.2	1.5	1.9	2.1	2.2	1.5
Commodity or service	Average weekly household expenditure (£)					
1 Food & non-alcoholic drinks	32.80	46.00	61.10	71.00	83.80	46.80
2 Alcoholic drinks, tobacco & narcotics	4.90	6.40	9.90	18.50	15.80	7.60
3 Clothing & footwear	6.10	10.80	17.30	25.40	27.60	11.80
4 Housing(net)[2], fuel & power	40.70	49.70	55.40	58.20	76.90	48.90
5 Household goods & services	13.90	28.30	39.30	43.60	63.10	27.00
6 Health	5.30	7.10	14.40	17.70	31.70	9.40
7 Transport	13.50	30.10	54.50	81.90	86.20	33.70
8 Communication	9.80	13.10	16.70	18.40	22.30	13.20
9 Recreation & culture	25.90	38.30	74.90	127.80	138.00	51.00
10 Education	..	..	..	..	..	[0.70]
11 Restaurants & hotels	11.40	20.40	38.70	57.20	82.10	24.80
12 Miscellaneous goods & services	19.40	38.80	49.80	61.00	80.80	36.20
1-12 All expenditure groups	183.80	289.20	432.30	582.10	723.90	311.20
13 Other expenditure items	27.20	39.90	63.40	73.00	154.90	45.60
Total expenditure	**211.00**	**329.20**	**495.70**	**655.10**	**878.80**	**356.80**
Average weekly expenditure per person (£)						
Total expenditure	**183.50**	**218.90**	**265.70**	**307.90**	**400.80**	**237.90**

Note: The commodity and service categories are not comparable to those in publications before 2001-02.

Please see background notes for symbols and conventions used in this report.

This table is based on a three year average.

1 Lower boundary of 2019-20 gross income quintile groups (£ per week).

2 Excluding mortgage interest payments, council tax and Northern Ireland rates.

Source: Office for National Statistics

Table A16DE

Household expenditure by equivalised disposable income quintile group (OECD-modified scale) where the household reference person is aged 75 or over

UK, financial year ending 2018 to financial year ending 2020

	Lowest twenty per cent	Second quintile group	Third quintile group	Fourth quintile group	Highest twenty per cent	All house-holds
Lower boundary of group (£ per week)[1]		240	342	462	629	
Average weighted number of households (thousands)	1,030	1,220	830	530	330	3,930
Total number of households in sample (over 3 years)	540	650	450	290	180	2,110
Total number of persons in sample (over 3 years)	750	970	750	490	290	3,240
Total number of adults in sample (over 3 years)	740	970	740	490	290	3,220
Weighted average number of persons per household	1.4	1.4	1.6	1.6	1.6	1.5

Commodity or service	Average weekly household expenditure (£)					
1 Food & non-alcoholic drinks	37.80	42.20	52.30	55.70	64.50	46.80
2 Alcoholic drinks, tobacco & narcotics	5.40	6.30	7.60	11.10	14.60	7.60
3 Clothing & footwear	7.40	9.30	14.40	17.50	19.50	11.80
4 Housing(net)[2], fuel & power	42.10	45.60	50.60	58.40	62.70	48.90
5 Household goods & services	15.20	22.30	31.70	40.00	48.60	27.00
6 Health	5.50	6.60	12.50	10.70	21.40	9.40
7 Transport	16.70	24.60	41.00	52.00	71.20	33.70
8 Communication	9.90	12.50	14.10	16.50	18.50	13.20
9 Recreation & culture	24.50	37.00	55.70	79.50	124.30	51.00
10 Education	:	..	..	..	..	[0.70]
11 Restaurants & hotels	13.10	18.20	29.30	36.50	56.60	24.80
12 Miscellaneous goods & services	20.10	24.10	54.60	48.60	64.30	36.20
1-12 All expenditure groups	197.50	248.70	363.80	427.10	573.70	311.20
13 Other expenditure items	24.10	38.80	48.60	57.50	112.50	45.60
Total expenditure	**221.60**	**287.50**	**412.40**	**484.60**	**686.30**	**356.80**
Average weekly expenditure per person (£)						
Total expenditure	**159.00**	**199.00**	**258.90**	**295.60**	**435.50**	**237.90**

Note: The commodity and service categories are not comparable to those in publications before 2001-02.

Please see background notes for symbols and conventions used in this report.

This table is based on a three year average.

1 Lower boundary of 2019-20 gross income quintile groups (£ per week).

2 Excluding mortgage interest payments, council tax and Northern Ireland rates.

Source: Office for National Statistics

Table A17

Household expenditure by economic activity status of the household reference person

UK, financial year ending 2020

Commodity or service	Employees Full-time	Employees Part-time	Employees All	Self-employed	All in employment[1]	Unemployed	All economically active[1]	Economically inactive Retired	Economically inactive Other	Economically inactive All	All households
Weighted number of households (thousands)	12,130	2,800	14,930	2,320	17,250	470	17,720	7,190	2,910	10,090	27,820
Total number of households in sample	2,250	570	2,810	440	3,250	80	3,330	1,510	600	2,110	5,440
Total number of persons in sample	6,160	1,470	7,620	1,130	8,750	170	8,930	2,460	1,290	3,740	12,670
Total number of adults in sample	4,460	1,000	5,460	850	6,310	130	6,440	2,430	1,010	3,440	9,880
Weighted average number of persons per household	2.7	2.6	2.7	2.7	2.7	2.1	2.7	1.6	2.2	1.8	2.4
Average weekly household expenditure (£)											
1 Food & non-alcoholic drinks	71.70	62.70	70.00	71.20	70.20	47.50	69.60	52.50	55.70	53.40	63.70
2 Alcoholic drinks, tobacco & narcotics	14.10	11.60	13.60	15.90	13.90	9.20	13.80	10.40	14.10	11.50	12.90
3 Clothing & footwear	31.20	22.10	29.50	23.00	28.60	13.90	28.30	13.70	17.60	14.80	23.40
4 Housing (net)[2], fuel & power	99.00	84.30	96.20	99.40	96.60	86.40	96.40	50.60	81.30	59.50	83.00
5 Household goods & services	45.10	31.40	42.60	41.10	42.40	19.30	41.70	27.00	28.20	27.30	36.50
6 Health	7.80	6.40	7.50	7.90	7.60	2.20	7.40	9.90	8.80	9.60	8.20
7 Transport	111.50	72.20	104.10	102.10	103.80	41.40	102.20	42.80	52.20	45.50	81.60
8 Communication	25.30	22.70	24.80	23.70	24.70	14.50	24.40	15.50	17.30	16.00	21.40
9 Recreation & culture	84.20	64.10	80.40	78.90	80.20	40.40	79.10	65.30	71.70	67.10	74.80
10 Education	7.10	7.80	7.20	2.50	6.60	..	6.40	..	[3.30]	1.20	4.50
11 Restaurants & hotels	68.50	49.00	64.80	58.10	63.90	23.70	62.80	32.80	41.50	35.30	52.90
12 Miscellaneous goods & services	56.80	41.40	53.90	52.50	53.70	22.70	52.90	34.90	28.10	33.00	45.70
1-12 All expenditure groups	622.20	475.70	594.70	576.40	592.20	321.50	585.00	355.90	419.70	374.30	508.50
13 Other expenditure items	106.20	69.50	99.30	98.00	99.10	54.80	98.00	48.70	41.30	46.60	79.30
Total expenditure	**728.40**	**545.10**	**694.00**	**674.30**	**691.30**	**376.40**	**683.00**	**404.70**	**461.00**	**420.90**	**587.90**
Average weekly expenditure per person (£)											
Total expenditure	**265.70**	**207.10**	**255.00**	**249.80**	**254.30**	**175.10**	**252.70**	**254.10**	**209.50**	**238.10**	**248.70**

Note: The commodity and service categories are not comparable to those in publications before 2001-02.

Please see background notes for symbols and conventions used in this report.

1 Includes households where household reference person was on a Government supported training scheme.

2 Excluding mortgage interest payments, council tax and Northern Ireland rates.

Source: Office for National Statistics

Table A18

Household expenditure by gross income: the household reference person is a full-time employee

UK, financial year ending 2020

	Lowest twenty per cent	Second quintile group	Third quintile group	Fourth quintile group	Highest twenty per cent	All house-holds
Lower boundary of group (£ per week)[1]		335	568	873	1,296	
Weighted number of households (thousands)	210	1,320	2,750	3,690	4,160	12,130
Total number of households in sample	40	260	520	690	740	2,250
Total number of persons in sample	60	470	1,300	1,980	2,350	6,160
Total number of adults in sample	50	360	930	1,420	1,700	4,460
Weighted average number of persons per household	1.6	1.8	2.4	2.9	3.2	2.7
Commodity or service	Average weekly household expenditure (£)					
1 Food & non-alcoholic drinks	40.50	42.30	57.50	72.80	90.90	71.70
2 Alcoholic drinks, tobacco & narcotics	17.10	10.30	10.40	13.30	18.20	14.10
3 Clothing & footwear	14.40	11.70	18.80	32.30	45.50	31.20
4 Housing (net)[2], fuel & power	85.90	97.50	99.50	92.20	105.80	99.00
5 Household goods & services	30.00	22.90	29.40	39.30	68.40	45.10
6 Health	1.60	3.20	5.00	7.70	11.40	7.80
7 Transport	41.80	47.10	83.90	103.40	160.70	111.50
8 Communication	19.40	18.20	22.00	25.40	30.00	25.30
9 Recreation & culture	50.60	37.00	52.60	78.60	126.50	84.20
10 Education	..	..	2.40	3.80	15.20	7.10
11 Restaurants & hotels	28.50	26.50	45.70	60.80	105.50	68.50
12 Miscellaneous goods & services	32.40	27.20	42.80	55.80	77.60	56.80
1-12 All expenditure groups	362.40	345.20	470.00	585.40	855.70	622.20
13 Other expenditure items	38.10	41.00	68.60	95.60	164.50	106.20
Total expenditure	**400.60**	**386.10**	**538.60**	**681.10**	**1,020.20**	**728.40**
Average weekly expenditure per person (£)						
Total expenditure	**252.20**	**217.30**	**221.00**	**238.60**	**318.20**	**265.70**

Note: The commodity and service categories are not comparable to those in publications before 2001-02.

Please see background notes for symbols and conventions used in this report.

1 Lower boundary of 2019-20 gross income quintile groups (£ per week).

2 Excluding mortgage interest payments, council tax and Northern Ireland rates.

Source: Office for National Statistics

Table A18DE

Household expenditure by equivalised disposable income (OECD-modified scale): the household reference person is a full-time employee

UK, financial year ending 2020

	Lowest twenty per cent	Second quintile group	Third quintile group	Fourth quintile group	Highest twenty per cent	All house-holds
Lower boundary of group (£ per week)[1]		240	342	462	629	
Weighted number of households (thousands)	510	1,560	2,800	3,450	3,820	12,130
Total number of households in sample	100	310	520	640	680	2,250
Total number of persons in sample	350	950	1,450	1,730	1,690	6,160
Total number of adults in sample	190	590	1,000	1,330	1,350	4,460
Weighted average number of persons per household	3.5	3.1	2.8	2.7	2.5	2.7
Commodity or service	Average weekly household expenditure (£)					
1 Food & non-alcoholic drinks	69.70	65.10	66.70	73.50	76.70	71.70
2 Alcoholic drinks, tobacco & narcotics	12.60	11.00	11.90	15.40	15.90	14.10
3 Clothing & footwear	24.00	18.90	27.70	32.40	38.80	31.20
4 Housing (net)[2], fuel & power	115.60	102.70	91.30	92.80	106.30	99.00
5 Household goods & services	33.20	30.20	34.40	44.50	61.30	45.10
6 Health	3.90	4.70	5.30	7.10	11.90	7.80
7 Transport	74.80	72.90	85.20	111.20	151.60	111.50
8 Communication	26.80	22.00	24.50	25.90	26.60	25.30
9 Recreation & culture	55.50	55.00	62.10	84.80	115.50	84.20
10 Education	..	[1.70]	4.70	5.80	12.80	7.10
11 Restaurants & hotels	42.50	38.60	48.70	72.20	95.30	68.50
12 Miscellaneous goods & services	40.20	37.50	47.40	57.70	73.10	56.80
1-12 All expenditure groups	500.50	460.30	510.00	623.20	785.90	622.20
13 Other expenditure items	54.50	69.70	76.40	95.60	159.60	106.20
Total expenditure	**555.00**	**530.10**	**586.40**	**718.80**	**945.50**	**728.40**
Average weekly expenditure per person (£)						
Total expenditure	**157.60**	**170.70**	**210.80**	**267.80**	**376.60**	**265.70**

Note: The commodity and service categories are not comparable to those in publications before 2001-02.

Please see background notes for symbols and conventions used in this report.

1 Lower boundary of 2019-20 equivalised disposable income quintile groups (£ per week).

2 Excluding mortgage interest payments, council tax and Northern Ireland rates.

Source: Office for National Statistics

Table A19

Household expenditure by gross income: the household reference person is self-employed

UK, financial year ending 2018 to financial year ending 2020

	Lowest twenty per cent	Second quintile group	Third quintile group	Fourth quintile group	Highest twenty per cent	All households
Lower boundary of group (£ per week)[1]		335	568	873	1,296	
Average weighted number of households (thousands)	360	430	490	530	550	2,360
Total number of households in sample (over 3 years)	210	260	290	290	300	1,350
Total number of persons in sample (over 3 years)	360	660	790	820	950	3,570
Total number of adults in sample (over 3 years)	280	450	560	630	750	2,680
Weighted average number of persons per household	1.8	2.6	2.7	3.0	3.2	2.7
Commodity or service	Average weekly household expenditure (£)					
1 Food & non-alcoholic drinks	43.90	61.90	67.90	78.20	93.70	71.60
2 Alcoholic drinks, tobacco & narcotics	7.60	11.60	14.60	17.70	21.50	15.20
3 Clothing & footwear	12.50	16.40	22.10	30.30	46.30	27.30
4 Housing (net)[2], fuel & power	76.70	94.30	83.50	98.30	104.40	92.90
5 Household goods & services	15.90	29.70	38.60	38.50	88.30	45.30
6 Health	4.90	7.90	4.80	9.60	10.90	7.80
7 Transport	49.70	75.80	91.30	124.70	179.20	110.40
8 Communication	14.60	18.50	19.40	25.00	31.20	22.50
9 Recreation & culture	42.10	51.30	69.20	94.50	145.50	85.00
10 Education	..	..	[3.40]	11.20	26.00	10.10
11 Restaurants & hotels	32.60	37.30	57.10	65.20	102.00	62.10
12 Miscellaneous goods & services	31.30	38.80	41.20	55.30	82.20	52.10
1-12 All expenditure groups	332.40	446.50	513.10	648.50	931.30	602.30
13 Other expenditure items	48.50	57.90	70.80	104.60	159.70	93.50
Total expenditure	**380.90**	**504.40**	**583.90**	**753.10**	**1,091.00**	**695.80**
Average weekly expenditure per person (£) **Total expenditure**	**212.40**	**195.10**	**219.30**	**250.50**	**338.60**	**255.40**

Note: The commodity and service categories are not comparable to those in publications before 2001-02.

Please see background notes for symbols and conventions used in this report.

This table is based on a three year average.

1 Lower boundary of 2019-20 gross income quintile groups (£ per week).

2 Excluding mortgage interest payments, council tax and Northern Ireland rates.

Source: Office for National Statistics

Table A19DE

Household expenditure by equivalised disposable income (OECD-modified scale):
the household reference person is self-employed

UK, financial year ending 2018 to financial year ending 2020

	Lowest twenty per cent	Second quintile group	Third quintile group	Fourth quintile group	Highest twenty per cent	All house-holds
Lower boundary of group (£ per week)[1]		240	342	462	629	
Average weighted number of households (thousands)	470	390	400	440	660	2,360
Total number of households in sample (over 3 years)	270	230	230	250	370	1,350
Total number of persons in sample (over 3 years)	720	660	640	660	890	3,570
Total number of adults in sample (over 3 years)	460	450	480	540	760	2,680
Weighted average number of persons per household	2.8	3.0	2.8	2.8	2.4	2.7
Commodity or service	Average weekly household expenditure (£)					
1 Food & non-alcoholic drinks	59.60	71.00	72.10	73.00	79.00	71.60
2 Alcoholic drinks, tobacco & narcotics	9.00	14.50	12.40	14.30	22.30	15.20
3 Clothing & footwear	17.70	20.40	23.70	35.70	34.90	27.30
4 Housing (net)[2], fuel & power	86.60	82.70	94.80	90.80	102.60	92.90
5 Household goods & services	23.60	36.50	29.70	40.90	77.70	45.30
6 Health	4.60	7.10	8.40	5.90	11.80	7.80
7 Transport	63.50	92.00	99.80	114.80	157.70	110.40
8 Communication	17.00	23.70	22.30	23.70	25.00	22.50
9 Recreation & culture	48.40	54.00	70.00	93.70	134.40	85.00
10 Education	[1.50]	[4.40]	[1.80]	7.10	25.30	10.10
11 Restaurants & hotels	38.20	46.80	55.50	64.30	91.40	62.10
12 Miscellaneous goods & services	36.50	40.80	49.20	50.00	73.10	52.10
1-12 All expenditure groups	406.30	494.00	539.80	614.20	835.20	602.30
13 Other expenditure items	51.70	72.70	73.30	91.50	148.90	93.50
Total expenditure	**458.10**	**566.70**	**613.10**	**705.60**	**984.00**	**695.80**
Average weekly expenditure per person (£)						
Total expenditure	**164.70**	**189.50**	**220.20**	**252.20**	**402.70**	**255.40**

Note: The commodity and service categories are not comparable to those in publications before 2001-02.

Please see background notes for symbols and conventions used in this report.

This table is based on a three year average.

1 Lower boundary of 2019-20 gross income quintile groups (£ per week).

2 Excluding mortgage interest payments, council tax and Northern Ireland rates.

Source: Office for National Statistics

Table A20

Household expenditure by number of persons working

UK, financial year ending 2020

	Number of persons working					All house-holds
	None	One	Two	Three	Four or more	
Weighted number of households (thousands)	9,050	7,590	9,200	1,490	490	27,820
Total number of households in sample	1,910	1,480	1,750	240	70	5,440
Total number of persons in sample	3,090	3,110	5,270	880	330	12,670
Total number of adults in sample	2,850	2,310	3,690	750	280	9,880
Weighted average number of persons per household	1.6	2.1	3.0	3.7	4.9	2.4
Weighted average age of head of household	69	49	43	51	50	54
Employment status of the household reference person[1]:						
- % working full-time or self-employed	0	62	86	86	90	49
- % working part-time	0	22	12	12	10	10
- % not working	100	16	2	2	0	40
Commodity or service	Average weekly household expenditure (£)					
1 Food & non-alcoholic drinks	48.40	55.40	76.90	96.90	126.20	63.70
2 Alcoholic drinks, tobacco & narcotics	10.00	11.40	15.20	21.30	22.10	12.90
3 Clothing & footwear	12.90	18.40	32.10	43.90	68.10	23.40
4 Housing (net)[2], fuel & power	55.20	91.50	94.80	118.90	132.30	83.00
5 Household goods & services	24.50	31.10	49.30	51.80	55.70	36.50
6 Health	8.70	6.50	9.00	7.70	11.60	8.20
7 Transport	39.20	69.70	118.70	134.80	191.80	81.60
8 Communication	14.50	19.60	26.80	32.70	38.40	21.40
9 Recreation & culture	61.70	59.30	92.80	98.80	144.40	74.80
10 Education	[0.70]	3.70	8.70	[6.40]	..	4.50
11 Restaurants & hotels	29.90	43.50	72.40	95.30	127.50	52.90
12 Miscellaneous goods & services	30.30	40.10	60.10	66.90	82.10	45.70
1-12 All expenditure groups	335.90	450.20	656.90	775.40	1003.80	508.50
13 Other expenditure items	40.60	74.70	112.10	111.40	152.30	79.30
Total expenditure	**376.60**	**524.90**	**769.10**	**886.80**	**1,156.10**	**587.90**
Average weekly expenditure per person (£)						
Total expenditure	**239.10**	**249.20**	**256.60**	**238.20**	**235.80**	**248.70**

Note: The commodity and service categories are not comparable to those in publications before 2001-02.

Please see background notes for symbols and conventions used in this report.

1 Excludes households where the household reference person was on a Government-supported training scheme.

2 Excluding mortgage interest payments, council tax and Northern Ireland rates.

Source: Office for National Statistics

Table A21

Household expenditure by age at which the household reference person completed continuous full-time education

UK, financial year ending 2020

	Aged 14 and under	Aged 15	Aged 16	Aged 17 and under 19	Aged 19 and under 22	Aged 22 or over
Weighted number of households (thousands)	260	1,650	6,360	4,780	4,290	4,000
Total number of households in sample	50	360	1,280	940	790	750
Total number of persons in sample	110	740	3,140	2,440	2,100	1,980
Total number of adults in sample	80	620	2,410	1,770	1,500	1,410
Weighted average number of persons per household	2.7	2.2	2.5	2.7	2.7	2.7
Weighted average age of head of household	53	57	50	46	44	44

Commodity or service	Average weekly household expenditure (£)					
1 Food & non-alcoholic drinks	71.40	58.20	62.20	69.20	69.50	74.20
2 Alcoholic drinks, tobacco & narcotics	12.10	15.40	15.10	14.90	12.20	12.90
3 Clothing & footwear	15.80	17.30	23.80	26.50	30.80	30.60
4 Housing (net)[1], fuel & power	90.60	69.10	76.10	86.40	101.00	111.00
5 Household goods & services	20.80	34.40	36.80	41.70	38.30	50.00
6 Health	[7.40]	5.50	6.40	7.90	8.80	9.50
7 Transport	47.90	64.70	86.00	98.90	99.40	108.80
8 Communication	17.70	18.80	23.10	23.30	24.00	23.90
9 Recreation & culture	39.50	53.30	74.50	78.70	88.10	93.60
10 Education	..	..	2.70	5.80	3.90	13.00
11 Restaurants & hotels	31.10	32.80	51.80	57.30	65.20	76.60
12 Miscellaneous goods & services	22.20	29.50	40.70	49.40	56.30	60.40
1-12 All expenditure groups	377.80	399.20	499.20	560.00	597.40	664.70
13 Other expenditure items	31.80	46.60	66.40	83.90	109.20	132.80
Total expenditure	**409.60**	**445.80**	**565.60**	**643.90**	**706.60**	**797.50**
Average weekly expenditure per person (£)						
Total expenditure	**152.40**	**206.10**	**225.40**	**241.50**	**264.80**	**299.20**

Note: The commodity and service categories are not comparable to those in publications before 2001-02.

Please see background notes for symbols and conventions used in this report.

1 Excluding mortgage interest payments, council tax and Northern Ireland rates.

Source: Office for National Statistics

Table A22

Household expenditure by socio-economic classification of household reference person

UK, financial year ending 2020

Commodity or service	Large employers and higher managerial	Higher professional	Lower managerial and professional	Intermediate	Small employers	Lower supervisory	Semi-routine	Routine	Long-term unemployed[1]	Students	Occupation not stated[2]	All households
Weighted number of households (thousands)	1,100	3,150	5,390	1,930	1,910	1,500	2,060	1,850	440	380	8,110	27,820
Total number of households in sample	200	570	1,030	390	350	290	410	360	90	70	1,700	5,440
Total number of persons in sample	570	1,530	2,720	940	920	810	1,060	900	190	180	2,850	12,670
Total number of adults in sample	410	1,100	2,000	720	690	560	740	650	120	140	2,750	9,880
Weighted average number of persons per household	2.9	2.7	2.6	2.5	2.8	2.7	2.7	2.5	2.3	2.7	1.7	2.4
Average weekly household expenditure (£)												
1 Food & non-alcoholic drinks	87.70	77.20	69.30	65.10	70.70	63.60	62.30	56.50	49.20	58.20	52.60	63.70
2 Alcoholic drinks, tobacco & narcotics	18.40	14.30	14.40	12.60	14.60	13.20	13.50	10.20	7.50	13.30	11.10	12.90
3 Clothing & footwear	36.60	34.00	31.50	26.70	22.20	22.70	19.20	22.00	11.20	24.10	13.70	23.40
4 Housing (net)[3], fuel & power	92.70	102.00	87.50	88.80	97.80	97.70	99.20	90.30	72.20	214.90	52.20	83.00
5 Household goods & services	58.50	51.00	41.10	38.60	40.00	43.10	35.40	29.80	12.80	18.80	26.20	36.50
6 Health	16.20	9.20	8.20	8.10	7.40	4.50	5.20	4.60	1.20	5.20	9.70	8.20
7 Transport	141.90	129.70	105.20	90.90	96.60	86.50	62.70	73.80	24.00	69.10	42.80	81.60
8 Communication	28.80	24.40	25.70	23.60	23.80	22.20	23.20	20.20	12.70	16.80	15.50	21.40
9 Recreation & culture	132.90	106.70	89.60	64.40	69.50	70.30	48.30	53.10	20.50	63.50	64.30	74.80
10 Education	[18.20]	11.20	5.40	5.60	[1.70]	4.40	2.30	[1.10]	..	[26.50]	[0.50]	4.50
11 Restaurants & hotels	95.80	84.90	71.30	50.00	54.40	47.10	36.20	36.30	19.60	75.80	32.50	52.90
12 Miscellaneous goods & services	70.30	62.80	59.90	46.60	45.50	43.80	34.80	33.60	11.90	49.20	33.50	45.70
1-12 All expenditure groups	798.10	707.50	609.20	521.00	544.20	519.10	442.50	431.50	243.80	635.40	354.50	508.50
13 Other expenditure items	153.50	142.90	104.60	70.90	80.10	75.50	56.80	51.20	16.60	51.30	47.20	79.30
Total expenditure	**951.70**	**850.40**	**713.80**	**591.80**	**624.40**	**594.50**	**499.20**	**482.70**	**260.40**	**686.70**	**401.80**	**587.90**
Average weekly expenditure per person (£)												
Total expenditure	**330.60**	**313.20**	**269.60**	**236.60**	**226.90**	**217.00**	**188.20**	**194.00**	**113.70**	**256.60**	**241.80**	**248.70**

Note: Changes to categories of socio-economic classification were made in 2011
The commodity and service categories are not comparable to those in publications before 2001-02.
Please see background notes for symbols and conventions used in this report.
1 Includes those who have never worked.
2 Includes those who are economically inactive.
3 Excludes mortgage interest payments, council tax and Northern Ireland rates.

Source: Office for National Statistics

Table A23

Expenditure by household composition

UK, financial year ending 2020

| | Retired households | | | | Non-retired | | Retired and non-retired households | | | | | | |
| | State pension[1] | | Other retired | | | | One adult | | Two adults | | | Three or more adults | |
	One person	Two adults	One person	Two adults	One person	Two adults	with one child	with two or more children	with one child	with two children	with three or more children	without children	with children
Weighted number of households (thousands)	770	470	2,780	2,770	4,370	6,220	620	540	2,190	2,540	960	2,520	1,080
Total number of households in sample	140	120	530	640	840	1,190	140	130	420	510	190	410	170
Total number of persons in sample	140	240	530	1,290	840	2,390	290	440	1,270	2,040	990	1,370	850
Total number of adults in sample	140	240	530	1,290	840	2,390	140	130	850	1,020	370	1,370	570
Weighted average number of persons per household	1.0	2.0	1.0	2.0	1.0	2.0	2.0	3.4	3.0	4.0	5.2	3.4	5.0
Commodity or service					Average weekly household expenditure (£)								
1 Food & non-alcoholic drinks	34.00	64.40	34.40	67.50	32.50	63.50	41.10	55.00	71.70	88.20	103.90	97.90	105.40
2 Alcoholic drinks, tobacco & narcotics	6.30	11.80	6.30	13.40	9.20	15.90	7.50	6.60	12.40	11.60	10.70	24.60	17.30
3 Clothing & footwear	7.90	9.50	8.00	19.10	11.00	24.00	16.90	23.80	31.40	33.50	31.10	40.10	55.30
4 Housing(net)[2], fuel & power	46.30	46.90	46.40	53.00	74.00	92.30	99.40	94.40	99.90	98.00	102.20	119.00	92.30
5 Household goods & services	13.70	33.20	16.90	39.70	19.10	42.50	21.90	21.20	50.70	46.70	49.70	51.70	48.70
6 Health	3.10	7.50	9.30	12.20	5.30	10.50	2.50	3.10	5.30	7.10	7.20	11.00	6.20
7 Transport	17.70	41.70	25.00	63.20	45.20	101.00	38.60	43.10	100.60	115.80	106.60	137.20	146.40
8 Communication	10.90	16.80	12.50	18.70	13.60	23.80	15.50	17.80	25.60	25.70	27.00	31.10	36.40
9 Recreation & culture	31.30	58.30	42.50	99.70	33.70	87.40	37.70	42.10	80.40	103.20	83.20	108.90	97.50
10 Education	:	:	:	:	[1.40]	2.70	[10.70]	[4.20]	5.30	13.60	17.30	6.70	11.10
11 Restaurants & hotels	11.70	29.10	18.10	50.40	27.10	63.30	21.70	31.70	61.60	74.30	61.00	93.90	90.20
12 Miscellaneous goods & services	42.80	25.90	22.30	45.50	27.40	47.50	29.60	28.00	60.80	64.90	58.90	62.40	71.20
1-12 All expenditure groups	225.70	345.10	241.70	483.40	299.40	574.40	342.90	371.00	605.70	682.70	658.80	784.40	778.00
13 Other expenditure items	31.30	40.10	33.00	67.80	57.20	90.10	39.80	37.10	102.60	118.50	113.90	110.40	107.80
Total expenditure	**257.00**	**385.20**	**274.70**	**551.10**	**356.60**	**664.50**	**382.80**	**408.10**	**708.30**	**801.20**	**772.70**	**894.80**	**885.80**
Average weekly expenditure per person (£)													
Total expenditure	**257.00**	**192.60**	**274.70**	**275.60**	**356.60**	**332.30**	**191.40**	**118.60**	**236.10**	**200.30**	**147.90**	**259.80**	**177.30**

Note: The commodity and service categories are not comparable to those in publications before 2001-02.

Please see background notes for symbols and conventions used in this report.

1 Mainly dependent on state pensions and not economically active.

2 Excluding mortgage interest payments, council tax and Northern Ireland rates.

Source: Office for National Statistics

Table A26

Expenditure of one adult non-retired households by gross income quintile group[1]

UK, financial year ending 2018 to financial year ending 2020

	Lowest twenty per cent	Second quintile group	Third quintile group	Fourth quintile group	Highest twenty per cent	All house-holds
Lower boundary of group (gross income: £ per week)[2]		335	568	873	1,296	
Average weighted number of households (thousands)	1,630	1,100	790	360	200	4,080
Total number of households in sample (over 3 years)	1,030	680	450	210	110	2,470
Total number of persons in sample (over 3 years)	1,030	680	450	210	110	2,470
Total number of adults in sample (over 3 years)	1,030	680	450	210	110	2,470
Weighted average number of persons per household	1.0	1.0	1.0	1.0	1.0	1.0
Commodity or service	Average weekly household expenditure (£)					
1 Food & non-alcoholic drinks	28.50	31.40	33.90	37.80	42.70	31.90
2 Alcoholic drinks, tobacco & narcotics	9.70	8.70	9.00	10.30	10.50	9.40
3 Clothing & footwear	6.70	11.20	11.80	17.20	25.60	10.80
4 Housing(net)[3], fuel & power	56.70	79.60	81.10	81.70	113.40	72.50
5 Household goods & services	13.70	20.70	27.80	37.70	74.30	23.40
6 Health	3.40	4.10	5.40	9.50	13.40	5.00
7 Transport	23.30	43.10	62.70	87.20	125.10	46.90
8 Communication	10.30	13.80	16.50	17.20	16.40	13.30
9 Recreation & culture	21.20	37.10	40.70	73.30	71.10	36.10
10 Education	..	[2.20]	[1.30]	..	..	3.00
11 Restaurants & hotels	14.70	23.20	38.90	47.30	69.80	27.20
12 Miscellaneous goods & services	13.80	25.30	29.40	38.30	44.30	23.60
1-12 All expenditure groups	205.20	300.30	358.50	467.20	609.00	303.10
13 Other expenditure items	23.40	45.30	64.00	92.30	163.10	50.50
Total expenditure	**228.60**	**345.60**	**422.50**	**559.50**	**772.20**	**353.60**
Average weekly expenditure per person (£)						
Total expenditure	**228.60**	**345.60**	**422.50**	**559.50**	**772.20**	**353.60**

Note: The commodity and service categories are not comparable to those in publications before 2001-02.

Please see background notes for symbols and conventions used in this report.

This table is based on a three year average.

1 Mainly dependent on state pensions and not economically active.

2 Lower boundary of 2016-17 gross income quintile groups (£ per week).

3 Excluding mortgage interest payments, council tax and Northern Ireland rates.

Source: Office for National Statistics

Table A29

Expenditure of two adult non-retired households by gross income quintile group[1]

UK, financial year ending 2018 to financial year ending 2020

	Lowest twenty per cent	Second quintile group	Third quintile group	Fourth quintile group	Highest twenty per cent	All house-holds
Lower boundary of group (gross income: £ per week)[2]		335	568	873	1,296	
Average weighted number of households (thousands)	490	830	1,390	1,790	1,560	6,060
Total number of households in sample (over 3 years)	300	530	840	1,050	900	3,600
Total number of persons in sample (over 3 years)	600	1,060	1,670	2,090	1,790	7,210
Total number of adults in sample (over 3 years)	600	1,060	1,670	2,090	1,790	7,210
Weighted average number of persons per household	2.0	2.0	2.0	2.0	2.0	2.0

Commodity or service	Average weekly household expenditure (£)					
1 Food & non-alcoholic drinks	51.50	55.50	59.90	61.60	69.40	61.60
2 Alcoholic drinks, tobacco & narcotics	13.60	14.30	15.60	15.90	16.70	15.60
3 Clothing & footwear	15.20	14.20	20.00	25.70	36.10	24.60
4 Housing(net)[3], fuel & power	72.70	79.20	92.20	90.10	89.70	87.70
5 Household goods & services	23.30	29.60	38.60	42.90	75.10	46.80
6 Health	4.40	7.50	5.20	9.10	12.80	8.50
7 Transport	47.20	65.10	84.50	102.30	146.50	100.10
8 Communication	14.70	18.40	21.40	22.90	25.60	21.90
9 Recreation & culture	53.40	52.40	71.20	89.40	131.10	88.00
10 Education	..	..	3.10	5.30	8.50	4.80
11 Restaurants & hotels	33.20	35.40	53.50	61.50	100.80	64.00
12 Miscellaneous goods & services	24.70	32.80	39.30	47.40	68.80	47.30
1-12 All expenditure groups	354.60	405.80	504.40	574.10	781.00	570.80
13 Other expenditure items	35.40	49.20	63.10	98.00	158.40	94.00
Total expenditure	**390.00**	**455.10**	**567.60**	**672.10**	**939.50**	**664.80**

Average weekly expenditure per person (£)						
Total expenditure	**195.00**	**227.50**	**283.80**	**336.00**	**469.70**	**332.40**

Note: The commodity and service categories are not comparable to those in publications before 2001-02.

Please see background notes for symbols and conventions used in this report.

This table is based on a three year average.

1 Mainly dependent on state pensions and not economically active.

2 Lower boundary of 2019-20 gross income quintile groups (£ per week).

3 Excluding mortgage interest payments, council tax and Northern Ireland rates.

Source: Office for National Statistics

Table A32

Household expenditure by tenure

UK, financial year ending 2020

	Owners			Social rented from			Rent free	Private rented[4]			All tenures
	Owned outright	Buying with a mortgage[1]	All	Council[2]	Registered Social Landlord[3]	All		Rent paid, unfurnished[5]	Rent paid, furnished	All	
Weighted number of households (thousands)	9,900	8,520	18,430	2,200	2,340	4,540	180	3,760	910	4,850	27,820
Total number of households in sample	2,060	1,630	3,680	450	440	890	40	690	130	860	5,440
Total number of persons in sample	3,930	4,690	8,620	1,030	920	1,950	90	1,690	320	2,090	12,670
Total number of adults in sample	3,710	3,270	6,970	730	680	1,410	60	1,170	270	1,500	9,880
Weighted average number of persons per house	1.9	2.9	2.4	2.4	2.1	2.3	2.0	2.5	2.5	2.4	2.4
Commodity or service					Average weekly household expenditure (£)						
1 Food & non-alcoholic drinks	62.50	76.20	68.80	52.80	48.20	50.40	55.90	56.90	56.00	56.70	63.70
2 Alcoholic drinks, tobacco & narcotics	12.70	15.30	13.90	11.70	9.70	10.70	[8.30]	12.20	9.80	11.60	12.90
3 Clothing & footwear	20.40	33.50	26.50	14.40	13.50	14.00	14.10	20.20	22.60	20.40	23.40
4 Housing(net)[6]. fuel & power	48.40	51.40	49.80	88.10	97.80	93.10	28.40	190.90	270.40	199.70	83.00
5 Household goods & services	37.60	54.40	45.40	17.80	17.80	17.80	11.70	22.40	14.10	20.40	36.50
6 Health	11.40	8.70	10.10	3.90	3.70	3.80	7.90	4.80	5.10	5.00	8.20
7 Transport	70.90	124.00	95.40	34.50	37.90	36.30	74.40	69.70	78.60	71.50	81.60
8 Communication	19.80	26.60	23.00	17.30	15.60	16.40	13.90	20.90	17.30	19.90	21.40
9 Recreation & culture	87.80	96.90	92.10	34.70	30.20	32.40	39.30	50.60	43.20	48.80	74.80
10 Education	3.20	6.80	4.90	[0.20]	[1.00]	0.60	..	6.20	..	6.80	4.50
11 Restaurants & hotels	50.10	74.60	61.40	23.60	23.70	23.60	41.80	44.00	63.90	47.70	52.90
12 Miscellaneous goods & services	46.40	60.60	52.90	22.10	18.10	20.10	26.70	44.10	36.30	42.00	45.70
1-12 All expenditure groups	471.10	629.00	544.10	321.20	317.20	319.10	347.50	542.80	623.00	550.50	508.50
13 Other expenditure items	62.80	140.20	98.60	24.20	25.60	24.90	62.40	52.30	75.70	57.00	79.30
Total expenditure	533.90	769.20	642.70	345.30	342.80	344.00	409.90	595.10	698.70	607.50	587.90
Average weekly expenditure per person (£)											
Total expenditure	280.20	264.50	271.30	143.80	161.90	152.60	209.60	242.40	279.90	248.60	248.70

Note: The commodity and service categories are not comparable to those in publications before 2001-02.
Please see background notes for symbols and conventions used in this report.
1 Including shared owners (who own part of the equity and pay mortgage, part rent).
2 "Council" includes local authorities, New Towns and Scottish Homes, but see note 3 below.
3 Formerly Housing Associations.
4 All tenants whose accommodation goes with the job of someone in the household are allocated to "rented privately", even if the landlord is a local authority or housing association or Housing Action Trust, or if the accommodation is rent free. Squatters are also included in this category.
5 "Unfurnished" includes the answers: "partly furnished".
6 Excluding mortgage interest payments, council tax and Northern Ireland rates.

Source: Office for National Statistics

Table A33

Household expenditure by countries and regions

UK, financial year ending 2018 to financial year ending 2020

	United Kingdom	England	North East	North West	Yorkshire and The Humber	East Midlands	West Midlands	East	London	South East	South West	Wales	Scotland	Northern Ireland
	K02000001	E92000001	E12000001	E12000002	E12000003	E12000004	E12000005	E12000006	E12000007	E12000008	E12000009	W92000004	S92000003	N92000002
Average weighted number of households (thousands)	27,480	22,920	1,170	3,100	2,370	1,980	2,420	2,580	3,290	3,660	2,340	1,360	2,450	760
Total number of households in sample (over 3 years)	16,320	12,120	690	1,650	1,330	1,190	1,240	1,460	1,260	1,850	1,450	730	2,330	1,150
Total number of persons in sample (over 3 years)	38,230	28,870	1,550	3,800	3,080	2,850	2,950	3,530	3,280	4,440	3,410	1,680	5,010	2,670
Total number of adults in sample (over 3 years)	29,800	22,440	1,240	2,960	2,410	2,220	2,290	2,730	2,460	3,450	2,680	1,320	4,010	2,030
Weighted average number of persons per household	2.4	2.4	2.2	2.3	2.3	2.4	2.4	2.4	2.7	2.5	2.3	2.3	2.2	2.4
Commodity or service					Average weekly household expenditure (£)									
1 Food & non-alcoholic drinks	62.20	62.90	57.10	57.80	56.10	62.20	60.40	63.50	69.90	68.70	63.10	57.40	57.60	65.10
2 Alcoholic drinks, tobacco & narcotics	12.80	12.60	13.40	13.50	12.80	13.00	11.90	13.30	11.00	12.70	12.60	11.80	14.90	14.60
3 Clothing & footwear	24.20	24.20	21.00	25.00	22.30	23.30	20.10	23.70	28.50	26.70	22.50	20.70	23.90	30.00
4 Housing (net)[1], fuel & power	79.50	82.70	60.20	68.50	64.30	67.20	71.10	82.30	136.10	84.90	78.70	64.80	65.70	54.10
5 Household goods & services	39.50	40.40	38.20	38.20	40.50	40.00	36.00	40.10	37.30	46.40	44.80	34.00	35.60	31.50
6 Health	7.70	8.00	5.30	5.30	6.50	7.30	8.70	9.00	8.90	10.20	8.70	6.20	6.00	7.00
7 Transport	82.60	84.00	73.90	70.70	76.90	84.70	73.50	90.60	82.30	100.30	93.80	78.10	75.30	73.70
8 Communication	20.20	20.40	18.80	19.20	18.70	19.80	19.90	20.50	21.70	22.50	19.90	18.90	19.30	20.00
9 Recreation & culture	75.60	77.40	72.20	66.70	72.80	75.80	68.40	81.20	64.90	103.70	82.30	74.40	67.00	51.70
10 Education	6.30	7.00	1.60	4.00	3.90	5.30	5.00	4.80	16.70	8.90	6.40	2.60	2.30	2.80
11 Restaurants & hotels	51.50	53.00	44.60	49.60	49.50	48.60	42.80	50.40	67.00	59.90	52.20	42.90	43.80	46.30
12 Miscellaneous goods & services	45.00	46.50	34.30	43.10	41.80	46.10	41.20	47.60	50.70	54.10	48.90	40.00	35.70	39.10
1-12 All expenditure groups	507.30	519.30	440.60	461.80	466.10	493.40	458.80	526.90	595.00	598.90	533.90	451.70	447.10	435.90
13 Other expenditure items	77.90	81.20	58.70	68.20	63.80	73.60	66.30	80.70	108.10	99.70	82.80	61.30	65.30	50.40
Total expenditure	585.20	600.50	499.30	530.00	529.90	567.00	525.20	607.70	703.10	698.60	616.60	513.00	512.40	486.40
Average weekly expenditure per person (£)														
Total expenditure	245.90	249.70	225.20	229.50	233.70	239.90	219.30	255.40	259.50	285.00	263.90	225.30	234.80	199.00

Note: The commodity and service categories are not comparable to those in publications before 2001-02.

Please see background notes for symbols and conventions used in this report.

This table is based on a three year average.

1 Excluding mortgage interest payments, council tax and Northern Ireland rates.

Source: Office for National Statistics

Table A34

Household expenditure as a percentage of total expenditure by countries and regions

UK, financial year ending 2018 to financial year ending 2020

Commodity or service	United Kingdom	England	North East	North West	Yorkshire and The Humber	East Midlands	West Midlands	East	London	South East	South West	Wales	Scotland	Northern Ireland
	K02000001	E92000001	E12000001	E12000002	E12000003	E12000004	E12000005	E12000006	E12000007	E12000008	E12000009	W92000004	S92000003	N92000002
Average weighted number of households (thousands)	27,480	22,920	1,170	3,100	2,370	1,980	2,420	2,580	3,290	3,660	2,340	1,360	2,450	760
Total number of households in sample (over 3 years)	16,320	12,120	690	1,650	1,330	1,190	1,240	1,460	1,260	1,850	1,450	730	2,330	1,150
Total number of persons in sample (over 3 years)	38,230	28,870	1,550	3,800	3,080	2,850	2,950	3,530	3,280	4,440	3,410	1,680	5,010	2,670
Total number of adults in sample (over 3 years)	29,800	22,440	1,240	2,960	2,410	2,220	2,290	2,730	2,460	3,450	2,680	1,320	4,010	2,030
Weighted average number of persons per household	2.4	2.4	2.2	2.3	2.3	2.4	2.4	2.4	2.7	2.5	2.3	2.3	2.2	2.4
Percentage of total expenditure														
1 Food & non-alcoholic drinks	11	10	11	11	11	11	11	10	10	10	10	11	11	13
2 Alcoholic drinks, tobacco & narcotics	2	2	3	3	2	2	2	2	2	2	2	2	3	3
3 Clothing & footwear	4	4	4	5	4	4	4	4	4	4	4	4	5	6
4 Housing (net)[1], fuel & power	14	14	12	13	12	12	14	14	19	12	13	13	13	11
5 Household goods & services	7	7	8	7	8	7	7	7	5	7	7	7	7	6
6 Health	1	1	1	1	1	1	2	1	1	1	1	1	1	1
7 Transport	14	14	15	13	15	15	14	15	12	14	15	15	15	15
8 Communication	3	3	4	4	4	3	4	3	3	3	3	4	4	4
9 Recreation & culture	13	13	14	13	14	13	13	13	9	15	13	15	13	11
10 Education	1	1	0	1	1	1	1	1	2	1	1	1	0	1
11 Restaurants & hotels	9	9	9	9	9	9	8	8	10	9	8	8	9	10
12 Miscellaneous goods & services	8	8	7	8	8	8	8	8	7	8	8	8	7	8
1-12 All expenditure groups	87	86	88	87	88	87	87	87	85	86	87	88	87	90
13 Other expenditure items	13	14	12	13	12	13	13	13	15	14	13	12	13	10
Total expenditure	100	100	100	100	100	100	100	100	100	100	100	100	100	100

Note: The commodity and service categories are not comparable to those in publications before 2001-02.
Please see background notes for symbols and conventions used in this report.
This table is based on a three year average.
1 Excluding mortgage interest payments, council tax and Northern Ireland rates.

Source: Office for National Statistics

Table A35

Detailed household expenditure by countries and regions

UK, financial year ending 2018 to financial year ending 2020

Commodity or service	United Kingdom	England	North East	North West	Yorkshire and the Humber	East Midlands	West Midlands	East	London	South East	South West	Wales	Scotland	Northern Ireland
	K02000001	E92000001	E12000001	E12000002	E12000003	E12000004	E12000005	E12000006	E12000007	E12000008	E12000009	W92000004	S92000003	N92000002
Average weighted number of households (thousands)	27,480	22,920	1,170	3,100	2,370	1,980	2,420	2,580	3,290	3,660	2,340	1,360	2,450	760
Total number of households in sample (over 3 years)	16,320	12,120	690	1,650	1,330	1,190	1,240	1,460	1,260	1,850	1,450	730	2,330	1,150
Total number of persons in sample (over 3 years)	38,230	28,870	1,550	3,800	3,080	2,850	2,950	3,530	3,280	4,440	3,410	1,680	5,010	2,670
Total number of adults in sample (over 3 years)	29,800	22,440	1,240	2,960	2,410	2,220	2,290	2,730	2,460	3,450	2,680	1,320	4,010	2,030
Weighted average number of persons per household	2.4	2.4	2.2	2.3	2.3	2.4	2.4	2.4	2.7	2.5	2.3	2.3	2.2	2.4
Commodity or service														
					Average weekly household expenditure (£)									
1 Food & non-alcoholic drinks	62.20	62.90	57.10	57.80	56.10	62.20	60.40	63.50	69.90	68.70	63.10	57.40	57.60	65.10
1.1 Food	57.00	57.70	52.10	53.00	51.50	56.90	55.20	58.20	64.30	63.20	58.10	52.40	52.10	59.20
1.1.1 Bread, rice and cereals	5.60	5.70	5.00	5.20	5.10	5.60	5.20	5.60	6.50	6.00	5.40	5.30	5.10	6.10
1.1.2 Pasta products	0.40	0.40	0.40	0.40	0.40	0.40	0.40	0.50	0.60	0.50	0.40	0.40	0.50	0.40
1.1.3 Buns, cakes, biscuits etc.	4.00	4.00	3.90	3.70	3.50	4.10	4.00	4.00	4.10	4.20	4.20	3.40	3.80	4.90
1.1.4 Pastry (savoury)	1.00	1.00	1.00	0.90	0.90	1.00	0.80	1.00	0.90	1.10	1.00	0.90	0.90	0.90
1.1.5 Beef (fresh, chilled or frozen)	1.90	1.90	2.10	1.90	1.80	2.00	2.00	2.00	1.70	1.90	1.80	1.80	1.90	3.20
1.1.6 Pork (fresh, chilled or frozen)	0.60	0.60	0.60	0.50	0.60	0.60	0.60	0.70	0.50	0.60	0.60	0.60	0.40	0.60
1.1.7 Lamb (fresh, chilled or frozen)	0.60	0.70	0.30	0.60	0.50	0.70	0.70	0.50	1.30	0.70	0.60	0.50	0.20	0.30
1.1.8 Poultry (fresh, chilled or frozen)	2.40	2.40	2.20	2.20	2.10	2.30	2.40	2.40	3.20	2.40	2.30	2.10	2.00	2.60
1.1.9 Bacon and ham	0.80	0.80	0.90	0.80	0.90	0.90	0.90	0.80	0.50	0.90	0.90	0.90	0.80	1.30
1.1.10 Other meat and meat preparations	6.50	6.50	7.30	6.60	6.30	6.60	6.30	6.60	5.50	6.90	6.50	6.60	6.80	7.80
1.1.11 Fish and fish products	3.00	3.10	2.50	2.70	2.80	2.70	2.60	3.30	4.20	3.60	3.00	2.40	2.50	2.20
1.1.12 Milk	2.20	2.20	1.90	2.20	2.10	2.10	2.30	2.10	2.10	2.20	2.40	2.20	2.00	2.50
1.1.13 Cheese and curd	2.10	2.20	1.80	1.80	1.90	2.10	2.10	2.30	2.30	2.50	2.30	1.80	1.80	1.70
1.1.14 Eggs	0.70	0.80	0.70	0.60	0.60	0.70	0.70	0.70	1.00	0.80	0.70	0.70	0.70	0.70
1.1.15 Other milk products	2.30	2.40	1.90	2.10	2.10	2.40	2.10	2.40	2.60	2.70	2.50	2.20	2.10	2.40
1.1.16 Butter	0.50	0.50	0.40	0.50	0.40	0.50	0.40	0.50	0.50	0.50	0.50	0.60	0.40	0.70
1.1.17 Margarine, other vegetable fats and peanut butter	0.60	0.60	0.60	0.60	0.60	0.70	0.60	0.60	0.50	0.70	0.60	0.60	0.70	0.50
1.1.18 Cooking oils and fats	0.40	0.40	0.30	0.30	0.40	0.30	0.30	0.30	0.70	0.40	0.30	0.30	0.20	0.30
1.1.19 Fresh fruit	4.00	4.10	3.30	3.50	3.30	3.90	3.70	4.10	5.30	4.70	4.30	3.50	3.50	3.70
1.1.20 Other fresh, chilled or frozen fruits	0.50	0.50	0.40	0.50	0.40	0.40	0.40	0.50	0.70	0.50	0.40	0.40	0.40	0.50
1.1.21 Dried fruit and nuts	0.90	0.90	0.60	0.70	0.70	0.80	0.70	0.90	1.40	1.10	1.00	0.70	0.60	0.50
1.1.22 Preserved fruit and fruit based products	0.20	0.20	0.10	0.10	0.10	0.20	0.20	0.20	0.20	0.20	0.10	0.10	0.10	0.10
1.1.23 Fresh vegetables	4.40	4.60	3.10	3.60	3.80	4.40	4.20	4.60	6.00	5.30	4.80	3.80	3.30	3.20
1.1.24 Dried vegetables	0.10	0.10	0.00-	0.00-	0.10	0.10	0.00-	0.00-	0.10	0.10	0.00-	0.00-	0.10	0.00-
1.1.25 Other preserved or processed vegetables	1.80	1.80	1.50	1.60	1.50	1.70	1.70	1.80	2.20	2.20	1.90	1.50	1.50	1.60
1.1.26 Potatoes	0.70	0.70	0.70	0.70	0.70	0.80	0.80	0.80	0.70	0.80	0.80	0.60	0.60	1.10
1.1.27 Other tubers and products of tuber vegetables	1.80	1.70	1.90	1.70	1.60	1.80	1.90	1.70	1.50	1.80	1.70	1.80	2.00	2.10
1.1.28 Sugar and sugar products	0.40	0.40	0.30	0.40	0.30	0.40	0.40	0.40	0.40	0.50	0.40	0.30	0.30	0.30
1.1.29 Jams, marmalades	0.30	0.30	0.20	0.30	0.20	0.30	0.30	0.30	0.40	0.40	0.30	0.30	0.30	0.40
1.1.30 Chocolate	2.20	2.20	2.20	2.00	2.00	2.10	2.10	2.30	1.90	2.50	2.20	2.20	2.20	2.30
1.1.31 Confectionery products	0.80	0.80	0.90	0.80	0.70	0.90	0.80	0.80	0.70	0.80	0.70	0.80	0.90	0.90
1.1.32 Edible ices and ice cream	0.70	0.70	0.70	0.70	0.60	0.70	0.70	0.80	0.80	0.80	0.70	0.80	0.70	0.70
1.1.33 Other food products	2.70	2.70	2.40	2.50	2.50	2.80	2.40	2.80	3.10	3.00	2.70	2.60	2.50	2.60
1.2 Non-alcoholic drinks	5.20	5.20	5.00	4.80	4.60	5.30	5.10	5.30	5.60	5.50	5.10	4.90	5.50	6.00
1.2.1 Coffee	1.00	1.00	1.00	1.00	0.90	1.10	1.00	1.00	0.80	1.20	1.10	1.10	0.90	1.00
1.2.2 Tea	0.50	0.50	0.40	0.40	0.40	0.40	0.50	0.50	0.50	0.50	0.50	0.40	0.40	0.50
1.2.3 Cocoa and powdered chocolate	0.10	0.10	0.10	0.10	0.10	0.10	0.10	0.10	0.10	0.20	0.10	0.10	0.10	0.10
1.2.4 Fruit and vegetable juices (inc. fruit squash)	1.10	1.10	0.80	1.00	0.90	1.00	1.00	1.20	1.30	1.20	1.00	0.90	1.10	1.00
1.2.5 Mineral or spring waters	0.40	0.40	0.30	0.40	0.30	0.30	0.30	0.40	0.70	0.30	0.30	0.30	0.30	0.50
1.2.6 Soft drinks (inc. fizzy and ready to drink fruit drinks)	2.20	2.10	2.40	2.00	2.00	2.30	2.20	2.10	2.20	2.00	2.00	2.10	2.70	2.90

Note: The commodity and service categories are not comparable to those in publications before 2001-02.
The numbering system is sequential, it does not use actual COICOP codes.
Please see background notes for symbols and conventions used in this report.
This table is based on a three year average.

Table A35

Detailed household expenditure by countries and regions (cont.)

UK, financial year ending 2018 to financial year ending 2020

Commodity or service	United Kingdom	England	North East	North West	Yorkshire and The Humber	East Midlands	West Midlands	East	London	South East	South West	Wales	Scotland	Northern Ireland
						Average weekly household expenditure (£)								
2 Alcoholic drink, tobacco & narcotics	**12.80**	**12.60**	**13.40**	**13.50**	**12.80**	**13.00**	**11.90**	**13.30**	**11.00**	**12.70**	**12.60**	**11.80**	**14.90**	**14.60**
2.1 Alcoholic drinks	9.10	9.10	9.10	9.80	9.00	9.20	8.80	10.20	7.50	9.40	9.20	8.70	9.10	8.10
2.1.1 Spirits and liqueurs (brought home)	2.10	2.00	2.50	2.20	1.90	2.20	2.00	2.40	1.30	1.90	2.00	2.30	2.90	2.20
2.1.2 Wines, fortified wines (brought home)	4.50	4.60	4.00	5.00	4.30	4.30	4.20	5.30	4.10	5.30	4.70	4.10	4.20	3.60
2.1.3 Beer, lager, ciders and perry (brought home)	2.40	2.40	2.60	2.60	2.80	2.70	2.50	2.40	2.10	2.20	2.50	2.20	2.00	2.20
2.1.4 Alcopops (brought home)	0.00~	0.00~	[0.10]	[0.00]	..	[0.00]	[0.00]	[0.00]	..	[0.00]	[0.00]	..	0.00~	0.10
2.2 Tobacco and narcotics	3.80	3.50	4.30	3.70	3.90	3.80	3.10	3.10	3.60	3.40	3.40	3.10	5.80	6.50
2.2.1 Cigarettes	2.60	2.40	3.10	2.70	2.70	2.30	2.10	2.10	2.60	2.40	1.90	1.70	4.70	5.20
2.2.2 Cigars, other tobacco products and narcotics	1.10	1.10	1.20	1.00	1.20	1.60	1.00	1.00	1.00	0.90	1.60	1.40	1.20	1.20
3 Clothing & footwear	**24.20**	**24.20**	**21.00**	**25.00**	**22.30**	**23.30**	**20.10**	**23.70**	**28.50**	**26.70**	**22.50**	**20.70**	**23.90**	**30.00**
3.1 Clothing	19.20	19.30	16.10	19.60	17.80	18.90	15.60	19.20	22.40	21.80	18.00	16.40	19.10	22.90
3.1.1 Men's outer garments	4.90	4.90	4.00	4.80	5.00	5.10	3.80	4.50	6.20	5.60	4.10	3.80	4.30	6.70
3.1.2 Men's under garments	0.50	0.50	0.50	0.50	0.40	0.70	0.40	0.70	0.50	0.60	0.50	0.50	0.50	0.60
3.1.3 Women's outer garments	8.40	8.40	7.30	8.60	7.30	7.90	6.70	8.20	9.90	9.40	8.20	7.40	8.50	8.80
3.1.4 Women's under garments	1.20	1.20	0.80	1.30	1.10	1.30	1.00	1.20	1.20	1.50	1.30	0.90	1.20	1.40
3.1.5 Boys' outer garments (5-15)	0.90	0.80	0.70	1.00	0.90	0.70	0.80	0.90	0.80	0.80	0.60	0.70	1.10	1.30
3.1.6 Girls' outer garments (5-15)	1.00	1.00	1.00	1.10	1.10	0.90	1.00	1.30	1.00	1.00	0.90	1.00	1.00	1.40
3.1.7 Infants' outer garments (under 5)	0.70	0.60	0.40	0.80	0.60	0.60	0.50	0.70	0.60	0.70	0.50	0.50	0.80	0.90
3.1.8 Children's under garments (under 16)	0.40	0.40	0.30	0.50	0.40	0.40	0.30	0.40	0.50	0.40	0.40	0.50	0.40	0.70
3.1.9 Accessories	0.80	0.80	0.60	0.50	0.70	1.00	0.70	0.80	0.80	1.00	0.90	0.50	0.70	0.70
3.1.10 Haberdashery, clothing materials and clothing hire	0.30	0.30	0.30	0.30	0.10	0.20	0.20	0.30	0.30	0.40	0.30	0.60	0.30	0.30
3.1.11 Dry cleaners, laundry and dyeing	0.20	0.20	[0.10]	0.10	0.10	[0.10]	[0.10]	0.20	0.60	0.30	0.10	[0.10]	0.20	0.20
3.2 Footwear	5.00	4.90	4.90	5.50	4.60	4.30	4.50	4.50	6.10	4.90	4.50	4.20	4.80	7.10
4 Housing (net)[1], fuel & power	**79.50**	**82.70**	**60.20**	**68.50**	**64.30**	**67.20**	**71.10**	**82.30**	**136.10**	**84.90**	**78.70**	**64.80**	**65.70**	**54.10**
4.1 Actual rentals for housing	51.00	53.70	39.60	40.10	38.80	36.50	41.80	48.80	118.20	48.70	43.30	35.80	39.50	34.00
4.1.1 Gross rent	51.00	53.70	39.60	39.90	38.80	36.50	41.80	48.80	118.20	48.70	43.30	35.50	39.40	34.00
4.1.2 *less housing benefit, rebates & allowances rec'd*	13.10	13.20	15.60	12.10	11.40	10.00	11.40	9.20	26.60	10.30	9.80	11.50	13.10	13.20
4.1.3 Net rent[2]	37.90	40.50	24.10	27.90	27.30	26.40	30.40	39.60	91.60	38.40	33.40	24.00	26.30	20.80
4.1.4 Second dwelling rent	..	..												
4.2 Maintenance and repair of dwelling	7.90	8.20	4.90	6.80	6.40	8.70	7.30	8.70	7.90	10.50	10.20	7.40	6.70	4.40
4.3 Water supply and miscellaneous services relating to the dwelling	9.80	10.40	9.30	9.70	8.90	8.60	9.60	9.80	13.50	10.90	10.90	8.90	8.20	0.60
4.4 Electricity, gas and other fuels	23.90	23.60	22.00	23.90	21.70	23.50	23.80	24.10	23.10	25.00	24.20	24.20	24.60	28.30
4.4.1 Electricity	12.10	12.00	10.40	12.00	10.80	12.00	11.90	12.30	11.90	12.60	12.90	11.80	12.80	12.60
4.4.2 Gas	10.20	10.50	10.60	11.40	10.10	10.30	10.80	9.80	11.10	11.10	8.60	9.60	10.00	4.00
4.4.3 Other fuels	1.60	1.20	0.90	0.50	0.80	1.20	1.10	2.10	0.10	1.30	2.70	2.80	1.80	11.70

Note: The commodity and service categories are not comparable to those in publications before 2001-02.

The numbering system is sequential, it does not use actual COICOP codes.

Please see background notes for symbols and conventions used in this report.

This table is based on a three year average.

1 Excluding mortgage interest payments, council tax and Northern Ireland rates.

2 The figure included in total expenditure is net rent as opposed to gross rent.

Table A35
Detailed household expenditure by countries and regions (cont.)

UK, financial year ending 2018 to financial year ending 2020

Commodity or service	United Kingdom	England	North East	North West	Yorkshire and The Humber	East Midlands	West Midlands	East	London	South East	South West	Wales	Scotland	Northern Ireland
					Average weekly household expenditure (£)									
5 Household goods & services	**39.50**	**40.40**	**38.20**	**38.20**	**40.50**	**40.00**	**36.00**	**40.10**	**37.30**	**46.40**	**44.80**	**34.00**	**35.60**	**31.50**
5.1 Furniture and furnishings, carpets and other floor coverings	21.90	22.50	24.50	22.20	24.30	22.30	19.70	20.00	20.10	26.20	23.30	18.70	19.70	16.60
5.1.1 Furniture and furnishings	18.00	18.60	21.20	18.20	19.60	17.00	16.10	16.70	17.30	21.10	20.40	16.00	15.40	14.40
5.1.2 Floor coverings	3.90	3.90	3.30	4.00	4.80	5.30	3.60	3.30	2.80	5.10	2.90	2.60	4.30	2.20
5.2 Household textiles	2.10	2.20	1.50	2.10	2.20	2.40	2.10	2.20	1.80	2.30	3.00	1.60	2.00	2.00
5.3 Household appliances	3.70	3.80	2.30	3.50	3.50	3.40	4.00	5.20	3.80	3.40	4.40	3.10	3.70	2.60
5.4 Glassware, tableware and household utensils	1.90	1.90	1.40	1.60	1.70	2.00	1.70	1.90	2.10	2.50	1.80	2.20	1.70	1.40
5.5 Tools and equipment for house and garden	2.90	3.00	2.10	2.60	2.80	3.30	2.90	2.80	2.00	3.20	4.90	3.40	2.40	2.40
5.6 Goods and services for routine household maintenance	6.90	7.10	6.40	6.30	5.90	6.70	5.60	8.00	7.60	8.90	7.40	5.00	6.10	6.50
5.6.1 Cleaning materials	2.50	2.60	2.50	2.30	2.40	2.70	2.30	2.60	2.70	2.80	2.60	2.30	2.30	2.70
5.6.2 Household goods and hardware	1.80	1.80	1.60	1.60	1.70	1.80	1.60	2.00	1.90	1.90	1.90	1.60	1.70	1.80
5.6.3 Domestic services, carpet cleaning and hire/repair of furniture/furnishings	2.60	2.80	2.30	2.40	1.80	2.10	1.70	3.40	3.00	4.20	2.80	1.20	2.10	2.00
6 Health	**7.70**	**8.00**	**5.30**	**5.30**	**6.50**	**7.30**	**8.70**	**9.00**	**8.90**	**10.20**	**8.70**	**6.20**	**6.00**	**7.00**
6.1 Medical products, appliances and equipment	4.20	4.30	3.00	3.20	3.40	4.40	4.80	5.40	3.90	4.80	5.30	3.80	3.60	3.70
6.1.1 Medicines, prescriptions, healthcare products and equipment	2.50	2.50	1.90	2.10	2.30	2.10	2.60	3.00	2.80	2.90	2.60	1.80	2.20	2.00
6.1.2 Spectacles, lenses, accessories and repairs	1.70	1.80	1.00	1.10	1.10	2.30	2.20	2.40	1.10	2.00	2.70	1.90	1.40	1.70
6.2 Hospital services	3.50	3.70	2.30	2.10	3.10	2.90	3.90	3.60	4.90	5.40	3.40	2.50	2.40	3.30
7 Transport	**82.60**	**84.00**	**73.90**	**70.70**	**76.90**	**84.70**	**73.50**	**90.60**	**82.30**	**100.30**	**93.80**	**78.10**	**75.30**	**73.70**
7.1 Purchase of vehicles	27.60	27.90	30.00	21.30	27.70	31.60	25.50	31.40	22.20	29.80	36.10	29.20	27.00	20.80
7.1.1 Purchase of new cars and vans	9.30	9.10	10.00	7.10	9.90	7.90	5.90	10.50	9.10	10.30	11.70	12.30	10.60	5.30
7.1.2 Purchase of second hand cars or vans	17.40	17.80	19.50	13.70	17.70	22.50	19.20	20.30	12.30	18.20	21.20	16.10	15.60	15.30
7.1.3 Purchase of motorcycles and other vehicles	0.90	1.00	::	[0.40]		[1.30]	[0.40]	[0.60]	[0.80]	1.30	3.20	[0.80]	0.80	::
7.2 Operation of personal transport	34.10	34.40	29.60	30.40	32.10	37.30	33.10	37.60	25.50	42.00	40.80	35.80	28.50	38.80
7.2.1 Spares and accessories	2.30	2.40	1.70	1.90	2.40	2.40	2.10	2.30	1.90	3.40	2.70	2.20	2.20	2.40
7.2.2 Petrol, diesel and other motor oils	22.30	22.30	21.30	20.50	21.60	24.90	22.70	25.20	15.20	24.90	25.40	24.10	19.70	30.00
7.2.3 Repairs and servicing	6.50	6.70	4.20	5.40	5.60	7.30	5.30	7.00	5.90	9.20	9.00	7.20	4.60	4.60
7.2.4 Other motoring costs	2.90	3.10	2.40	2.50	2.40	2.60	3.00	3.10	2.50	4.40	3.60	2.30	2.00	1.80
7.3 Transport services	20.90	21.70	14.30	19.00	17.10	15.80	14.90	21.60	34.60	28.60	16.90	13.00	19.70	14.00
7.3.1 Rail and tube fares	4.50	5.00	1.80	2.70	1.80	2.00	2.70	7.10	9.10	9.30	2.50	1.90	2.80	1.00
7.3.2 Bus and coach fares	1.60	1.60	1.90	1.80	1.80	1.60	1.50	1.00	2.10	1.40	1.30	1.30	1.60	1.40
7.3.3 Combined fares	0.70	0.90					[0.20]	0.60	4.90	0.30				
7.3.4 Other travel and transport	14.10	14.30	10.40	14.50	13.40	12.20	10.40	13.00	18.50	17.50	13.10	9.80	15.20	11.60
8 Communication	**20.20**	**20.40**	**18.80**	**19.20**	**18.70**	**19.80**	**19.90**	**20.50**	**21.70**	**22.50**	**19.90**	**18.90**	**19.30**	**20.00**
8.1 Postal services	0.60	0.60	0.40	0.50	0.50	0.70	0.50	0.60	0.60	0.80	0.80	0.80	0.70	0.40
8.2 Telephone and telefax equipment	1.20	1.20	1.20	1.10	0.90	0.90	1.50	0.80	1.40	1.90	1.00	0.80	1.10	2.00
8.3 Telephone and telefax services[3]	9.90	10.00	8.90	9.50	9.50	9.70	9.50	10.10	11.60	10.60	9.70	9.10	8.70	10.00
8.4 Internet subscription fees (ex. combined packages)	1.70	1.70	1.60	1.50	1.70	1.60	1.70	1.90	2.00	1.90	1.60	1.60	1.70	1.90
8.5 Combined telecom services[4]	6.70	6.70	6.70	6.70	6.10	7.00	6.70	7.20	6.10	7.30	6.80	6.50	7.00	5.70

Note: The commodity and service categories are not comparable to those in publications before 2001-02.
The numbering system is sequential, it does not use actual COICOP codes.
Please see background notes for symbols and conventions used in this report.
This table is based on a three year average.
3 For FYE 2019 onwards, excludes payments made as part of a combined bill.
4 New for FYE 2019. This encompasses all telecoms bills that include more than one service. Due to the nature of combined packages, this also includes packages that includes television services.

Table A35

Detailed household expenditure by countries and regions (cont.)

UK, financial year ending 2018 to financial year ending 2020

Commodity or service		United Kingdom	England	North East	North West	Yorkshire and The Humber	East Midlands	West Midlands	East	London	South East	South West	Wales	Scotland	Northern Ireland
		Average weekly household expenditure (£)													
9	**Recreation & culture**	**75.60**	**77.40**	**72.20**	**66.70**	**72.80**	**75.80**	**68.40**	**81.20**	**64.90**	**103.70**	**82.30**	**74.40**	**67.00**	**51.70**
9.1	Audio-visual, photographic and information processing equipment	4.90	4.80	4.10	4.70	5.20	4.10	3.30	5.50	4.30	6.70	3.70	6.10	5.80	2.50
9.1.1	Audio equipment and accessories, CD players	1.10	1.10	1.30	0.90	0.80	1.00	0.80	0.90	1.10	1.60	1.20	1.50	0.80	0.60
9.1.2	TV, video and computers	3.30	3.20	2.60	3.60	4.00	2.80	2.40	3.90	2.60	3.80	2.20	3.60	4.80	1.80
9.1.3	Photographic, cine and optical equipment	0.50	0.50	..	[0.20]	[0.40]	[0.30]	..	0.70	[0.60]	1.20	[0.30]	[1.00]	[0.20]	[0.20]
9.2	Other major durables for recreation and culture	2.50	2.70	..	3.80	2.20	2.60	1.20	4.00	[0.40]	4.10	3.50	..	1.00	[0.30]
9.3	Other recreational items and equipment, gardens and pets	14.40	14.60	12.90	12.90	13.90	15.10	13.80	16.50	9.60	18.30	18.30	14.90	12.50	11.40
9.3.1	Games, toys and hobbies	3.10	3.10	2.40	3.00	3.20	2.40	3.00	4.30	2.20	3.40	3.30	3.00	3.10	2.60
9.3.2	Computer software and games	1.00	1.10	1.60	1.20	1.00	1.10	0.90	1.00	0.60	1.40	1.10	1.10	0.60	0.90
9.3.3	Equipment for sport, camping and open-air recreation	1.30	1.30	0.80	0.90	0.80	1.80	2.00	1.20	1.10	1.30	1.80	2.30	1.20	1.20
9.3.4	Horticultural goods, garden equipment and plants	2.90	3.00	2.40	2.60	2.30	3.00	2.70	3.50	2.20	4.00	3.70	2.40	2.30	2.20
9.3.5	Pets and pet food	6.10	6.20	5.70	5.10	6.50	6.90	5.30	6.60	3.40	8.30	8.40	6.10	5.40	4.40
9.4	Recreational and cultural services	20.20	21.00	16.70	18.10	18.50	21.20	17.30	20.80	24.20	26.20	20.60	15.90	17.30	15.20
9.4.1	Sports admissions, subscriptions, leisure class fees and equipment hire	7.30	7.80	4.00	6.60	5.70	7.70	5.20	6.50	11.00	11.40	7.80	4.30	5.30	4.20
9.4.2	Cinema, theatre and museums etc.	3.30	3.50	2.00	2.40	3.20	3.10	3.20	3.70	5.10	3.70	3.40	2.40	2.80	2.20
9.4.3	TV, video, satellite rental, cable subscriptions and TV licences[5]	5.40	5.40	5.30	5.10	5.20	5.50	5.10	5.70	4.90	6.20	5.40	5.70	5.30	4.80
9.4.4	Miscellaneous entertainments	1.50	1.50	0.90	1.30	1.40	1.60	1.20	1.80	1.20	1.90	2.20	1.00	1.10	1.10
9.4.5	Development of film, deposit for film development, passport photos, holiday and school photos	0.20	0.20	[0.10]	0.10	0.20	0.30	0.10	0.20	0.20	0.30	0.30	0.30	0.20	0.20
9.4.6	Gambling payments	2.50	2.50	4.40	2.50	2.80	3.00	2.40	2.90	1.80	2.70	1.60	2.20	2.50	2.80
9.5	Newspapers, books and stationery	5.40	5.40	4.80	4.80	4.80	5.20	5.10	5.80	5.30	6.70	5.60	5.30	5.20	4.80
9.5.1	Books	1.20	1.30	0.90	1.00	1.00	1.10	1.30	1.50	1.40	1.50	1.20	1.40	1.10	0.90
9.5.2	Diaries, address books, cards etc.	2.20	2.20	1.80	2.00	1.80	2.20	2.10	2.50	2.40	2.70	2.20	1.90	1.90	1.70
9.5.3	Newspapers	1.30	1.30	1.30	1.20	1.30	1.30	1.20	1.20	0.90	1.60	1.40	1.20	1.60	1.60
9.5.4	Magazines and periodicals	0.70	0.70	0.60	0.60	0.60	0.60	0.60	0.60	0.50	0.80	0.80	0.70	0.60	0.60
9.6	Package holidays	28.30	28.90	31.00	22.30	28.20	27.60	27.80	28.50	21.10	41.80	30.60	29.70	25.30	17.50
9.6.1	Package holidays - UK	1.90	2.10	2.20	2.10	2.10	1.80	2.50	2.00	1.00	2.60	2.40	1.40	0.90	[0.70]
9.6.2	Package holidays - abroad	26.40	26.80	28.90	20.20	26.10	25.80	25.30	26.50	20.10	39.10	28.20	28.30	24.40	16.80
10	**Education**	**6.30**	**7.00**	**1.60**	**4.00**	**3.90**	**5.30**	**5.00**	**4.80**	**16.70**	**8.90**	**6.40**	**2.60**	**2.30**	**2.80**
10	Education fees	5.80	6.50	[1.50]	3.60	3.70	4.90	4.80	4.30	15.10	8.30	6.00	[2.30]	2.00	1.70
10	Payments for school trips, other ad-hoc expenditure	0.50	0.50	[0.10]	0.40	0.20	0.40	[0.20]	0.40	1.60	0.60	0.50	[0.30]	0.30	1.10
11	**Restaurants & hotels**	**51.50**	**53.00**	**44.60**	**49.60**	**49.50**	**48.60**	**42.80**	**50.40**	**67.00**	**59.90**	**52.20**	**42.90**	**43.80**	**46.30**
11	Catering services	40.50	41.50	37.40	39.80	38.00	36.80	34.40	41.00	53.10	44.20	39.40	34.90	34.40	41.10
11.1.1	Restaurant and café meals	19.50	20.00	15.90	18.00	18.00	18.40	16.40	21.30	24.00	22.50	20.70	16.80	16.50	18.00
11.1.2	Alcoholic drinks (away from home)	8.20	8.50	9.40	9.80	8.40	7.60	7.30	7.20	10.00	8.90	7.40	6.70	6.30	6.40
11.1.3	Take away meals eaten at home	5.40	5.30	5.60	4.60	5.50	4.90	4.80	5.20	7.30	5.20	4.60	4.50	5.40	7.80
11.1.4	Other take-away and snack food	5.40	5.40	4.60	4.80	5.00	4.20	4.10	5.10	8.80	5.60	4.90	4.90	4.80	6.30
11.1.5	Contract catering (food) and canteens	2.10	2.20	1.90	2.50	2.00	1.80	1.90	2.00	3.00	2.10	1.80	1.90	1.50	2.60
11	Accommodation services	11.00	11.60	7.30	9.80	10.60	11.70	8.40	9.50	13.90	15.60	12.80	8.10	9.40	5.10
11.2.1	Holiday in the UK	6.00	6.20	4.80	5.40	7.00	7.50	5.40	5.90	4.40	7.40	7.50	6.20	5.30	2.10
11.2.2	Holiday abroad	4.90	5.20	2.40	4.30	3.50	4.00	2.80	3.50	9.30	8.00	5.10	1.80	4.10	3.00
11.2.3	Room hire	0.10	0.20	..	[0.20]	..	..	..	..	[0.20]	[0.20]	..	..	..	..

Note: The commodity and service categories are not comparable to those in publications before 2001-02.
The numbering system is sequential, it does not use actual COICOP codes.
Please see background notes for symbols and conventions used in this report.
This table is based on a three year average.
5 For FYE 2019 onwards, excludes payments made as part of a combined bill.

Table A35

Detailed household expenditure by countries and regions (cont.)

UK, financial year ending 2018 to financial year ending 2020

Commodity or service	United Kingdom	England	North East	North West	Yorkshire and The Humber	East Midlands	West Midlands	East	London	South East	South West	Wales	Scotland	Northern Ireland
	Average weekly household expenditure (£)													
12 Miscellaneous goods & services	**45.00**	**46.50**	**34.30**	**43.10**	**41.80**	**46.10**	**41.20**	**47.60**	**50.70**	**54.10**	**48.90**	**40.00**	**35.70**	**39.10**
12 Personal care	13.00	13.30	10.80	13.30	12.00	13.50	12.20	13.40	14.70	14.00	13.20	10.60	11.80	13.70
12.1.1 Hairdressing, beauty treatment	4.20	4.30	3.70	4.10	4.00	4.30	3.50	4.30	4.30	5.20	4.70	3.20	3.80	4.90
12.1.2 Toilet paper	0.90	0.90	0.80	0.90	0.80	0.80	0.90	0.90	0.90	0.90	1.00	0.90	0.90	1.10
12.1.3 Toiletries and soap	2.50	2.60	2.20	2.50	2.20	2.50	2.40	2.80	3.10	2.80	2.50	2.10	2.30	2.70
12.1.4 Baby toiletries and accessories (disposable)	0.60	0.70	0.30	1.00	0.60	0.60	0.50	0.80	0.70	0.60	0.50	0.60	0.50	0.70
12.1.5 Hair products, cosmetics and electrical personal appliances	4.70	4.80	3.90	4.90	4.40	5.30	4.80	4.70	5.80	4.60	4.50	3.90	4.30	4.40
12 Personal effects	4.00	4.10	3.00	4.10	3.40	3.70	4.70	4.00	4.00	5.10	3.50	3.40	3.60	3.50
12 Social protection	3.80	3.90	2.20	3.40	5.30	2.90	2.40	1.90	5.80	4.40	5.40	2.90	2.80	4.00
12 Insurance	19.00	19.70	16.00	18.50	17.70	18.70	18.60	20.20	21.10	23.40	19.00	17.60	14.10	15.90
12.4.1 Household insurances - structural, contents and appliances	4.80	4.90	4.10	4.40	4.40	4.70	4.60	5.30	4.80	5.80	5.00	5.30	4.50	4.00
12.4.2 Medical insurance premiums[6]	2.40	2.60	1.10	1.50	1.70	1.60	1.50	2.10	3.90	4.90	2.50	1.40	1.10	1.20
12.4.3 Vehicle insurance including boat insurance	11.10	11.50	10.20	11.90	10.50	11.90	12.00	12.20	11.50	11.70	10.60	10.40	7.70	10.30
12.4.4 Non-package holiday, other travel insurance[7]	0.70	0.80	0.60	0.60	1.00	0.60	0.60	0.60	0.90	1.00	0.90	0.50	0.70	0.40
13 Other services	5.30	5.60	2.40	3.80	3.40	7.30	3.30	8.10	5.00	7.30	7.80	5.40	3.30	2.00
12.5.1 Moving house	2.80	3.00	1.10	2.00	2.20	2.50	1.60	3.40	2.70	4.60	5.00	3.30	1.70	0.70
12.5.2 Bank, building society, post office, credit card charges	0.50	0.60	0.30	0.50	0.50	0.50	0.40	0.60	0.70	0.70	0.70	0.60	0.50	0.20
12.5.3 Other services and professional fees	1.90	2.00	1.00	1.30	0.70	4.30	1.30	4.10	1.70	2.00	2.10	1.60	1.20	1.10
1-12 All expenditure groups	**507.30**	**519.30**	**440.60**	**461.80**	**466.10**	**493.40**	**458.80**	**526.90**	**595.00**	**598.90**	**533.90**	**451.70**	**447.10**	**435.90**
13 Other expenditure items	**77.90**	**81.20**	**58.70**	**68.20**	**63.80**	**73.60**	**66.30**	**80.70**	**108.10**	**99.70**	**82.80**	**61.30**	**65.30**	**50.40**
13.1 Housing: mortgage interest payments, council tax etc.	48.10	50.10	35.70	42.80	40.10	46.40	44.40	54.10	59.50	60.50	52.50	39.60	40.50	26.00
13.2 Licences, fines and transfers	3.90	4.10	2.90	3.30	3.20	4.30	3.90	4.40	4.70	4.60	4.30	3.60	2.70	3.30
13.3 Holiday spending	12.40	12.70	8.20	9.40	10.30	9.30	8.80	9.90	26.10	14.10	11.00	7.60	12.90	9.60
13.4 Money transfers and credit	13.60	14.30	11.90	12.80	10.20	13.70	9.20	12.30	17.80	20.50	15.00	10.60	9.20	11.50
13.4.1 Money, cash gifts given to children	0.20	0.20		[0.10]	[0.10]	[0.10]	0.30	0.50	[0.10]	[0.70]	[0.70]	[0.20]	0.10	0.10
13.4.2 Cash gifts and donations	12.30	13.00	11.30	11.90	9.20	12.20	8.10	10.50	16.40	19.10	12.70	9.40	8.30	10.90
13.4.3 Club instalment payments (child) and interest on credit cards	1.00	1.10	0.50	0.80	0.90	1.30	0.70	1.30	1.30	1.30	1.60	0.90	0.80	0.50
Total expenditure	**585.20**	**600.50**	**499.30**	**530.00**	**529.90**	**567.00**	**525.20**	**607.70**	**703.10**	**698.60**	**616.60**	**513.00**	**512.40**	**486.40**
14 Other items recorded														
14.1 Life assurance, contributions to pension funds	29.30	30.00	19.30	26.10	23.00	23.70	28.60	33.10	40.40	38.70	23.50	23.70	26.70	24.10
14.2 Other insurance inc. friendly societies	2.20	2.30	1.60	1.90	2.00	3.00	1.90	2.30	1.80	3.10	2.80	1.80	1.80	0.60
14.3 Income tax, payments less refunds	103.60	109.70	63.90	84.20	85.90	84.20	83.10	117.20	163.80	147.50	96.30	72.20	77.40	60.90
14.4 National insurance contributions	37.00	38.40	28.00	33.40	30.50	33.10	33.60	41.60	54.30	45.30	31.20	29.50	30.90	28.60
14.5 Purchase or alteration of dwellings, mortgages	69.80	74.20	34.80	88.80	49.30	57.70	54.30	82.40	94.30	86.90	77.10	69.80	41.20	29.60
14.6 Savings and investments	7.90	8.70	4.80	7.20	6.60	8.30	4.80	5.90	7.80	17.80	9.10	3.60	5.50	1.90
14.7 Pay off loan to clear other debt	2.10	2.20	2.10	2.30	2.00	2.20	1.60	1.60	2.60	2.30	2.80	1.60	1.90	0.90
14.8 Windfall receipts from gambling etc[8]	1.30	1.30	1.90	1.70	1.40	1.40	1.00	1.80	1.10	1.30	0.40	1.00	1.40	1.40

Note: The commodity and service categories are not comparable to those in publications before 2001-02.

The numbering system is sequential, it does not use actual COICOP codes.

Please see background notes for symbols and conventions used in this report.

This table is based on a three year average.

6 For FYE 2019, critical illness cover, personal accident insurance and other medical insurance are included here. They were not included in previous years.

7 For FYE 2019, information about insurance for non-package holiday and other travel insurance was collected in the questionnaire in addition to the diary. In previous years, this was based on diary data only.

8 Expressed as an income figure as opposed to an expenditure figure.

Source: Office for National Statistics

Table A36

Household expenditure by urban/rural areas

Great Britain[1], financial year ending 2018 to financial year ending 2020

	Urban	Rural
Average number of weighted households (thousands)	20,700	6,020
Total number of households in sample (over 3 years)	11,390	3,780
Total number of persons in sample (over 3 years)	26,870	8,690
Total number of adults in sample (over 3 years)	20,770	7,000
Weighted average number of persons per household	2.4	2.3

Commodity or service	Average weekly household expenditure (£)	
1 Food & non-alcoholic drinks	61.50	64.50
2 Alcoholic drinks, tobacco & narcotics	12.20	14.90
3 Clothing & footwear	24.20	23.30
4 Housing (net)[2], fuel & power	82.80	71.40
5 Household goods & services	37.20	48.10
6 Health	7.30	9.30
7 Transport	76.40	105.00
8 Communication	20.20	20.20
9 Recreation & culture	72.10	90.90
10 Education	6.60	5.60
11 Restaurants & hotels	51.20	53.50
12 Miscellaneous goods & services	44.20	48.60
1-12 All expenditure groups	495.90	555.30
13 Other expenditure items	76.90	84.80
Total expenditure	**572.90**	**640.10**

Average weekly expenditure per person (£)		
Total expenditure	**238.90**	**277.10**

Note: The commodity and service categories are not comparable to those in publications before 2001-02.

Please see background notes for symbols and conventions used in this report.

This table is based on a three year average.

1 Combined urban/rural classification for England & Wales and Scotland.

2 Excludes mortgage interest payments, council tax.

Source: Office for National Statistics

Table A45

Percentage of households with durable goods[1]

UK, 1970 to financial year ending 2020

	Car/ van	Central heating[2]	Tumble dryer[3]	Dish- washer[3]	Tele- phone	Mobile phone[4]	Home computer	Internet connec- tion
1970	52	30	--	--	35	--	--	--
1975	57	47	--	--	52	--	--	--
1980	60	59	--	--	72	--	--	--
1985	63	69	--	--	81	--	13	--
1990	67	79	--	--	87	--	17	--
1994-95	69	84	50	18	91	--	--	--
1995-96	70	85	50	20	92	--	--	--
1996-97	69	87	51	20	93	16	27	--
1997-98	70	89	51	22	94	20	29	--
1998-99	72	89	51	24	95	26	32	9
1998-99[5]	72	89	51	23	95	27	33	10
1999-2000	71	90	52	23	95	44	38	19
2000-01	72	91	53	25	93	47	44	32
2001-02[6]	74	92	54	27	94	64	49	39
2002-03	74	93	56	29	94	70	55	45
2003-04	75	94	57	31	92	76	58	49
2004-05	75	95	58	33	93	78	62	53
2005-06	74	94	58	35	92	79	65	55
2006[7]	76	95	59	38	91	80	67	59
2006[8]	74	95	59	37	91	79	67	58
2007	75	95	57	37	89	78	70	61
2008	74	95	59	37	90	79	72	66
2009	76	95	58	39	88	81	75	71
2010	75	96	57	40	87	80	77	73
2011	75	96	56	41	88	87	79	77
2012	75	96	56	42	88	87	81	79
2013	76	96	56	42	89	92	83	82
2014	76	96	56	44	88	94	85	84
2014-15	76	96	56	44	88	94	85	84
2015-16	78	95	56	45	88	95	88	88
2016-17	79	95	56	46	89	95	88	89
2017-18	78	95	58	49	85	95	88	89
2018-19	79	97	58	48	83	96	89	91
Latest year	80	96	57	50	82	90	89	94

Please see background notes for symbols and conventions used in this report.

-- Data not available.

1 The questions asking about ownership of washing machines, microwaves and DVD players were removed from the FYE 2020 questionnaire.

2 Full or partial.

3 For FYE 2020, the placement of the dishwashers and tumble driers ownership questions were moved to the household improvements section of the questionnaire.

4 From FYE 2020 onwards, the calculation of whether a household owns a landline/mobile/internet connection is based on whether they report any spending on these services in the questionnaire. Prior to FYE 2020, households were explicitly asked whether they owned these goods.

5 From this version of 1998-99, figures shown are based on weighted data and including children's expenditure.

6 From 2001-02 onwards, weighting is based on the population figures from the 2001 census.

7 From 1998-99 to this version of 2006, figures shown are based on weighted data using non-response weights based on the 1991 Census and population figures from the 1991 and 2001 Census.

8 From this version of 2006, figures shown are based on weighted data using updated weights, with non-response weights and population figures based on the 2001 Census.

Source: Office for National Statistics

Table A46

Percentage[1] of households with durable goods[2] by income group and household composition

UK, financial year ending 2020

	Central heating[3]	Tumble dryer[4]	Dish-washer[4]	Home computer	Internet connection	Tele-phone	Mobile phone[5]
All households	**96**	**57**	**50**	**89**	**94**	**82**	**90**
Gross income decile group							
Lowest ten per cent	94	36	21	59	74	66	81
Second decile group	95	49	27	78	85	83	84
Third decile group	96	47	33	82	91	84	87
Fourth decile group	95	58	44	90	95	85	90
Fifth decile group	98	55	45	94	97	82	91
Sixth decile group	96	61	50	96	99	82	93
Seventh decile group	97	62	58	98	99	85	93
Eighth decile group	96	65	64	98	99	82	93
Ninth decile group	95	66	74	100	99	87	93
Highest ten per cent	97	73	85	100	99	90	92
Household composition							
One adult, retired mainly dependent on state pensions[6]	96	43	30	58	69	87	77
One adult, other retired	96	44	34	68	73	88	74
One adult, non-retired	94	41	31	82	92	69	90
One adult, one child	97	46	26	86	96	68	92
One adult, two or more children	94	54	35	87	99	77	98
Two adults, retired mainly dependent on state pensions[6]	96	53	34	82	86	96	80
Two adults, other retired	97	67	66	91	93	97	87
Two adults, non-retired	96	57	56	97	99	81	92
Two adults, one child	98	63	55	97	100	83	95
Two adults, two children	97	72	63	97	99	83	94
Two adults, three children	94	67	58	95	99	82	94
Two adults, four or more children	100	83	63	95	89	74	92
Three adults	94	72	61	97	99	88	95
Three adults, one or more children	96	72	68	100	99	84	91
All other households without children	91	67	64	100	100	83	93
All other households with children	100	65	53	97	100	94	100

Please see background notes for symbols and conventions used in this report.

1 See table A47 for number of recording households.

2 The questions asking about ownership of washing machines, microwaves and DVD players were removed from the FYE 2020 questionnaire.

3 Full or partial.

4 For FYE 2020, the placement of the dishwashers and tumble driers ownership questions were moved to the household improvements section of the questionnaire.

5 From FYE 2020 onwards, the calculation of whether a household owns a landline/mobile/internet connection is based on whether they report any spending on these services in the questionnaire. Prior to FYE 2020, households were explicitly asked whether they owned these goods.

6 Mainly dependent on state pensions and not economically active

Source: Office for National Statistics

Table A47

Percentage of households with cars by income group, tenure and household composition

UK, financial year ending 2020

	One car/van	Two cars/vans	Three or more cars/vans	All with cars/vans	Weighted number of house-holds (000s)	House-holds in the sample (number)
All households	**46**	**27**	**7**	**80**	**27,820**	**5,440**
Gross income decile group						
Lowest ten per cent	35	4	..	39	2,780	550
Second decile group	50	6	..	57	2,780	550
Third decile group	58	11	..	70	2,780	570
Fourth decile group	64	15	[3]	82	2,780	580
Fifth decile group	58	24	[3]	86	2,780	570
Sixth decile group	52	31	6	89	2,780	560
Seventh decile group	43	43	8	94	2,780	530
Eighth decile group	33	46	12	91	2,780	530
Ninth decile group	32	46	15	94	2,780	520
Highest ten per cent	29	46	20	94	2,780	480
Tenure of dwelling[1]						
Owners						
Owned outright	50	28	8	85	9,900	2,060
Buying with a mortgage	40	44	12	95	8,520	1,630
All	45	35	9	90	18,430	3,680
Social rented from						
Council	41	6	..	49	2,200	450
Registered social landlord [2]	44	7	..	52	2,340	440
All	43	7	[1]	51	4,540	890
Private rented						
Rent free	62	..	..	81	180	40
Rent paid, unfurnished	50	19	3	72	3,760	690
Rent paid, furnished	41	[6]	..	50	910	130
All	49	17	3	68	4,850	860
Household composition						
One adult, retired mainly dependent on state pensions[3]	47	..	:	48	770	140
One adult, other retired	54	[2]	..	56	2,780	530
One adult, non-retired	58	4	..	64	4,370	840
One adult, one child	57	..	:	61	620	140
One adult, two or more children	55	..	:	58	540	130
Two adults, retired mainly dependent on state pensions[3]	64	21	:	85	470	120
Two adults, other retired	55	33	5	92	2,770	640
Two adults, non-retired	38	42	6	87	6,220	1,190
Two adults, one child	44	41	5	90	2,190	420
Two adults, two children	41	49	4	95	2,540	510
Two adults, three children	39	40	[7]	86	790	140
Two adults, four or more children	[33]	52	..	89	180	40
Three adults	27	32	30	89	1,720	290
Three adults, one or more children	31	40	23	94	780	130
All other households without children	29	17	38	85	800	120
All other households with children	[33]	[30]	[31]	94	300	40

Please see background notes for symbols and conventions used in this report.

1 See footnotes in Table A32.

2 Formerly housing association.

3 Mainly dependent on state pensions and not economically active.

Source: Office for National Statistics

Table A48

Percentage of households with durable goods[1] by countries and regions

UK, financial year ending 2018 to financial year ending 2020

	United Kingdom	England	North East	North West	Yorkshire and the Humber	East Midlands	West Midlands	East	London	South East	South West	Wales	Scotland	Northern Ireland
	K02000001	E92000001	E12000001	E12000002	E12000003	E12000004	E12000005	E12000006	E12000007	E12000008	E12000009	W92000004	S92000003	N92000002
Average weighted number of households (thousands)	27,480	22,920	1,170	3,100	2,370	1,980	2,420	2,580	3,290	3,660	2,340	1,360	2,450	760
Total number of households in sample (over 3 years)	16,320	12,120	690	1,650	1,330	1,190	1,240	1,460	1,260	1,850	1,450	730	2,330	1,150
Percentage of households by region and Country														
Car/van	79	79	74	76	78	82	81	86	65	86	86	84	73	79
One	44	44	41	44	46	39	44	47	45	43	42	44	46	44
Two	27	28	25	26	26	33	29	30	16	33	33	30	23	28
Three or more	7	8	7	6	6	10	8	9	4	9	11	10	4	7
Central heating full or partial	96	96	97	96	96	97	97	97	93	97	96	97	96	96
Fridge-freezer or deep freezer	65	65	65	64	64	65	65	65	66	65	64	65	66	66
Tumble dryer[2]	58	58	56	60	56	62	62	59	44	62	60	63	55	65
Dishwasher[2]	49	50	36	41	40	50	45	56	50	61	57	46	44	51
Telephone	83	83	81	82	80	83	83	84	78	87	87	87	84	77
Mobile phone[3]	94	94	92	92	94	96	93	94	95	94	95	91	92	94
Home computer	89	89	83	86	86	90	86	92	93	93	92	87	87	81
Internet connection	91	92	88	89	88	91	89	93	94	94	94	90	90	87

Please see background notes for symbols and conventions used in this report.

This table is based on a three year average.

1 The questions asking about ownership of washing machines, microwaves and DVD players were removed from the FYE 2020 questionnaire.
2 For FYE 2020, the placement of the dishwashers and tumble driers ownership questions were moved to the household improvements section of the questionnaire.
3 From FYE 2020 onwards, the calculation of whether a household owns a landline/mobile/internet connection is based on whether they report any spending on these services in the questionnaire. Prior to FYE 2020, households were explicitly asked whether they owned these goods.

Source: Office for National Statistics

Table A49

Percentage of households by size, composition and age in each gross income decile group
UK, financial year ending 2020

	Lowest ten per cent	Second decile group	Third decile group	Fourth decile group	Fifth decile group	Sixth decile group	Seventh decile group	Eighth decile group	Ninth decile group	Highest ten per cent	All house-holds
Lower boundary of group (£ per week)		228	335	446	568	708	873	1,051	1,296	1,733	
Weighted number of households (thousands)	2,780	2,780	2,780	2,780	2,780	2,780	2,780	2,780	2,780	2,780	27,820
Number of households in the sample	550	550	570	580	570	560	530	530	520	480	5,440
Size of household											
One person	81	61	42	33	24	17	9	6	5	5	28
Two persons	12	26	39	45	45	46	42	43	39	26	36
Three persons	4	7	10	10	18	16	21	23	24	22	15
Four persons	..	4	5	5	10	13	18	21	24	28	13
Five persons	..	..	[3]	6	[3]	6	7	5	6	13	5
Six or more persons	:	..	..	..	..	[2]	[3]	..	[3]	[5]	2
All sizes	100	100	100	100	100	100	100	100	100	100	100
Household composition											
One adult, retired mainly dependent on state pensions[1]	18	7	[3]	..	:	..	:	:	:	:	3
One adult, other retired	25	32	18	13	6	[4]	..	..	..	..	10
One adult, non-retired	39	23	21	20	18	13	9	6	[4]	5	16
One adult, one child	4	5	5	[3]	[2]	[2]	..	..	..	..	2
One adult, two or more children	3	5	4	3	[2]	..	..	..	..	:	2
Two adults, retired mainly dependent on state pensions[1]	..	4	9	3	..	:	:	:	:	:	2
Two adults, other retired	..	8	13	20	18	15	10	8	6	[2]	10
Two adults, non-retired	7	10	13	19	25	29	31	34	32	24	22
Two adults, one child	..	[3]	5	6	10	9	10	11	12	12	8
Two adults, two children	..	..	[3]	4	8	11	14	14	15	19	9
Two adults, three children	..	..	[2]	4	[3]	[4]	[4]	[2]	[3]	5	3
Two adults, four or more children	:	..	..	..	..	[2]	..	..	..	..	1
Three adults	..	..	..	[2]	6	6	11	11	12	11	6
Three adults, one or more children	..	..	..	..	..	[2]	5	5	5	7	3
All other households without children	:	:	..	..	..	..	[2]	[3]	8	12	3
All other households with children	:	:	..	..	:	..	..	..	[2]	[3]	1
All compositions	100	100	100	100	100	100	100	100	100	100	100
Age of household reference person											
15 and under 20 years	..	..	..	..	..	..	:	:	:	:	[0]
20 and under 25 years	[3]	[3]	[4]	..	[3]	[3]	..	..	..	..	2
25 and under 30 years	[4]	5	4	5	8	11	8	9	7	[4]	6
30 and under 35 years	[3]	6	5	6	9	10	10	11	10	7	8
35 and under 40 years	5	4	6	4	7	8	10	12	14	13	8
40 and under 45 years	[3]	4	7	6	7	9	12	12	11	14	8
45 and under 50 years	7	4	7	9	9	7	10	11	12	16	9
50 and under 55 years	9	6	8	9	9	8	11	11	13	18	10
55 and under 60 years	10	7	4	8	8	10	9	8	14	13	9
60 and under 65 years	12	9	7	9	10	9	9	9	7	8	9
65 and under 70 years	10	10	10	10	9	8	8	6	5	5	8
70 and under 75 years	12	11	11	10	8	6	6	4	3	..	7
75 and under 80 years	10	13	8	8	6	5	3	[3]	..	..	6
80 and under 85 years	8	13	10	6	4	5	[2]	..	..	..	5
85 and under 90 years	..	6	6	5	[2]	..	:	..	..	..	2
90 years or more	[4]	..	..	..	..	..	..	:	:	:	1
All ages	100	100	100	100	100	100	100	100	100	100	100

Please see background notes for symbols and conventions used in this report.
1 Mainly dependent on state pensions and not economically active.

Source: Office for National Statistics

Table A50

Percentage of households by economic activity, tenure and socio-economic classification in each gross income decile group

UK, financial year ending 2020

	Lowest ten per cent	Second decile group	Third decile group	Fourth decile group	Fifth decile group	Sixth decile group	Seventh decile group	Eighth decile group	Ninth decile group	Highest ten per cent	All house-holds
Lower boundary of group (£ per week)		228	335	446	568	708	873	1,051	1,296	1,733	
Weighted number of households (thousands)	2,780	2,780	2,780	2,780	2,780	2,780	2,780	2,780	2,780	2,780	27,820
Number of households in the sample	550	550	570	580	570	560	530	530	520	480	5,440
Number of economically active persons in household											
No person	76	68	50	40	24	20	11	8	7	[2]	31
One person	23	26	37	42	43	30	26	17	13	15	27
Two persons	..	5	11	17	32	43	53	61	61	57	34
Three persons	:	..	..	..	..	6	10	10	13	15	6
Four or more persons	:	:	..	:	:	..	..	[3]	6	10	2
All economically active persons	100	100	100	100	100	100	100	100	100	100	100
Tenure of dwelling[1]											
Owners											
Owned outright	36	44	43	50	42	35	31	27	25	23	36
Buying with a mortgage	5	6	11	13	24	32	43	53	57	63	31
All	41	50	54	63	66	67	74	80	82	86	66
Social rented from											
Council	19	17	12	11	7	5	[3]	[2]	..	..	8
Registered social landlord[2]	22	17	15	9	7	5	5	[2]	..	..	8
All	41	33	27	20	14	10	8	4	[3]	..	16
Private rented											
Rent free	..	[2]	..	..	..	..	..	..	..	..	1
Rent paid, unfurnished	15	12	16	13	16	19	15	11	11	8	14
Rent paid, furnished	[2]	..	[3]	[4]	[3]	[4]	[2]	[5]	[4]	[4]	3
All	18	16	19	18	20	23	18	16	15	12	17
All tenures	100	100	100	100	100	100	100	100	100	100	100
Socio-economic classification											
Higher managerial and professional											
Large employers/higher managerial	..	..	..	..	..	[2]	[3]	4	9	16	4
Higher professional	[2]	..	[2]	[3]	7	9	14	21	21	34	11
Lower managerial and professional	4	6	11	14	19	22	26	29	32	30	19
Intermediate	5	3	7	8	9	10	9	11	5	[3]	7
Small employers	6	7	8	8	7	5	10	7	7	5	7
Lower supervisory	[3]	[2]	5	7	7	9	10	6	4	[2]	5
Semi-routine	6	11	9	10	11	10	7	[3]	5	[2]	7
Routine	8	7	7	7	9	9	7	5	5	..	7
Long-term unemployed[3]	8	6	..	..	..	..	:	:	:	:	2
Students	[2]	..	..	..	..	..	..	..	[3]	..	1
Occupation not stated[4]	54	57	49	41	28	22	14	12	9	4	29
All occupational groups	100	100	100	100	100	100	100	100	100	100	100

Note: Changes to categories of socio-economic classification were made in 2011.

Please see background notes for symbols and conventions used in this report.

1 See footnotes in Table A32.

2 Formerly housing association.

3 Includes those who have never worked.

4 Includes those who are economically inactive.

Source: Office for National Statistics

Table A51

Average weekly household expenditure by Output Area Classification (OAC) supergroup

UK, financial year ending 2020

	Rural residents	Cosmopolitans	Ethnicity central	Multicultural metropolitans	Urbanites	Suburbanites	Constrained city dwellers	Hard-pressed living	
	OAC Super-group 1	OAC Super-group 2	OAC Super-group 3	OAC Super-group 4	OAC Super-group 5	OAC Super-group 6	OAC Super-group 7	OAC Super-group 8	All house-holds
Weighted number of households (thousands)	3,250	1,370	1,400	2,940	5,250	6,280	2,440	4,880	27,820
Total number of households in sample	720	220	180	460	1,020	1,290	540	1,020	5,440
Total number of persons in sample	1,710	470	440	1,200	2,300	3,130	1,100	2,320	12,670
Total number of adults in sample	1,360	390	330	860	1,820	2,490	850	1,780	9,880
Weighted average number of persons per household	2.4	2.2	2.6	2.7	2.3	2.5	2.1	2.3	2.4

Commodity or service	Average weekly household expenditure (£)								
1 Food & non-alcoholic drinks	70.30	52.60	68.70	66.50	63.50	71.70	50.00	56.10	63.70
2 Alcoholic drinks, tobacco & narcotics	14.20	9.60	6.70	11.60	13.20	14.70	12.50	13.30	12.90
3 Clothing & footwear	23.80	23.20	25.50	23.20	23.30	30.10	16.00	17.80	23.40
4 Housing (net)[1], fuel & power	73.90	162.70	160.10	98.00	83.10	58.80	76.70	69.40	83.00
5 Household goods & services	47.00	20.50	17.20	28.20	40.10	51.90	23.60	27.40	36.50
6 Health	9.90	6.90	10.10	5.80	8.50	12.00	5.40	4.50	8.20
7 Transport	116.30	63.50	62.40	71.30	88.40	99.30	40.70	65.80	81.60
8 Communication	20.70	19.10	18.60	22.20	21.50	24.50	17.80	20.20	21.40
9 Recreation & culture	97.90	55.90	45.80	52.60	85.30	102.30	42.40	55.70	74.80
10 Education	6.60	[11.20]	[1.80]	3.40	2.80	7.40	1.40	2.50	4.50
11 Restaurants & hotels	60.50	66.40	58.50	49.80	55.20	65.10	32.00	36.30	52.90
12 Miscellaneous goods & services	51.80	40.10	50.80	40.70	50.00	58.60	27.00	32.70	45.70
1-12 All expenditure groups	593.00	531.50	526.10	473.20	535.10	596.50	345.70	401.70	508.50
13 Other expenditure items	92.80	104.20	80.70	83.10	88.90	96.00	37.00	50.00	79.30
Total expenditure	**685.70**	**635.70**	**606.80**	**556.30**	**624.00**	**692.50**	**382.70**	**451.70**	**587.90**
Average weekly expenditure per person (£)									
Total expenditure	**290.60**	**294.10**	**233.50**	**204.90**	**273.40**	**282.50**	**186.10**	**198.80**	**248.70**

Please see background notes for symbols and conventions used in this report.

1 Excluding mortgage interest payments, council tax and Northern Ireland rates.

Source: Office for National Statistics

Table A52

Average weekly household expenditure by Output Area Classification (OAC) group
UK, financial year ending 2020

Commodity or service	Farming Communities OAC group 1A	Rural Tenants OAC group 1B	Ageing Rural Dwellers OAC group 1C	Students Around Campus OAC group 2A	Inner-City Students OAC group 2B	Comfortable Cosmopolitans OAC group 2C	Aspiring and Affluent OAC group 2D	Ethnic Family Life OAC group 3A	Endeavouring Ethnic Mix OAC group 3B	Ethnic Dynamics OAC group 3C	Aspirational Techies OAC group 3D	Rented Family Living OAC group 4A	Challenged Asian Terraces OAC group 4B
Weighted number of households (thousands)	1,000	1,800	450	310	280	340	430	520	290	60	540	1,420	630
Total number of households in sample	260	370	90	50	40	70	60	60	40	10	70	230	100
Total number of persons in sample	640	860	220	110	80	130	140	170	100	20	150	600	280
Total number of adults in sample	510	680	170	100	80	120	100	120	70	20	120	430	200
Weighted average number of persons per household	2.3	2.3	2.5	2.2	2.2	1.7	2.5	2.7	2.9	2.5	2.3	2.7	2.9
Commodity or service						Average weekly household expenditure (£)							
1 Food & non-alcoholic drinks	70.90	70.50	68.30	53.40	43.00	40.90	67.80	60.20	69.60	[43.40]	79.40	65.10	59.50
2 Alcoholic drinks, tobacco & narcotics	12.80	14.90	14.70	13.30	9.40	8.30	8.00	6.40	[3.40]	:	8.60	12.70	8.00
3 Clothing & footwear	25.70	24.70	16.20	28.40	29.00	12.60	23.90	27.00	23.80	:	26.60	26.30	16.60
4 Housing (net)[1], fuel & power	79.90	69.80	76.90	135.30	201.40	120.80	190.60	169.80	171.50	[110.60]	150.60	104.20	103.80
5 Household goods & services	45.90	46.40	51.90	14.80	16.60	21.90	26.10	11.60	15.50	[20.30]	23.10	30.40	18.40
6 Health	11.90	9.00	8.90	5.20	[10.70]	2.20	9.20	8.30	2.00	:	16.50	5.80	5.30
7 Transport	124.10	112.00	115.80	45.90	67.00	43.70	89.80	71.10	47.80	[26.20]	66.10	66.20	57.80
8 Communication	18.80	20.90	24.10	19.30	17.10	14.80	23.70	21.30	13.40	[15.40]	19.20	21.40	24.70
9 Recreation & culture	110.60	86.80	114.40	56.50	69.10	29.80	67.50	57.70	32.70	[17.40]	44.90	56.50	25.40
10 Education	[2.60]	9.80	:	:	:	:	:	:	:	:	:	:	:
11 Restaurants & hotels	65.30	56.70	64.60	71.50	66.80	51.50	74.20	53.00	56.10	:	70.80	52.90	38.10
12 Miscellaneous goods & services	49.40	54.40	46.60	39.40	48.40	28.80	44.00	31.80	59.60	[16.90]	68.40	35.20	47.10
1-12 All expenditure groups	618.00	576.00	605.00	507.90	581.70	382.30	634.50	519.90	495.90	[288.40]	577.00	482.10	406.60
13 Other expenditure items	101.70	83.70	109.20	80.60	138.00	53.30	140.00	92.60	37.60	:	99.20	81.90	54.20
Total expenditure	**719.70**	**659.70**	**714.10**	**588.50**	**719.60**	**435.60**	**774.50**	**612.50**	**533.60**	**[311.00]**	**676.20**	**563.90**	**460.80**
Average weekly expenditure per person (£) **Total expenditure**	**308.50**	**280.80**	**290.30**	**271.20**	**328.80**	**256.70**	**308.70**	**225.00**	**185.90**	**125.50**	**288.00**	**211.30**	**161.00**

Please see background notes for symbols and conventions used in this report.
1 Excluding mortgage interest payments, council tax and Northern Ireland rates.

Source: Office for National Statistics

Table A52

Average weekly household expenditure by Output Area Classification (OAC) group

UK, financial year ending 2020

	Asian Traits	Urban Professionals and Families	Ageing Urban Living	Suburban Achievers	Semi-Detached Suburbia	Challenged Diversity	Constrained Flat Dwellers	White Communities	Ageing City Dwellers	Industrious Communities	Challenged Terraced Workers	Hard-Pressed Ageing Workers	Migration and Churn	All house-holds
	OAC group 4C	OAC group 5A	OAC group 5B	OAC group 6A	OAC group 6B	OAC group 7A	OAC group 7B	OAC group 7C	OAC group 7D	OAC group 8A	OAC group 8B	OAC group 8C	OAC group 8D	OAC
Weighted number of households (thousands)	880	2,820	2,440	2,440	3,840	1,110	260	790	270	1,440	870	1,360	1,210	27,820
Total number of households in sample	120	530	480	530	760	210	70	190	70	290	200	300	230	5,440
Total number of persons in sample	310	1,240	1,050	1,300	1,840	460	130	410	100	680	420	650	580	12,670
Total number of adults in sample	230	960	860	1,020	1,470	350	110	310	90	520	330	510	420	9,880
Weighted average number of persons per household	2.7	2.3	2.2	2.5	2.4	2.2	1.8	2.1	1.5	2.3	2.1	2.1	2.5	2.4
Commodity or service						Average weekly household expenditure (£)								
1 Food & non-alcoholic drinks	73.70	62.50	64.60	75.70	69.10	51.70	37.80	52.00	49.30	60.70	53.90	51.40	57.40	63.70
2 Alcoholic drinks, tobacco & narcotics	12.40	12.80	13.70	15.50	14.20	11.60	13.40	13.30	13.20	13.20	13.30	11.60	15.30	12.90
3 Clothing & footwear	23.10	24.70	21.60	31.00	29.50	19.40	11.80	13.40	13.80	20.50	16.70	14.70	18.90	23.40
4 Housing(net)[1], fuel & power	83.80	80.80	85.90	63.80	55.70	84.20	72.80	69.00	72.40	64.20	63.10	69.50	80.20	83.00
5 Household goods & services	31.60	38.40	42.10	56.60	49.00	21.50	13.80	28.70	27.30	30.80	30.00	27.70	20.90	36.50
6 Health	6.00	8.40	8.60	14.50	10.50	7.50	2.60	4.50	2.40	4.50	4.10	4.40	5.00	8.20
7 Transport	89.20	84.30	93.20	118.40	87.10	43.10	32.60	42.70	32.60	71.40	45.00	70.10	69.00	81.60
8 Communication	21.60	21.50	21.60	23.60	25.10	18.50	15.70	18.70	14.40	20.10	21.20	18.60	21.60	21.40
9 Recreation & culture	66.00	77.40	94.50	118.00	92.30	56.10	28.70	32.50	28.30	72.50	51.70	48.60	46.50	74.80
10 Education	..	3.60	1.90	15.40	2.30	..	..	[1.00]	..	[2.90]	..	[4.50]	..	4.50
11 Restaurants & hotels	53.00	55.20	55.30	74.30	59.30	36.10	26.70	28.30	31.20	40.30	37.20	30.90	37.20	52.90
12 Miscellaneous goods & services	44.90	48.80	51.50	65.90	54.10	30.30	15.20	25.40	29.20	37.30	30.00	28.40	33.80	45.70
1-12 All expenditure groups	506.70	518.30	554.50	672.70	548.10	382.20	271.50	329.60	314.20	438.40	366.50	380.40	407.30	508.50
13 Other expenditure items	106.00	82.60	96.10	108.00	88.40	38.20	25.50	39.70	35.20	59.30	49.50	46.30	43.60	79.30
Total expenditure	**612.70**	**600.90**	**650.60**	**780.70**	**636.50**	**420.40**	**297.10**	**369.30**	**349.50**	**497.70**	**416.00**	**426.70**	**450.80**	**587.90**
Average weekly expenditure per person (£) **Total expenditure**	**228.20**	**256.80**	**293.60**	**311.40**	**263.50**	**192.10**	**163.40**	**173.50**	**228.70**	**217.70**	**193.70**	**199.60**	**180.50**	**248.70**

Please see background notes for symbols and conventions used in this report.

1 Excluding mortgage interest payments, council tax and Northern Ireland rates.

Source: Office for National Statistics

Table A56

Expenditure of households with children
by gross income quintile group

UK, financial year ending 2018 to financial year ending 2020

	Lowest twenty per cent	Second quintile group	Third quintile group	Fourth quintile group	Highest twenty per cent	All house-holds
Lower boundary of group (gross income: £ per week)[1]		335	568	873	1,296	
Average weighted number of households (thousands)	770	1,300	1,640	2,070	2,290	8,060
Total number of households in sample (over 3 years)	490	810	990	1,230	1,290	4,800
Total number of persons in sample (over 3 years)	1,420	2,840	3,720	4,790	5,180	17,950
Total number of adults in sample (over 3 years)	630	1,370	1,940	2,640	2,930	9,510
Weighted average number of persons per household	3.0	3.6	3.8	3.9	4.1	3.8

Commodity or service	Average weekly household expenditure (£)					
1 Food & non-alcoholic drinks	50.10	62.60	73.60	82.90	103.40	80.40
2 Alcoholic drinks, tobacco & narcotics	7.20	9.70	11.10	12.20	15.90	12.20
3 Clothing & footwear	16.70	23.90	26.40	34.50	54.30	35.00
4 Housing (net)[2], fuel & power	77.80	103.90	100.60	87.20	93.00	93.40
5 Household goods & services	21.60	27.10	33.20	45.20	77.50	46.70
6 Health	1.70	3.20	4.20	5.80	11.70	6.30
7 Transport	32.10	55.00	77.30	109.50	171.30	104.20
8 Communication	14.50	20.30	23.30	25.60	32.00	25.00
9 Recreation & culture	33.40	43.10	58.20	78.80	150.70	84.80
10 Education	3.70	3.60	3.50	8.40	27.80	11.70
11 Restaurants & hotels	21.80	31.30	45.80	60.50	105.00	61.70
12 Miscellaneous goods & services	22.50	32.30	44.00	58.20	91.50	57.20
1-12 All expenditure groups	303.20	415.90	501.10	608.80	934.00	618.50
13 Other expenditure items	27.90	40.70	72.20	100.50	164.00	96.30
Total expenditure	**331.10**	**456.60**	**573.20**	**709.30**	**1,098.10**	**714.80**
Average weekly expenditure per person (£)						
Total expenditure	**111.10**	**128.00**	**151.20**	**181.10**	**267.50**	**188.20**

Note: The commodity and service categories are not comparable to those in publications before 2001-02.

Please see background notes for symbols and conventions used in this report.

This table is based on a three year average.

1 Lower boundary of 2019-20 gross income quintile groups (£ per week).

2 Excluding mortgage interest payments, council tax and Northern Ireland rates.

Source: Office for National Statistics

Table A57

Expenditure of households without children
by gross income quintile group

UK, financial year ending 2018 to financial year ending 2020

	Lowest twenty per cent	Second quintile group	Third quintile group	Fourth quintile group	Highest twenty per cent	All house-holds
Lower boundary of group (gross income: £ per week)[1]		335	568	873	1,296	
Average weighted number of households (thousands)	4,730	4,200	3,860	3,430	3,210	19,420
Total number of households in sample (over 3 years)	2,840	2,620	2,350	1,990	1,730	11,520
Total number of persons in sample (over 3 years)	3,450	4,150	4,310	4,190	4,180	20,280
Total number of adults in sample (over 3 years)	3,450	4,150	4,310	4,190	4,180	20,280
Weighted average number of persons per household	1.2	1.6	1.8	2.1	2.5	1.8
Commodity or service			Average weekly household expenditure (£)			
1 Food & non-alcoholic drinks	34.50	46.60	56.70	65.80	80.40	54.70
2 Alcoholic drinks, tobacco & narcotics	8.50	10.10	13.30	16.70	19.80	13.10
3 Clothing & footwear	7.80	12.10	18.60	27.30	40.50	19.70
4 Housing (net)[2], fuel & power	51.70	63.80	75.40	87.60	102.70	73.80
5 Household goods & services	15.20	27.00	36.70	43.40	72.20	36.40
6 Health	4.10	6.50	8.70	11.00	13.60	8.30
7 Transport	22.60	46.10	75.50	103.20	151.20	73.70
8 Communication	10.70	15.00	19.20	22.80	27.30	18.20
9 Recreation & culture	28.10	46.30	74.70	100.30	135.50	71.80
10 Education	1.20	[1.10]	2.10	8.00	10.30	4.10
11 Restaurants & hotels	16.00	27.60	46.70	62.80	103.60	47.30
12 Miscellaneous goods & services	17.50	31.50	40.90	50.10	72.30	40.00
1-12 All expenditure groups	218.00	333.60	468.60	598.90	829.40	461.00
13 Other expenditure items	26.10	43.70	67.10	91.60	151.70	70.30
Total expenditure	**244.10**	**377.30**	**535.70**	**690.50**	**981.10**	**531.40**
Average weekly expenditure per person (£)						
Total expenditure	**201.30**	**241.10**	**293.10**	**323.20**	**388.50**	**296.70**

Note: The commodity and service categories are not comparable to those in publications before 2001-02.

Please see background notes for symbols and conventions used in this report.

This table is based on a three year average.

1 Lower boundary of 2019-20 gross income quintile groups (£ per week).

2 Excluding mortgage interest payments, council tax and Northern Ireland rates.

Source: Office for National Statistics

Office for
National Statistics

Living Costs and Food Survey QMI

Contact:

socialsurveys@ons.gov.uk

Release date:
20 December 2012

Next release:
To be announced

Table of contents

1 . Methodology background

National Statistic	
Survey name	XXXXX
Frequency	XXXXX
How compiled	XXXXX
Geographic coverage	UK
Sample size	XXXXX
Last revised	XXXXX

2 . Executive summary

The Living Costs and Food Survey (LCF) is an annual survey, designed primarily to measure household expenditure on goods and services. It also gathers information about the income of household members. Respondents, including children, keep a detailed diary of expenditure for 2 weeks. Respondents also record the weights and volumes of food and drink items bought.

A household expenditure survey has been conducted each year in the UK since 1957. From 1957 to March 2001, the Family Expenditure Survey (FES) and National Food Survey (NFS) provided information on household expenditure patterns and food consumption. Both surveys were well-established important sources of information for government and the wider community, charting changes and patterns in the UK's spending and food consumption since the 1950s. In April 2001, these surveys were combined to form the Expenditure and Food Survey (EFS). The EFS was renamed as the Living Costs and Food (LCF) survey in January 2008 when it became part of the Integrated Household Survey (IHS). The change saw the insertion of a core set of questions, common to all of the separate surveys that together comprise the IHS.

The long history of the survey has inevitably meant that discontinuities have been introduced. More information on this can be found in the section on Comparability and coherence.

The LCF sample for Great Britain is a multi-stage stratified random sample. Addresses are drawn from the Postcode Address File (PAF). In Northern Ireland, the companion survey to the Great Britain LCF is conducted by the Central Survey Unit of the Northern Ireland Statistics and Research Agency (NISRA). A systematic random sample of private addresses is drawn from the Land and Property Services Agency's database.

Results from the LCF are published in two main publications: Family spending and Family Food. Family spending, produced by Office for National Statistics (ONS), provides a comprehensive overview of household expenditure and income and also includes background information on the survey's history and methodology. Family Food, produced by the Department for Environment, Food and Rural Affairs (DEFRA), provides detailed statistical information on the purchase and consumption of food and drink.

The UK Data Archive at Essex University provides free access to the various LCF datasets, and can be contacted via the UK Data Archive website. The archive also provides detailed user guides on the survey.

This report contains the following sections:

- Output quality

- About the output

- How the output is created

- Validation and quality assurance

- Concepts and definitions

- Other information, relating to quality trade-offs and user needs

- Sources for further information or advice

3 . Output quality

This report provides a range of information that describes the quality of the output and details any points that should be noted when using the output.

We have developed Guidelines for Measuring Statistical Quality; these are based upon the five European Statistical System (ESS) quality dimensions. This report addresses the quality dimensions and important quality characteristics, which are:

- relevance

- timeliness and punctuality

- coherence and comparability

- accuracy

- output quality trade-offs

- assessment of user needs and perceptions

- accessibility and clarity

More information is provided about these quality dimensions in the following sections.

4 . About the output

Relevance

(The degree to which the statistical outputs meet users' needs.)

The LCF meets the needs of a range of users. These are summarised in this section.

One of the main purposes of the LCF is to define the basket of goods for the Consumer Prices Index (CPI) and the Retail Prices Index (RPI). The CPI is the main UK domestic measure of consumer price inflation for macroeconomic purposes. It forms the basis for the government's target for inflation that the Bank of England's Monetary Policy Committee (MPC) is required to achieve. The CPI is also used to uprate benefits, tax credits and public service pensions. The RPI is the most long-standing general purpose measure of inflation in the UK.

Information from the LCF is also a major source for estimates of household expenditure in the UK National Accounts.

LCF information on expenditure and income is used by HM Treasury and HM Revenue and Customs to study how taxes and benefits affect household incomes and to analyse the effects of policy in these areas.

Regional LCF information is one of the sources of regional estimates of consumer spending and other regional statistics.

Department for Environment, Food and Rural Affairs (DEFRA), which sponsors the collection of specialist food data, uses LCF data in its Family Food publication and other reports. Many other government departments use LCF data as a basis for policy-making, for example, in the areas of housing and transport.

Users outside government include independent research institutes, academic researchers and business and market researchers.

The main results from the survey are published by ONS in the annual Family spending statistical bulletin.

The LCF is the primary source of official information on household expenditure on goods and services and is also an important and detailed source of income data. The survey design and outputs are tailored to user needs (see the section on How the output is created). This is reflected in feedback obtained from main users, as detailed under Assessment of user needs and perceptions. However, some limitations are noted.

The survey does not provide a balance sheet of income and expenditure, either for individual households or for groups of households. The majority of expenditure information collected relates to the 2-week period immediately following the interview, whereas income components refer to a much longer period.

Experience of household surveys in the UK and in other countries indicates that reported expenditure on a few items (notably tobacco and alcohol) is below the levels that might be

expected by comparison with other sources of information. National Lottery spending has also been under-recorded in the LCF, particularly for scratch cards.

Timeliness and punctuality

(Timeliness refers to the lapse of time between publication and the period to which the data refer. Punctuality refers to the gap between planned and actual publication dates.)

ONS - Family spending

Family spending is timetabled to be published 11 months after the end of the reporting year. Once published, several deliveries of LCF data are released to other divisions of ONS and to other government departments.

Household Income and Expenditure (HIE) Branch

Processed data are supplied to HIE Branch of ONS both quarterly and annually. Quarterly files are timetabled to be delivered approximately 10 to 11 weeks after the end of the reporting period. The data contained in the quarterly files are only used for checking the income data and not for publication.

Annual files are timetabled to be delivered approximately 6 months after the end of the reporting period. The data are used for the Effects of Taxes and Benefits on Household Income publication.

Household and Non-Profit Institutions Serving Households (HNPISH) Branch

Processed data are timetabled to be supplied to the HNPISH Branch on a quarterly basis approximately 9 to 10 weeks after the end of the reporting period. The data are used for the Consumer trends publication.

RPI Production and Commodity Analysis Branch

Processed data are timetabled to be supplied to the RPI Production and Commodity Analysis Branch on an annual basis. These are timetabled to be delivered approximately 2 months after the end of the reporting period.

DEFRA

DEFRA receives raw data from the LCF on a monthly basis. DEFRA is timetabled to receive an initial supply of data for quality assurance purposes 10 weeks after the end of the reporting period and a re-supply of the data 6 weeks later, which includes any amendments made to the food coding arising from the quality assurance process.

Eurostat

Eurostat receives LCF data every 5 years for inclusion in the European Household Budget Survey.

Other annual outputs

ONS has a service level agreement with Department for Business, Energy and Industrial Strategy (BEIS). ONS send BEIS data on fuel expenditure following the publication of Family spending.

Punctuality

Deliveries to DEFRA, HIE Branch, HNPISH Branch and the RPI Production and Commodity Analysis Branch are usually made to timetable. Publication of the 2009 edition of Family spending was delayed because of procedural problems encountered in preparing the data. The delay was

conducted in compliance with the Code of Practice for Official Statistics, Protocol 2: Release Practices. The decision was appropriately authorised and publicised.

For more details on related releases, the GOV.UK release calendar provides 12 months' advance notice of release dates. If there are any changes to the pre-announced release schedule, public attention will be drawn to the change and the reasons for the change will be explained fully at the same time, as set out in the Code of Practice for Official Statistics.

5 . How the output is created

(This section outlines the methods used to produce LCF outputs. More information is available in the publication Family spending and the user guides deposited with the UK Data Archive.)

Overview

The LCF is a voluntary sample survey of private households. The basic unit of the survey is the household. The LCF (in line with other government social surveys) uses the harmonised definition of a household: a group of people (not necessarily related) living at the same address who share cooking facilities and share a living room or sitting room or dining area.

Each individual aged 16 or over in the household visited is asked to keep diary records of daily expenditure for 2 weeks. Information about regular expenditure, such as rent and mortgage payments, is obtained from a household interview along with retrospective information on certain large, infrequent expenditures such as those on vehicles. Children aged between 7 and 15 keep a simplified diary.

Detailed questions are asked about the income of each adult member of the household. In addition, personal information such as age, sex and marital status is recorded for each household member.

The fieldwork, and the editing and coding of data are carried out on a monthly basis. Interim monthly datasets are compiled and quality assured before being delivered to Department for Environment, Food and Rural Affairs (DEFRA). Additional quality assurance checks are carried out at the completion of each quarter and quarterly datasets are produced. Once the fieldwork for the calendar year has been completed, further quality assurance of the data is carried out before producing the annual dataset.

Sampling

Sample size

Approximately 6,000 responding households in the UK per year.

Sampling frame

Postcode Address File (PAF).

Sample design

The LCF sample for Great Britain is a multi-stage stratified random sample. Addresses on the PAF with "small user" postcodes are used as the sample frame. Postal sectors are used as the Primary Sampling Units (PSUs), with 18 addresses selected from each PSU to form the monthly interviewer quota. A total of 638 PSUs are selected annually after being arranged in strata defined by government regions and two 2001 Census variables: socio-economic group of the head of household and ownership of cars.

In Northern Ireland, the companion survey to the Great Britain LCF is conducted by the Central Survey Unit of the Northern Ireland Statistics and Research Agency (NISRA). A systematic random sample of private addresses is drawn from the Land and Property Services Agency's database.

Fieldwork

The fieldwork is conducted by ONS in Great Britain and by NISRA for the Department of Finance and Personnel in Northern Ireland using largely identical questionnaires. Differences between the two questionnaires reflect the country-specific harmonised standards for ethnicity, nationality and national identity, and the different systems of local taxation used in Great Britain and Northern Ireland.

Households at the selected addresses are visited and asked to co-operate in the survey. In order to maximise response, interviewers make at least four separate calls and sometimes many more, at different times of the day to households that are difficult to contact.

Interviews are conducted by Computer Assisted Personal Interviewing (CAPI) using laptop computers. Respondents complete a face-to-face interview and each individual aged 16 or over in the visited household is asked to keep a diary of daily expenditure for 2 weeks.

Weighting

A detailed description of the weighting process and its effects can be found in the Living Costs and Food Survey Technical Report.

The weighting procedure comprises two stages. First, a non-response adjustment is made using weighting classes derived from an analysis of respondent and non-respondent LCF households using addresses linking LCF response status to the 2001 Census data; for LCF addresses selected around the time of the census. Second, the non-response weights are calibrated to population totals for a set of calibration groups constructed from the numbers of males and females in different age groups and, separately, for regions.

From 2007, the results from the 2001 Census-linked study of non-respondents have been used to carry out the non-response weighting. The LCF took part in the Census Non-Response Linked Study from the 2011 Census, the results of which may be used to update non-response weighting in due course.

Calibration is used to adjust the non-response weights in such a way that weighted totals in the calibration groups match their counterpart population totals, based on a population definition of people living in private households. From 2006 onwards, the population totals have been projections based on estimates rolled forward from the 2001 Census using births and deaths registrations data and migration estimates.

Definitions of response outcome categories

A full response denotes a household in which:

- all adults aged 16 and over co-operated with the interview

- no income questions in the questionnaire were refused

- all adults kept a 2-week record of their expenditure

- the information given was complete and usable

There are three types of partial responses on the LCF:

- one or more adults, that are not the Main Diary Keeper (MDK) in the household refuse to keep the diary, but all adults complete the full income section of the interview

- one or more adults refuse the full income section but all adults in the household keep the diary and main income information is collected for all adults

- one or more adults (that are not the MDK) refuse to keep the diary and one or more adults refuse the full income section but main income information is collected for all adults

All partial responses must contain a diary from the MDK. If the MDK refuses to complete the diary, the household is classified as a refusal.

An outright refusal is a household that refuses to respond to the survey and the interviewer feels that there is no chance of an interview at the given time. In addition to outright refusals, there are also refusals when some of the information has not been collected. Refusals on the LCF are defined as:

- all adults complete the full income section, but the MDK of the household refuses to keep the diary

- one adult refuses to give the main income information in the questionnaire

A non-contact arises when an address is occupied but where it has not been possible to contact any member of the household in the field period.

A re-issue is an address where the interviewer has been unable to make contact or the household has refused to take part in the survey, but an interviewer has judged that the household is suitable for re-issue in a later field period month. These cases are re-distributed to field managers for assignment to interviewers at a later date. Re-issues are allocated on an ad- hoc basis to interviewers who are able to accept them alongside their main quota of work. Interviewers are expected to complete the re-issues within the field period of their main quota. Re-issued addresses are processed independently of the routinely collected interviews and diaries and then added to the annual dataset.

Proxy interview

Ideally, all adult members of the household should be present during the interview, so that the income section can be asked personally. However, where a member of the household is not present during the interview, another member of the household (such as spouse) may be able to provide documentary information about the absent person. The individual interview is then identified as a proxy interview.

From 2001to 2002 the EFS or LCF has included households that contained a proxy interview. Around a fifth of LCF households contain at least one proxy interview. Additional information on proxy interviews is available in the Living Costs and Food Survey Technical Report.

Disclosure

Statistical disclosure control methodology is also applied to LCF data. This ensures that information attributable to an individual is not disclosed in any publication. The Code of Practice for Official Statistics and specifically Principle 5: Confidentiality, sets out practices for how we protect data from being disclosed. The Principle includes a guarantee to survey respondents to "ensure that official statistics do not reveal the identity of an individual or organisation, or any private information relating to them".

6 . Validation and quality assurance

Accuracy

The degree of closeness between an estimate and the true value.

Response rates

The LCF is conducted with people who volunteer their time to answer questions about themselves and keep a diary for 2 weeks. The voluntary nature of the survey means that people who do not wish to take part in the survey can refuse to do so. Reasons for not participating in the survey include people who "can't be bothered" and those with a "bad experience of a previous survey". The sample is designed to ensure that the results of the survey represent the population of the UK. The risk of the survey not being representative may increase with every refusal or non-contact with a sampled household (survey non-response). One measure of the quality of survey results is therefore the response rate.

Response rates are available in the Living Costs and Food Survey Technical Report. In 2015 to 2016, the response rate was 46% in Great Britain. A long-term decline in response has been observed for the LCF, in common with other social surveys. Non-response weighting is applied to help mitigate non-response bias.

Quality assurance

Prior to publication LCF data are subjected to a rigorous process of quality assurance. An initial series of automatic checks are applied to raw household and income data as they are collected from respondents and entered onto the CAPI version of the questionnaire. These data are further checked by a team of editors within ONS who also impute for missing values. Missing data are imputed using a combination of the following methods:

- by reference to tables based on external (non-LCF) data published elsewhere

- by reference to tables based on LCF data from previous years showing average amounts according to household income

- by using information collected elsewhere in the questionnaire or by referring back to the interviewers

Respondents' diaries are checked after a few days to ensure the process of recording daily expenditure has been understood and before they are returned to ONS to ensure recorded information is complete. In manually entering diary data to ONS systems, further checks are made to these data.

Prior to the initial supply of data to Department for Environment, Food and Rural Affairs (DEFRA), further checks are made to raw data to ensure consistency between household, person and diary files and to check the coding of specific products known to have been coded incorrectly in the past.

DEFRA complete further checks of the data, feeding back their observations to ONS, before final versions of these raw datasets are supplied to DEFRA.

Further quality assurance is also undertaken once the data have been aggregated into quarterly and annual datasets. Household and Non-Profit Institutions Serving Households (HNPISH) Branch, of National Accounts Group, identify unusual movements in the aggregate data and HIE carry out detailed checks on the income and benefits data. Suspicious data are further investigated by the LCF team and may be corrected if found to be in error.

The LCF team also carries out a series of checks on the time series data to identify odd movements and to identify extreme values or outliers in household and person level datasets. In general, outliers are not treated on the LCF, with the exception of extreme values of income. However, only a few cases are treated each year by using the "surprise stratum" method. This method treats each outlier as if it were the only extreme unit in the stratum population and involves giving the outlying case a weight of one. This technique effectively reduces the impact of the outlying value without deleting it altogether.

Sources of error

Survey results are subject to various sources of error. The total error in a survey estimate is the difference between the estimate derived from the data collected and the true value for the population. It is helpful to distinguish between systematic and random error.

Systematic error

Systematic error, or bias, covers those sources of error that will not be expected to average to zero over repeats of the survey. Bias may occur, for example, if a certain section of the population is excluded from the sampling frame, because non-respondents to the survey have different characteristics to respondents, or if interviewers systematically influence responses in one way or another.

Substantial efforts are made to avoid systematic errors and these include:

- processes to ensure that households are selected in accordance with the sample design

- extensive measures to minimise non-response

- training to ensure that interviewers ask questions in such a way as to avoid biasing response

Additionally, the data are weighted to compensate for non-response; each respondent is given a weight so that they represent the non-respondents that are similar to them in terms of the survey characteristics. The sample distribution is weighted so that it matches the population distribution in terms of region, age group and sex.

Census Non-Response Linked Study (CNRLS)

Along with several other social surveys, the LCF is taking part in the CNRLS using data from the 2011 Census. The CNRLS matches census returns to recent sampled addresses from select ONS social surveys. The characteristics of survey responders and non-responders will be compared and evaluated using census data, providing an estimate of non-response bias. Where appropriate, this may be used to redesign the weighting methods that are used to correct for non-response bias in social surveys such including LCF.

Random error

Random error is the difference from the estimates derived using the sample data from the true values for the population that occur through chance occurrences. Random error may result from sources such as variation in a respondent's interpretation of the survey questions, or interviewer inconsistencies in asking questions. Efforts are made to minimise these effects through pilot work to ensure questions are understood by respondents and through interviewer training emphasising the need for consistency in dealing with selected sample members.

Sampling error

An important component of random error is sampling error, which arises because the estimate is based on a sample rather than a full census of the population. The results obtained for any single sample may, by chance, vary from the true values for the population but the variation would be expected to zero over many hypothetical repeats of the survey under the same conditions. Precision is usually estimated through the calculation of standard errors. Standard errors are estimated for some of the main variables on LCF. These are published in the Living Costs and Food Survey Technical Report.

The LCF uses a multi-stage stratified sample design. Consequently, it is inappropriate to estimate standard errors on the basis of a simple random design, as this will not reflect the true

sampling variation because of the complex sample design. The two-stage sample of addresses can lead to a substantial increase in standard error if the households or individuals within Primary Sampling Units (PSUs) are relatively homogeneous but the PSUs differ from one another. Stratification tends to reduce sampling error and is of most advantage where the stratification factor is strongly related to characteristics of interest in the survey.

Design factors

The design factor, or deft, is the ratio of the standard error of an estimate calculated taking into account the complex design relative to the standard error that would have resulted had the survey design been a simple random sample of the same size. Design factors are estimated for some of the main variables on LCF. These are published in the Living Costs and Food Survey Technical Report.

The size of the deft varies between survey variables according to the degree to which a characteristic is clustered within PSUs, or is distributed between strata, and the impact of the weighting. For a single variable, the size of the deft also varies according to the size of the subgroup on which the estimate is based and on the distribution of the subgroup between PSUs and strata.

Defts below 1.0 show that the standard errors associated with the complex design are lower than those associated with the simple random design due probably to the benefits of stratification. Defts greater than 1.0 show the survey has produced less precise estimates than would be obtained from a comparable simple random sample because of the effects of clustering and weighting.

Comparability and coherence

(Comparability is the degree to which data can be compared over time and domain, such as geographic level. Coherence is the degree to which data that are derived from different sources or methods, but refer to the same topic, are similar.)

Comparability

As already noted, a household expenditure survey has been conducted each year in the UK since 1957. A methodological discontinuity was introduced when the Family Expenditure Survey (FES) and National Food Survey (NFS) were combined to form the Expenditure and Food Survey (EFS) in April 2001. At the same time, the survey adopted the Classification of Individual Consumption by Purpose (COICOP), outlined in the section on Concepts and definitions. This meant a significant change to the categorisation of expenditure.

Until 2005 to 2006, annual data were collected and published on a financial year basis; from 2006 data were collected on a calendar year basis.

In 2008, the EFS was renamed as the Living Costs and Food Survey and became part of the Integrated Household Survey. This involved the insertion of a core set of questions, common to all of the separate modules that together comprise the IHS. However, collection of data on income and expenditure underwent little discontinuity over this transition.

Other more minor changes to definitions used in the survey have been introduced. Changes made since 1991 are documented in the Living Costs and Food Survey Technical Report.

Coherence

The main comparator for LCF estimates of expenditure data are the figures on final household consumption expenditure (HHFCE) published in Consumer trends and used in UK National Accounts. LCF data feed into some of the estimates published in Consumer trends, but other sources are also used. While differences occur in the estimates published, the differences are credible. Research is ongoing into the different estimates produced and their causes.

7 . Concepts and definitions

(Concepts and definitions describe the legislation governing the output, and a description of the classifications used in the output.)

The LCF utilises a suite of standard concepts and definitions. Some of the main terms are defined in this section, while a list of definitions and changes to these definitions can be found in the Living Costs and Food Survey Technical Report. These classifications reflect the needs of the users and also the survey's inclusion in the National Statistics Harmonisation Programme.

Classification of Individual Consumption by Purpose (COICOP)

The COICOP coding frame for expenditure items was introduced in 2001 to 2002. COICOP has been adapted to the needs of the Household Budget Survey (HBS) across the EU and is therefore compatible with similar national accounts and consumer prices indices. This allows the production of indicators which are comparable Europe-wide, such as the Harmonised Indices of Consumer Prices (CPI in the UK).

National Statistics Socio-economic Classification (NS-SEC)

In 2001 to 2002, the NS-SEC was adopted for all official surveys, replacing the social class based on occupation and socio-economic group. The long-term unemployed, which fall into a separate category, are defined as those unemployed and seeking work for 12 months or more.

Household Reference Person (HRP)

The HRP is defined as the person who:

- owns the household accommodation, or

- is legally responsible for the rent of the accommodation, or

- has the household accommodation as an emolument or perquisite, or

- has the household accommodation by virtue of some relationship to the owner who is not a member of the household

If there are joint householders the HRP is the one with the highest income; if the income is the same, then the eldest householder is taken. The concept of the HRP replaced the previous concept of the head of household in 2001 to 2002.

Household definition

A household is defined as one person living alone or a group of people (not necessarily related) living at the same address who share cooking facilities and share a living room or sitting room or dining area.

8 . Other information

Output quality trade-offs

(Trade-offs are the extent to which different dimensions of quality are balanced against each other.)

Publication of Family spending and the final LCF annual datasets, is completed as soon as possible, compatible with completing rigorous quality assurance conducted after all data have been collected and processed (see the section on Timeliness and punctuality).

Internal customers are provided with provisional datasets to provide data to feed into main outputs. Datasets are delivered quarterly as an input to the household expenditure component of UK National Accounts and quarterly GDP estimates; a final annual dataset is later delivered. Annual mid-year data are supplied to the RPI approximately 2 months after the reporting period, also representing provisional data for part of the relevant period covered by the data.

Assessment of user needs and perceptions

(The processes for finding out about users and uses, and their views on the statistical products.)

The LCF convenes a steering group of important customers in ONS and other government departments. Meetings are usually held biennially. The steering group is also consulted between meetings on proposals and developments, for example, on variable usage and questionnaire changes. A recent consultation of the steering group revealed positive views about the survey's products, though some concerns were expressed about the observed decline in response rates.

The LCF held a user engagement event in 2012 aimed at the academic and wider user community. This enabled users to communicate their uses of the data, and provided an opportunity for feedback and discussion. Views from users have also been obtained via a facility on the ONS website.

Views obtained from the wider user community also feed into formulation of outputs. For example, feedback from users of Family spending indicated that comprehensive coverage of housing costs would be useful to the user community. This led to a chapter on housing being included in the publication each year since 2004.

9 . Sources for further information or advice

Accessibility and clarity

(Accessibility is the ease with which users are able to access the data, also reflecting the format in which the data are available and the availability of supporting information. Clarity refers to the quality and sufficiency of the release details, illustrations and accompanying advice.)

Our recommended format for accessible content is a combination of HTML webpages for narrative, charts and graphs, with data being provided in usable formats such as CSV and Excel. Our website also offers users the option to download the narrative in PDF format. In some instances other software may be used, or may be available on request. Available formats for content published on our website but not produced by us, or referenced on our website but stored elsewhere, may vary. For further information please refer to the contact details at the beginning of this report.

For information regarding conditions of access to data, please refer to the following links:

- Terms and conditions (for data on the website)

- Copyright and reuse of published data

- Pre-release access (ended from 1 July 2017)

- Virtual Microdata Laboratory (VML)

Accessibility

Further methodology information is available on the Living Costs and Food Survey methodology pages, including access to datasets and the technical report.

A National Statistics Quality Review of the Living Costs and Food Survey was published in May 2016 and an ONS response in December 2016.

Living costs and food survey

User guidance and technical information for the Living Costs and Food Survey.

Contact:
Jo Bulman
joanna.bulman@ons.gov.uk
+44 (0)1633 455914

Release date:
16 February 2017

Next release:
To be announced

Table of contents

1 . Summary

The Living Costs and Food Survey (LCF) collects information on spending patterns and the cost of living that reflect household budgets. It is conducted throughout the year, across the whole of the UK, and is the most significant survey on household spending in the UK.

The survey provides essential information for key social and economic measures, such as:

- household spending patterns for the consumer prices index and for GDP figures

- detailed information on food consumption and nutrition for the Department for Environment, Food and Rural Affairs (Defra)

It is also an important source of economic and social data for a range of government and other research agencies.

The results are essential for understanding society and planning to meet its needs.

Information about the LCF is available for people selected to take part in the survey.

2 . Latest publications

The LCF releases data on an annual basis. The latest release can be seen on the ONS website.

3 . Access to LCF datasets

LCF data are made available through the End User Licence at the UK Data Service. The End User Licence is an agreement between the user and the University of Essex to provide users with the right to use the data held at the UK Data Service, this includes LCF data. The End User Licence dataset can be accessed through the UK Data Service (UKDS) website.

To find out more about the types of datasets available and how to apply for access, please contact access2data@ons.gov.uk.

4 . Technical report

The technical report describes technical aspects of the sampling, fieldwork and data processing for the LCF:

- Living Costs and Food Survey technical report for survey year April 2015 to March 2016

- Living Costs and Food Survey technical report for survey year January to December 2014 (Pdf 713Kb)

- Living Costs and Food Survey technical report for survey year January to December 2013 (529.7 Kb Pdf)

- Living Costs and Food Survey technical report for survey year January to December 2012 (345.6 Kb Pdf)

5 . Quality report

- Quality and methodology information for living costs and food survey (LCF) (117.9 Kb Pdf)